Endgame

Crucial Conversations
A Reckoning
Anger
The Magnificent Spinster
The Education of Harriet Hatfield

Wild Knoll in May

Endgame

A Journal of the Seventy-ninth Year

By *May Sarton*

W · W · Norton & Company   ·   New York   ·   London

Endpiece–CREDIT: SUSAN SHERMAN

First published as a Norton paperback 1995

The text of this book is composed in Caledonia
with the display set in Garamond Italic.
Manufacturing by the Haddon Craftsmen, Inc.

Library of Congress Cataloging-in-Publication Data
Sarton, May, 1912-1995.
    Endgame : a journal of the seventy-ninth year / by May Sarton.
        p.   cm.
    1. Sarton, May, 1912-1995–Diaries. 2. Authors, American–20th
century–Diaries. I. Title.
    PS3537.A832Z465   1992
    818´.5203–dc20
    [B] 91-30172

ISBN 0-393-31388-3

W. W. Norton & Company, Inc., 500 Fifth Avenue, New York, N.Y. 10110
W. W. Norton & Company Ltd., 10 Coptic Street, London WC1A 1PU

1 2 3 4 5 6 7 8 9 0

To Nancy Hartley

who has worked with me for
thirteen years as secretary,
librarian, and devoted friend
of the work.
Hail and farewell!

Preface

I ALWAYS IMAGINED a journal that would take me through my seventy-ninth year to meet my eightieth birthday at its end. I had imagined a philosophical journal, dealing with the joys and problems, the doors opening out from old age to unknown efforts and surprises. I looked forward to the year as a potent harvest.

I could not foresee that I would struggle through it with constant pain and increasing frailty. I lost fifty pounds, could not garden at all, and by Labor Day could no longer type. I kept believing that I would feel better in a month, in two months. But by late March I was facing the likelihood that I might never feel better. There appeared to be no future.

What was wrong? *First*, the fibrillating heart; *second*, the lining of my left lung filled up with fluid and made breathing difficult (it has to be drained about every three months); *third*, the cause of my despair: irritable bowel syndrome. That is what gave me six to eight hours of acute pain every day. I was hospitalized two or three times—to no avail. Doctors could only prescribe painkillers: Tylenol with codeine. It helped but did not cure, of course. The M.D.s are not interested in chronic pain; my general practitioner never even suggested diet.

After four months, on Labor Day, September 3, it was clear that I could no longer type, and with Susan Sherman's and Nancy Hartley's help I began to dictate into a cassette recorder that Nancy transcribes. I wish I could say that my dictation produces such subtle and complex results as Henry

James's did at the end of his life, but it is not at all like that, alas!

I have been correcting and rereading the dictated text these past weeks and at first was dismayed. Often there is no sentence structure. I can mend that, of course, but there is always the problem of how much about illness itself is relevant. How boring can I be? How self-enclosed in pain? More important, the style in this journal does not have strong imaginative images. Poets think in images, I have always said, but since the stroke something is locked up in the subconscious now. Since the stroke five years ago, I cannot listen to records because they open the locked places and then unstoppable tears flow.

Should I publish this journal at all? What value does it have, coming from a diminished old Sarton? I hope I am right in thinking that flawed though it is, it does have value, if only in suggesting how one old lady has dealt over a year with chronic pain; what the rewards are of living here by the sea, even old and ill; how I have had to learn to be dependent. Perhaps this *Endgame* will give some comfort to fellow sufferers.

For me it has been a lifesaver, and I am going on now with one more journal, which I began the day after my birthday, because I need to sum up and, in a way, discover what is going on around me and inside me.

Life would seem empty and without purpose without it.

MAY SARTON
June 3, 1991

Endgame

Thursday, May 3, 1990

MY SEVENTY-EIGHTH BIRTHDAY. It's hard to believe I am still around to be glad the sun is out at last and the daffodils crowding the wood's edge with abundant grace, all things moving toward opening and flowering after the imprisoning winter we have somehow survived. To write these few stumbling words is an event for me, as the months of illness caused by my fibrillating heart have meant putting a stop to any writing at all. Even a postcard has become a Herculean effort, which I think about in bed around five when Pierrot, the gorgeous Himalayan, decides it is time to go out. I let him out and go back to inventing a wonderful postcard, which rarely gets written, because by the time I have put out the bird feeder, watered the plant window, made my breakfast and washed up after it, made my bed, and dressed, my little store of energy has vanished.

Is that the truth or is the truth that the side effects of the medicines prescribed for my heart blur my mind in some way? I never feel fully awake, alive to the tremor of wind, except at night when the ecstatic peeping of the frogs prevents sleep but is so welcome, so thrilling after the silent winter, that I am glad to listen for hours.

I always imagined I would begin a last journal on this birthday, but when I tried as an experiment after Christmas and again near Easter, it was clear that the curious connection between what goes on in the head and its expression in words was simply not working. This is scary even when CAT scans show no brain damage and I am assured by the doctors that all is well. "Only," says wonderful Dr. Petrovich, "your heart is very, very tired and has also lost strength in the past year." So I am to settle, or so it seems, for a semilife, or the life of a semi-invalid. This has been the struggle of the last months, to learn to accept that my life as a writer is probably over and to learn to accept dependence.

Friday, May 4

ANOTHER BLUE SKY, another real spring day. We are right to tremble, as it will rain again tonight and all day tomorrow when the friends I think of as family, Anne Woodson and Barbara Barton, come for champagne and lobster rolls—a feast reduced to the minimum, as all things must be these days.

But as I write this I smile, for my birthday yesterday could hardly have been called austere or in any way diminished, trucks driving up every hour or so with extraordinary gifts of plants and flowers—one of these, two towering stems of white orchids, making together an orchid tree, which I lie under like an East Indian princess—these from dear extravagant Susan Sherman. Maggie Vaughan came bringing a delicious lunch of shrimp, salad, and her special strawberry sherbet with marinated strawberries and homemade cake, so I could lie on my chaise and answer phone calls and drink a whiskey sour. And among the more than six hundred cards and letters that had accumulated since last week I found that Polly Starr had copied out the following passage from Teilhard de Chardin, which hit me like an arrow to the heart, so exact is it for my present state:

This hostile force that lays him low and disintegrates him can become for him a loving principle of renewal, if he accepts it with faith, while never ceasing to struggle against it. On the experimental plane, everything is lost. But in the realm of the supernatural, as it is called, there is a further dimension, . . . which achieves a mysterious reversal of evil into good. Leaving the zone of human successes and failures behind him, . . . he accedes by an effort of trust in the greater than himself to the region of suprasensible transformations and growth. His resignation is no more than the thrust which lifts the field of his activity higher.

. . . There is a time for growth and a time for diminishment in the lives of each one of us. At one moment the dominant note is one of constructive human effort, and at another . . . annihilation. . . .

All these attitudes spring from the same inner orientation of the mind, from a single law which combines the twofold movement of the natural personalization of man and his supernatural depersonalization. . . .—*The Divine Milieu*

I have had *The Divine Milieu* by my desk (in a revolving bookcase with other treasures) but have not opened it to re-read for years, so Polly's copying it came like a present—key to a door that has been closed for months. It is enough to copy it out myself for the day and to affirm what Sheri, the visiting nurse, who came to give me a sponge bath today, told me: "You're getting better and I can tell because you smile, and you didn't when I first came."

Yesterday I forgot to say that when I drove down to get the mail I saw the marsh marigolds are in flower—that bright gold startles the eyes. It was one of my best presents for the day.

Monday, May 7

PRETTY DEPRESSING to find it raining again early this morning when I let Pierrot in—he had insisted on going out at five. We have had a mournful spring of rain, day after day, rain and wind, good for the garden but hard on people who long to be able to be outdoors. Sometimes I wonder why I have chosen to live in Maine, then something happens that lets me know why.

But the day itself, May 3, was peaceful.

When one florist had delivered three or four times I was a little embarrassed and explained to the middle-aged woman who brought the final arrangement late in the afternoon, "It's my seventy-eighth birthday, you know." Her answer: "Your friends don't let you forget it, do they?" This pure Maine remark filled me with joy, and I know why I live in Maine. That tart sense of humor is good medicine.

Wednesday, May 9

EVERY FALL I put in twenty or more tiny fritillary bulbs. Only one or two ever flower, because it is difficult to find the right root end, which may show a few tiny hairs or may not. This year three or four have flowered, and they are magic. I have

CREDIT: SUSAN SHERMAN

two in a tiny blue jug which belonged to Pat Chasse's grandmother; she has added this treasure from her family to the
weekly supply of custard she makes for me. Since my birthday
the house is full of small presents like this, and they are heart
medicine.

It is the sixth month now of being so debilitated that I
cannot work. Writing a single letter becomes a huge effort. I
am sure it is partly the effect of the heart medicine, which
makes me as drowsy as a bumblebee. But I must be a little
better, since I have written these few sentences. I could not
have done it a month ago.

My desire for fritillaries goes back to before World War II
in England when I saw them for the first time and was
enchanted. They were at Dorothy Wellesley's house, Penns-
in-the-Rocks, near Tunbridge Wells. As the car swung
across an ancient low stone bridge I saw that the meadow

on each side of us was pricked by hundreds of these small precise bells, each with checkered petals nodding on a single stem.

That was the start of a strange, illuminating weekend.

Friday, May 11

TODAY, after wild wind and rain all night, is a real blue-and-gold May day, the ocean rough, a deep molten blue in the distance, and the field so garlanded in daffodils that anyone walking here and coming on the scene by accident would have her breath taken away. "Imagine living here, living with this glory."

I have been wanting to write about the wonderful Friday morning last week when my efforts to accept dependency bore fruit. It happened in a few hours that laid to rest anxieties that had been keeping me awake and gave me a deep breath of peace. My neighbor Karen Kozlowski cleared out the liquor cupboard, a closet in the porch room where I sit and watch the birds and read in a chaise longue. It had accumulated years of stuff, "a glory hole," my mother would have called it. Amongst other things there were shelves of vases that had to be sorted out and many discarded.

Months ago, Karen K. called out of the blue to ask whether I needed any help, for she was free and could drive me to do shopping or whatever I needed. A few months ago I would have thanked her and told her I did not need help. But when she called I was feeling very ill. The weekends, when Nancy Hartley, my secretary, is not here, are the hardest days, of course, and also I am finding it difficult to eat anything, so I asked Karen whether she could make me some Jell-O. And lo and behold, trays of lemon and orange Jell-O began to appear. And now, lo and behold, the glory hole was being tidied up and cleaned out. Great day!

Meanwhile Nancy was out on the terrace planting the lobelia which we had bought two weeks ago to edge the little border inside the terrace wall. Birthday money had given me a big flat of bright blue violas, and those too were put in. Six miniature roses, a present from Edythe Haddaway, were still to be planted—and that Nancy achieved today. I had been so anxious that the lobelias might not survive that it was bliss to see them all along the border, perky and close to flowering.

The third wonder of that day was Diane Yorke, who gardens for me, but we have had so much rain that she has not been able to do a lot of things that need doing. On that good Friday, she was out there raking leaves from the flower beds, edging, and in general tidying up. It was such a cruel winter that I have lost a lot of plants, but at least what is left looks cherished.

So there I was on Friday morning accepting my new dependency and watching without a qualm while three women worked wonders in my behalf. I lay there and enjoyed! So in six months I have made a start at learning the lesson. The joke was finally on me, for Nancy, Karen, and Diane had worked here for half a day and seemed as fresh as daisies and I, who had simply sat and watched and given advice, was so exhausted I went to bed at seven!

CREDIT: SUSAN SHERMAN

Sunday, May 13

THE DREARIEST Mother's Day imaginable, a steady heavy rain.
I did not want to get up. Pierrot went out just after four and
came in at six, soaking wet from nose to tail, and then, of all
things, had his breakfast and asked to go out again. I went

back to bed, but got up again in half an hour, and sure enough, there he was waiting at the front door and meowing mournfully.

The battle is on every day against extreme fatigue and lassitude. It took me four days to be able finally to write about the day. All the work got done, but the journal is a relentless pressure and I have not got into a viable routine that includes it. Dr. Gilroy sparkled when I told him I was keeping one and said, "That's what will cure you . . . I am certain of it." Many other friends say the same thing, but they cannot know the effort it takes to write even a line. I may try a microrecorder if I ever have the energy to go to Portsmouth and get one. It is months since I have been to town, although yesterday I bought some sneakers here in York, quite an event.

Yesterday was a true spring day, blue ocean, emerald grass, and all . . . and I picked a small bunch of white violets. Suddenly they are back and carpet every free space in the borders, especially along the fence. The garden is full of riches, such as the lily of the valley, for one, but there are also losses because of our frightfully cold December. The white bleeding heart has survived in several places, and also the blue hydrangea from Winterthur that Huldah Sharp gave me for my birthday last year. They will remind me if they do well of our trip to the island of Sark together. I had explored it alone two years before, and my hunch that Huldah would love it was not wrong. We had Beatrix Potter days there, picnics among bluebells and primroses on meadows so high up on the cliffs we looked down on gulls flying far below.

Monday, May 14

THERE IS SUCH a continual interleaving of joys these days it is easy to forget one or the other of them, take it for granted, and let it go unregistered. Right now two wood pigeons are cooing compulsively, and a high wind rumples the ocean. What would it be like here without the birds? A suffocating silence.

But also the constant weaving in and out of wings at the feeder keeps the air alive. There are sometimes twenty dazzling goldfinches at a time coming and going to the feeder from the ornamental cherries which provide such good, safe perches. There are purple finches, nuthatches (both white, small, and rose-breasted), woodpeckers (hairy and downy), titmice, redwing blackbirds, grackles, pine siskins.

In these months when I have almost never felt well, going down early in the morning to put out the bird feeder is one thing that has kept me alive, been a reason for getting up.

The worst part of the struggle has been that sometimes there seems to be no reason for getting up. But now that I do write a little in the journal, I have, as it were, put on my work clothes again, am a functioning person for a change. It is forcing a change in me toward life. High time.

Thursday, May 17

ON MONDAY I had a fit of feeling better. Nancy was not here, and I woke up and decided to do the laundry that had piled up, get the job done before having breakfast or making my bed, only do the necessary chores, putting out the bird feeder and letting Pierrot in and feeding him. He had woken me at quarter to four to go out. "Once more into the breach, dear friends," but I should have paid attention to objections making themselves felt inside my chest and abdomen. After the wash was done and the sheets dried and folded and I got myself in gear to make my bed, I felt suddenly so weak it was as though I had no blood in my body. I could hardly make it to my bedroom down the hall and creep into bed, scared and furious. There I stayed for two hours and slept. After that, nothing whatever of any use got done that day.

Since then I have felt exceptionally tottery and depressed. Partly, the weather is odious. It is now raining very hard and will do so all night. Again the daffodils will be beaten down.

Dr. Petrovich, whom I saw Monday afternoon, thinks my heart is doing well. I do breathe more easily and do not have to pause quite as long halfway up the stairs. But I feel so ill and frail all the time it is not a real life anymore.

When I began this journal, which so many friends had begged me to do, which everyone imagined could be useful and not only help me through the dark but perhaps help its readers also, I thought maybe I could manage not to talk about ill health much or even at all. But how not to talk about something which frustrates every hopeful impulse toward some kind of life? I am lonely, but people tire me after even a short visit. Any physical effort such as watering the plants in the plant window ends in exhaustion. And this miserable journal is keeping me from writing the one letter a day I was able to manage. Pat Carroll's birthday is May 5.

Monday, May 21

I DID MANAGE to write Pat, who is going to play Falstaff at the Folger and whose life and art are bursting at the seams with that sovereign laughter reaching the rafters wherever she may be. But I realized that she is a good deal younger than I am, so I must not allow myself to quiver with dismay that she is achieving so much this year while I consider it a triumph to write a single paragraph or a letter a day.

It has been a wasted week. The weather is demoralizing, and too often when I have planned to get something done at my desk, I have had instead to curl up with diverticulitis, as I did yesterday from two in the morning till noon. I still have not managed to write Bea Hunter about Lotte Jacobi, who died more than a week ago. I have not written, but I have thought about Lotte a lot. She took the best photographs of me—they are on many of my book jackets. She was also a life-enhancing friend. A visit to see her in Deering was an event. She not only listened with absolute attention, she heard and understood, and out of that genius for getting inside a problem, always brought lifesaving wisdom and laughter to bear. When I was feeling old in my sixties she teased me unmercifully. She grew old in the way of a fairy godmother, more charming and irresistible with every year—until the very end, when for a few years she was not quite herself, though still a creature of joy and lightning response, a mischievous smile, a sense of herself as having much to give. This seems to me quite unusual and touching, for she was a great giver to the end and she did not deny that to herself. And the people who had come to her for years for wisdom and a taste of that rich life still came when the life had become a little askew, because, not quite all there, she was more there than most people ever are.

Thursday, May 24

THE SUN IS OUT! This, after twenty days of rain, fog, drizzle, cold east wind, the month of May that never happened. It is hard to get used to not seeing sun sparkle the new leaves, not to wake to banners of sunlight on the white walls of my bedroom, and up here in my study not to look down on the brilliant emerald path curving down the field to the rough blue sea. It has been a strange limbo all these days, the limbo in my head meeting the limbo of weather that has held us in thrall.

Just now I went out for a short walk around the terrace garden to see what was coming up, for soon Nancy and I are going for our yearly pilgrimage to get perennials. Since all the columbine died in our icy December, that is the one thing I must replace. Lots of things are flourishing—the white violets make a rich border around every plot and along the fence. The ordinary peonies have survived, but the tree peonies, my

CREDIT: SUSAN SHERMAN

greatest joy, have suffered a lot. There are just a few strong
woody stalks with very few buds to show for all the years, but
I look on each bud, especially of the white ones, as a god.
They are awesome. Some iris is in bud; all the roses, except
the big mound of a pink rugosa, have died. It is a mosaic of
losses but nevertheless rich in promise.

Perhaps that is rather like my life these days. I am certainly somewhat better, have less difficulty breathing, and have quiet nights of sleep whereas for months I could not sleep, and I enjoy seeing people. That is an improvement. Now I do not collapse after a half hour of talk. Seeing a friend for a real talk over lunch or tea is the most creative thing I do.

But where does the day go? Little gets done. I imagine that I'll write to so-and-so but sit dreaming at my desk and it doesn't get done. I am better but my head is not well. There is a gap between a thought and the words to express it. So thinking dangles.

Monday, May 28, Memorial Day

YESTERDAY WAS a spectacular day—for the third time I woke to sunlight in the window frame in my bedroom with the day opening out like some marvelous flower of brightness and hope. At eleven-thirty Susan Sherman arrived, having driven all the way from New York, to have lunch with me and to bring me the lovely blue, white, and black hood from the graduation ceremony at Centenary College, where she had represented me as the citation for my honorary degree was read. Angela Elliott gave the commencement address, a stirring weaving together of her assessment of some of my work with an address to the graduating class. I feel bad that I could not be present, this sixteenth time of being so honored. Centenary College had made a point of making my work known to some of the students, so I was far more included than one usually is on these occasions. It was awfully kind of Susan to go for me.

Cybèle

She arrived with not only these emblems from the college but with jars of marvelous yellow and a strange deep pink roses—such a festive avalanche of sweetness and rarity filling the house. She brought crème brulée custard and meringues and cheese and French bread.

All the while Cybèle II, her entrancing tiny poodle, a shock of curly white hair with deep brown eyes looking out from it, was waiting in the car in her bed, as good as gold. I suddenly longed to see the little animal free, to see her run, because she is never off the leash in New York. So Susan with

some trepidation let her out, and suddenly that ball of white
fluff was catapulting all over the lawn, around the terrace
behind the house, in an ecstasy of pleasure. It gave me a few
moments of pure joy.

I took Susan to Captain Simeon's Galley in Kittery Point.
Lately it has become my regular "joint" and I go there sometimes alone to read the mail, but more often with a friend, for
whom sitting looking out on the dockside full of boats, and
way off to the two lighthouses, is a treat.

Wednesday, May 30

IT WAS SUCH a splendid weekend, three sunny days, and such a
fine time with Susan. Why then did I go into a tailspin last
evening? Every now and then during these months of never
being well it has happened, a wild attack of misery because I
have no family.

The holidays, when most people are with family, intensify
this sense of loss, of deprivation. Quite irrational, of course.

When I was a child I made a beeline for families I could
adopt or who would adopt me. First among these was Bon
Bon Baekeland and sitting on the porch at Yonkers shelling
peas with her, with Buster and Teddy lying beside us; the
Copley Greenes, whose "Uncle Frank" taught us to ride ponies during summer stays at Rowley; the Ernest Hockings on
a lake in Vermont, where I heard Dickens read aloud su-
perbly; and, of course, the Limbosches in Belgium, with
whom I had a home for years—I could turn up at any time for
a month and be welcomed as a child of the family. I am aware
that family life is never as easy as it may look to an outsider.

Gide's *"Je hais les familles"* sprang from the pain of leading a
life far from family life, in a way as an antagonist. I am aware
also that those who adopt families as I have done do not pay
the price.

Saturday, June 2

IT IS SIMPLY perhaps that, to a point, family can be taken for
granted. "Home is the place where, when you have to go
there, they have to take you in," as Robert Frost said. So it is
when one is ill that the absence of a sister or brother is keenly
felt.

Wednesday, June 6

MY HEART is doing a lot better and Dr. Petrovich is pleased. I
don't have as much difficulty breathing, and I sleep well. But I
am frightfully tired all the time. Yesterday I lay down on my
bed after breakfast and slept till eleven, and then felt so shaky
I asked Nancy to drive me to fetch the mail.

What can I do about the daily defeat through fatigue?
This morning I began a new regime in the hope I may be able
to plan the morning hours better and so get an hour or so at
my desk. It is now eight. As usual Pierrot meowed to go out

Le Pignon Rouge, the Limbosch house near Brussels

May at seven years old between Claire and Jacques Limbosch

and jumped off and on my bed to tell me he wanted to go out. This was at three forty-five! I stumbled downstairs to open the door for him and then enjoyed getting back into bed for two hours or more. I aimed for six-fifteen.

It's another great blue sunny day, with birds singing their heads off. So down I went at six to let Pierrot in and feed him, and fill and hang the heavy bird feeder. Then I got things ready for my breakfast, milk ready to warm for coffee, muffin ready to be heated up in the electric toaster-oven. I watered the big impatiens in the plant window, which simply falls apart like a person in a faint if it needs water. Then—this is the new routine I am trying—I came back upstairs and ran a bath while I was making the bed. Making the bed has been the energy-eater lately, and my idea is to relax in the bath after doing it, and then get dressed. This I did and was downstairs getting my breakfast at just after seven, turned on the *Today Show* and prepared for a quiet half hour or so . . . with quite a lot already accomplished. And I don't feel that awful exhaustion which drove me to lie down again at eight yesterday. Nancy and I are going to try to find perennials, which will be fun, and a perfect day for it as it is not too hot.

Great news of the garden. Diane rototilled the annual garden on Saturday and sowed all the annual seeds on Sunday. This is a job I used to take a week to do even with Nancy's help, so it is astonishing to see what Diane can do in two days! Things are under control again as she even managed to turn on the outdoor water and set up the hoses.

The garden is lovely at the moment, the intermediate iris I decided to try two years ago really beautiful at the edge of the perennial border. They do not need to be staked and have survived the winter better than the few tall ones did. The great charm right now is the huge purple allium scattered through the border. They punctuate with startling majesty.

Thursday, June 7

I PAID for that good morning yesterday with four hours of cramps, so the afternoon was pure waste. But I am going on with the new routine, come hell or high water. Neither of those today, but cold (fifty-five when I went down at six), and in less than an hour Nancy will help me take Pierrot for his rabies shot.

It is strange that I have not spoken of what I have been reading this lamentable spring, for books are what have kept me alive. They and the English weeklies, the *Manchester Guardian* and the *New Statesman*, and a long read every day of the *New York Times*, keep me aware of the world beyond this safe green-and-blue enclosure.

Last night I finished a remarkable book by Christabel Bielenberg, *The Past Is Myself,* It is the painful story of her years in Germany as the English wife of a German lawyer. All through the Nazi years he was active in the group who made the attempt to assassinate Hitler, most of whom were hanged or shot when the attempt failed. Her husband, Peter, was finally released after months of prison and interrogation, the lone survivor of that brave group of Germans. How dreadfully hard it must have been to live always in fear of being arrested, bombed, starved, never daring to open your heart for fear of being reported! Marcie Hershman is writing a series of stories laid inside Germany, using what we know now about how many guillotines the Nazis had inside Berlin and how many suspect Germans were beheaded in those horrifying cellars.

And of course it was much the same in Stalin's Russia.

All through May I found myself for some reason imagining and marveling at my parents' courage when they arrived here in 1916 as refugees from battered Belgium. Some things live under the skin of a grown-up for years. I must have buried all memory of our arrival, my mother's and mine, through Ellis Island. I have no actual memory myself of this, but under the skin I know that my mother was frightfully humiliated there, perhaps by the brutal way everyone was stripped. She would never speak of it, never told anything about it, but I simply *know*, under my skin, that it was traumatic. My father had come over a few months earlier with one hundred dollars in his pocket and his dream of writing the history of science. How utterly naked to the world and brave they both were! Luckily, of course, English was my mother's native tongue, but my father spoke it very badly indeed. So learning to write and lecture in English, a foreign language for him, was only a small part of what he faced.

Friday, June 8

THE DAZZLING STRAWBERRY moon rose in a perfectly clear sky around eight last night, showering a golden path. Pierrot was far too absorbed to think of coming in—until one-thirty this morning, when he meowed very loudly. Oh dear, by then I had been fast asleep and could not get back to it. So I am rather a wreck this morning, though I have maintained the new routine and it is working. Will is now operative again, as it was not for months. I feel I am my own master, and that is a big boost to my morale.

I want to talk about another book I have read lately with great enjoyment, Bob Hale's *The Elm at the Edge of the Earth*. Bob for years ran Hathaway House, a marvelous bookstore in Wellesley, and also organized a yearly series of authors' readings to which I was occasionally invited, once to fill in at one dominated by Irma Bombeck. I had never heard of her, unbelievable though that might seem, found her charming, but was still unaware when we walked into the hall jammed with Bombeck fans that I was no one and she was the queen—and, I might add, deserved to be. At the signing afterwards there were long lines for Bombeck, and a few compassionate readers of mine lined up to assure me that to them I was a great success. Luckily I could laugh at all this when I got home to share it with Judy Matlack. Pride comes before a fall!

Bob's book is a masterpiece. It is laid in a county home somewhere in New England and is seen through the eyes of an eight-year-old boy. This version of a sensitive boy's world never wavers and more extraordinarily never bores, so involved do we get in David's explorations of his world and all the people in it: old, crippled, the prisoners of inevitable decline. I devoured the book partly for the joy of being brought back close to the seasons on a farm, close to nature, communicated through a wonderfully vivid, unpretentious style.

Monday, June 11

FEW BOOKS are nourishing these days, but that is what Bob's book is. I must try this morning to write and tell him so. Yesterday, another gloomy rainy day like this one, I did not write a single letter, only ferreted out the estimated-tax vouchers

for the IRS and made out checks. At least this is off my mind.
Many times during the day I murmured, "I wasted time and
now doth time waste me." But there is no spur these days,
and this horse refuses to run but is quite content to nibble and
saunter along.

I have regained self-respect by devising the new routine,
which has made it possible to come up here to my study at
eight or half past and write a little in the journal. I had
reached a point where will was not operative. Every day I
watched myself go to seed and settle for lying around doing
next to nothing. Now at least there is a small achievement
every day. If I could extend the work time to an hour or two
after my nap then it would be possible to catch up on letters,
but by then my store of energy has been squandered and I
settle for watching the birds at the feeder. Yesterday there
was the charming sight of a purple finch feeding his wife on a
branch of the cherry.

The speed with which I have gone downhill since late
November is amazing and a little frightening. Loss of memory
is part of it. Words get mixed up in the card index of my brain,
so all of a sudden columbine has become clematis. Certain
words and/or names drop out for long periods of time. One is
"Seattle," which disappeared a day after Nancy and I flew
back to Portland from there. How could that be, and why?
One day last week I spent an hour going through my address
book to try to find the name of Carol Ebbs, who had made me
a charming sachet for my birthday with exquisite embroidered bluebells on it. I did find it—sometimes such a hunt
simply fails. Every one tells me, "Oh, don't worry, I forget
everything myself these days." True, no doubt, but what it
does to me is to make me feel disoriented, as though words
were markers on maps that tell me where I am or was a short
time ago. Without them I am not sure where I am or who I
am. I have to trust that it is not Alzheimer's.

Thursday, June 14

TUESDAY TURNED out to be a perfect day, cool, wind making the fresh leaves shine as though they were wet, a dazzling bright blue ocean, *the* day for planting the perennials Nancy and I bought last week. So I was terribly frustrated when the worst attack of diverticulitis I have suffered lately took over and I spent the day in acute pain lying on my bed. At such times Pierrot, who turns over on his back to be caressed, is a great comfort. His big flossy paws never put claws out and his soft tummy is a pleasure to stroke.

Diverticulitis is a fairly common complaint, and there appears to be little one can do for it. With me it always is the result of fatigue and tension—on Tuesday because I had had an unexpected guest that afternoon when I was already overtired, for Nancy and I had used rainy Monday to go and get birdseed.

Yesterday I was still tired and queasy so got nothing much done, but now it is Thursday, the week almost gone, and I am ready to resume life. Nancy put in about half the perennials for me—such a boon, as I woke wondering whether I could ask her to do it. Then she reminded me that the perennials had been a birthday present that included planting them.

Last night I finished an extraordinary book, *The Road from Coorain*, by Jill Ker Conway, who was president of Smith for ten years. This is the story of her childhood, helping to run a sheep farm in Australia. Not many college presidents begin life herding thousands of sheep! For the first time I begin to understand the pull that immense treeless land has on its inhabitants, as late in the book she describes her first visit to England and her disappointment with its damp, enclosed world and how she missed the empty dry desert. In a small way I experienced the same thing when I came home from Santa Fe and drove across the country. When I came to Ohio and then New England I felt suddenly imprisoned by all the green and cared-for lawns and gardens and missed the light and the space of the Southwest. Towns began to be only a few miles apart, and soon I was arrested for speeding!

It is light now when I let Pierrot out at four, and when I am back in bed I luxuriate in the two hours I still have before I have to get up. Lately a single bird has carried on a brisk loud monologue for about an hour and kept me awake. It is not a song. It is simply "chirp, chirp, chirp," loud and flat. It is nerve-racking. Sometimes the wood pigeons repeat themselves endlessly as one is doing at this very moment, and it has the same effect on a listener. "Do be quiet, friend," I want to say.

Friday, June 15

YESTERDAY TURNED into a wonderful and even productive day for a change. It was still bright sunshine and a stiff ocean breeze to keep mosquitoes away, and after an elegant lunch with Mary-Leigh Smart and Beverly Hallam, and a short rest,

I pulled on old jeans and went out and planted the columbine Nancy and I bought last week. As always when one begins a gardening job, a hundred others spring up. Peonies needed staking, as they are about to bloom, and some of the bleeding heart has grown very high and needed straightening. Worst of all, very tall tough grass has about taken over the perennial border. The triumph was that in an hour I did manage to get the essentials done and discovered that if I pull the tall grass out stem by stem it comes out very easily—whereas when, one day lately, I tried to dig it out I hadn't the strength to do it. The hazard was falling, as I had to go into the center of the garden on very uneven ground and lost my balance several times, but I did manage to stay on my feet.

I was out working for just over an hour, but when I came in at five I was too exhausted even to change and just lay down for a half hour. But it was good to be tired after gardening for the first time in months!

Earlier in the morning I wrote a few thank-you notes that have been on my mind—notes of thanks for birthday presents. And I wrote one letter I really wanted to write, to answer a good one from Joan Palevsky in Los Angeles.

Today there is fog and I am "under the weather," and only want to go back to bed and sleep, which I may do for an hour before I get the mail. Thank goodness there is no one for lunch and I can mosey along at my own snail-like pace. Peace, it's wonderful!

Monday, June 18

Two REAL EVENTS lately have made me see what a doldrum I
am in. The first on Saturday was the gathering of Lotte
Jacobi's friends to celebrate her. Karen K. kindly drove me
there—good to have someone to leave me at the door with my
cane and then find a parking space. I could have driven myself
but could not have walked from the car to the arts building
even with my cane. Bea Hunter welcomed the guests and
asked each one of us to sign the book. Several people came up
to speak to me, including, to my great joy, Marilyn Shiffrin,
the composer, with whom Kay Martin shared a house for
many years. Marilyn, her hair white, looked stunning, but the
white hair did give me a start.

The walls were hung with Lotte's photos, many of them
well-known, as they have appeared in the book about her.
What I looked forward to greatly was the showing of a short
videotape made in her last years at the studio in Hillsboro,
where we had so many good talks in the kitchen while she
made coffee and where she had spread out cheese and bread
and nuts.

It was bad luck and poor organization that there were far
too few chairs for the video and the fifty or so people who
could not see it went on talking in the background so loudly
that we who were watching heard absolutely nothing. Still, it
was moving to see Lotte's tiny figure and think of the daring
adventures she took on at Hillsboro, including keeping bees.
Also one could see her beautiful and expressive hands as she

talked, sitting on a bench in the garden. I felt myself vividly there in the past and Lotte so vivid in my consciousness that it seemed as though I had been with her for a good talk.

The second event was a phone call from Carolyn Heilbrun. She and Jim were just back from a trip to Scandinavia and Paris. She always succeeds in making me laugh at myself and, in the kindliest possible way, gives me renewed courage. Without Carol, would I have managed to sustain this curious life? She has been able to help keep the compass set accurately.

Tuesday, June 19

IT WAS EXCITING yesterday morning in the fog to know that Frances Minturn Howard, the poet and my old friend, would be coming for lunch bearing crabmeat sandwiches, driven here by a friend of hers from Boston. It made me realize that I very seldom meet anyone these days who is my equal. That sounds snobbish as I write it, but why not be honest? The reason I miss my parents so much these days is partly the lack now of any conversation resembling theirs in depth and width. I am always eager for news of lives that have touched mine in some way and I listen to the tales about what has been happening, but it mostly leaves my imagination untouched, half asleep. Susan Sherman is one exception, because she lived in France so much as a young woman, and I have to confess also because she now knows more about me than I do about myself, since she has been immersed in the Sarton archive at the Berg for four years and will remind me on a postal card that she and I met just seven years ago (can it be that long ago?) and that I first met Virginia Woolf on June 14, 1937. She keeps a running commentary going on the past, much of which I have forgotten, so it is full of surprises, often joyful.

What a moment when, right on time, a car drove up and there were Frances and her friend Jeanne MacMillan. It seemed preposterously fortunate to welcome such dear people who had never seen the place, and soon we were settled in the library drinking a bottle of Mumm's champagne that Beverly Hallam had given me for my birthday. Frances is recently widowed and had sent me poignant poems from this time in her life, wonderful poems which I envy, for, a good deal older than I am, she still writes poems. We talked some about how we manage housekeeping now we are old. Frances was a great cook, Jeanne told me. The conversation rippled along, no plunging deeply, which is next to impossible, I find, with three people, but with true enjoyment and much laughter.

Jeanne had never seen tree peonies and was dazzled by the two I had picked, one immense single white one, the one I think of as a god, and one double yellow with petals edged in pink. It looks like a huge powder puff and is interesting but not, to my eyes, beautiful and arresting, as the grand white one is.

Saturday, June 21

This is the fourth cold, drizzly, miserable day. Having had no spring we are now, it would seem, to be deprived of summer. But yesterday anyway was lit up by my yearly reunion with Christopher De Vinck, the young poet Fred Rogers chose to be with me on *Mr. Rogers' Neighborhood*. He and I have a lot in common besides being poets. One thing is that his background is Belgian and when I talk about my parents and the kind of talk we shared at teatime, he recognizes it at once. He had a retarded brother, and his first book was the moving recounting of what that caretaking did for him and the family. He writes a series of essays about family life and life in general, and these will be a book. His great news is that he has an agent. Curiously enough, he is only the third writing friend of mine to have an agent, in all three cases one promising a large advance. Such great news after all the struggles to be *heard*.

Chris teaches in a public high school, four classes a day, and thus supports his family. He and his wife have three children, a boy ten and two younger daughters. I have been aware of how hard a balance it must be to support this beloved family and still be the poet and writer who needs more time than he can wrest out of the days. So maybe the newfound agent can help provide the answer. I never made enough money to live on from writing alone until I was sixty-five. Teaching and poetry readings helped. It is ironic that now I earn substantial royalties but cannot use the blessed time that gives me because I am not well.

Sunday, June 22

WHEN I WOKE UP to the fifth wet foggy day, I wanted to stay in bed and not make the effort to cope. I am demoralized by living what is on the surface a good life. I have seen good old friends this week and written a page of this journal a day. But under the surface it is not a good life, but a singularly dull and depressed one in which simply doing the daily chores is all I can manage. I am living, I sense, against the stream, against the tide of life itself. I don't know how to wake up and get going, because when I try it ends in exhaustion and having to accept that there is very little I can get out of such nonbeing.

Yet I am constantly made aware of what a spoiled person I am. For instance, on *The Today Show* this morning there was a poignant segment on three middle-aged women who have had to become full-time caretakers of their mothers—one had brought up ten children and had looked forward to some time of her own. And here I am wading around in oceans of time and wasting it! I should be struck by lightning.

The only saving moments lately have been the appearances of Nelson Mandela as he takes on a wildly exhausting schedule and manages to stay the same quiet, open presence devoured by multitudes of eyes. At the Cathedral of St. John the Divine yesterday there was a wonderful moment after the service when the whole audience joined in an African dance of triumph and suddenly Mandela's face lit up in a delighted smile as he joined in, and he looked released from all the stress and the demands. He has come into power after twenty-seven years deprived of it, and perhaps that has kept him so untrammeled, so pure, has made him, as one of his introducers said at the cathedral, "the morning star." He is not smirched by the cloud of political strife, not worn down by pressures and demands from opposing political segments. But for how long can this innocence be maintained? Even as tears came to my eyes as I watched, I had to wonder.

Saturday, June 23

IF SOMEONE FOUND their way here, as has only happened once since I moved in seventeen years ago, and said they were looking for May Sarton my answer would have to be "She did live here but she is not here now." People read the books and imagine I am the person who wrote them, sometimes as long as seventeen years ago *(Journal of a Solitude)*. My values have not changed and my way of life has changed very little, yet I am no longer the person who wrote those books. Truly that person does not live here in the present. So every day I disappoint someone I cannot answer, and disappoint myself. Reason enough, it occurs to me, to be depressed.

Monday, June 25

I SPENT most of Saturday afternoon watching the Mandela celebrations in Boston—twenty-five thousand waited hours on the Esplanade and no one else in the world perhaps could draw that many. It is a pity in many ways that in Boston, at least, it became a day of triumph for blacks. At last they have a true hero, but Mandela transcends race, and his extraordinary presence with so much stillness in it brings hope to all of

us, of all races and all ages. But nothing brought the tears to
my eyes as did the short walk he and Winnie made from the
prison to the waiting car when he was released—an unforgettable moment of intimacy and pure joy and love.

It's the first morning in days when I have woken to a clear
sky, no fog and drizzle, and a blue sea. I did a laundry to
celebrate, but unfortunately that extra effort always seems to
cost extreme fatigue, so I must now go and lie down.

I do feel a lot better than I did even a month ago. That
means that I am becoming again a person one can lean on,
and the mail brings needs, so many people distressed and/or
ill who turn to me with the idea that I am a friend.

Tuesday, June 26

THE SECOND DAY of sun and waking to a clear sky—wonderful.
I am savoring now the coming into their own of shrubs and
perennials I planted ten or more years ago. A gardener lives
in the future as much as in the present. The rugosa has been a
huge mound of elegant pink roses for two weeks, alive with
bees, such a triumphant sight. Rugosas love this climate, survive bitter cold, and are firm under wind and rain, but just
when this one was in its glory we had two deluges of heavy
rain and that pristine glory was blotted. Deer ate four or five
lilies, breaking off the stiff stems at about three feet from the
ground and eating the buds—they are fearless this year.

But the tree peonies survived icy December, and those in
front of the house have done well—such a joy! I planted eight
tiny tree peonies ten years ago. Five have survived and grow
stronger and more treelike each year.

The lilac, given as a small twig by the Arnold Arboretum, has grown to be twenty feet tall in less than five years. It flowers a week or two after the Persian lilacs and amazes by the speed of its growing. I really must subscribe again to the Arboretum, as they send you a sample like this every year. Fothergill, a bush with brilliant autumn color, came to me from them and has flourished—a bit of magic. The name alone makes me smile and even laugh.

A more recent acquisition is the white bleeding heart, which last longer than the classic pink-and-white one and has been glorious this spring. In fact it has not stopped flowering yet. Iris has done surprisingly well although the iris bed is simply a field of grass at the moment. Diane is here weeding today, so things are looking up, and yesterday Chris Cote came at last to take off the storm windows.

Wednesday, June 27

LAST NIGHT, lying awake for hours as Pierrot refused to come in till half-past one, I kept thinking of more shrubs and plants I had planted which now rejoice my heart. I forgot the de Rothschild azaleas. There is one very tall one against a spruce, a waterfall of yellow flowers this week, and across the lawn from it a tall white one that has a sweet pungent scent that reaches me in a wave when I walk past. A more recent acquisition is a kousa, the Chinese dogwood, which will flower as far north as here. Although in shade and shaping itself perpendicularly it is doing very well and is now covered with flowers. The little plum tree I planted behind the house flowers early and makes a cloud of white when there is nothing else in flower. The two forsythias I planted nearby on that same slope, too shady for most things, are growing fast and look right, unlike the one along the fence, which is shaped rigorously and hardly flowers at all. That is why I ordered two others which can be free, and this year they looked splendid.

But all these days have been devoted to Mandela. Yesterday by great good luck Alysan Hooper arrived for lunch just as he was addressing Congress, and she was glad to listen to it all, and I was happy for once to have a friend to share such an experience with.

The strength, the actual power, one feels while watching and listening to this man are amazing. Not since Martin Luther King. King was a great orator, of course. But Mandela, so unchangeably himself, so crucially honest even about not being willing to give up the possibility of violence against apartheid as long as it continues to use violence against the blacks, is most moving. He is adamant on what he will not yield.

But it becomes clearer with every national television program, such as Jennings and Rather last night, that the media are deliberately playing down Mandela. We had been told that many members of Congress were not enthusiastic about his speaking to them. It is only the third time a civilian who was not a head of government has addressed them, but not once was this fact mentioned last night. Far more important, several times the packed house rose to its feet. Applause was continual and sustained, interrupting Mandela many times. Nothing was told of this. The general drift was to emphasize his demand for an end to apartheid, but not once did either newscaster allude to the extraordinary power of this man. It

makes me uncomfortable and angry, because this kind of obfuscation has happened before. I realize more and more that I
am being led to believe what "they" want me to believe. It's a
dirty business, as usual.

Thursday, June 28

IT CAME TO ME last night as I lay awake with severe intestinal
pain, caused no doubt by a ragged, interrupted day yesterday,
that the emphasis lately on Mandela insisting that the NFA
will have to use violence if the government's violence against
them through apartheid does not diminish, has been a partial
and not historically accurate comparison with Martin Luther
King's brilliant victory through nonviolence during the civil
rights struggle. It was the Civil War in 1860 that freed the
slaves and gave blacks some entry into our society as human
beings who could vote. The Civil War, the worst war ever at
that time, was brutally violent and opened wounds that have
never healed. Coming one hundred years later, Martin Luther King could stand on some laws at least. And he proved
that nonviolence could succeed, but it could not have succeeded in freeing the slaves in the 1860s. And that is where
South Africa now stands, embedded in an adamant stand by
the whites against any compromise. There is nothing but tragedy ahead, but it is part of Mandela's quiet strength that he
will not pretend that a new democratic nonracist state can be
built in South Africa without terrifying struggle. I have not
cried for months, but Mandela has made me cry tears of
something like joy, the recognition of such purity and power

and hope. He hopes so fervently that I find myself hoping again, believing again, that goodness and mercy can prevail.

Another fine June day, the third in a row. I had planned on this one day, with no visitors expected, to go to the vegetable place in Kittery and pick up some fruit and vegetables, especially fresh artichokes. I never liked them very much, but now when there is very little I wish to eat I am enamored of the slow progress through an artichoke! Eating is hard for me still, and more often than not I settle for dry cereal for supper. I do not feel well, but Eleanor Perkins is here cleaning and it looks like the thing to do, so for the first time in months, off I go, shopping outside the York IGA.

Friday, June 29

IT WAS a wild-goose chase for artichokes, but I did find them in Portsmouth at my old haunt, the A&P. The best find was three tuberous begonias in splendid flower with thick healthy stems at the Golden Harvest—worth the whole trip. I used always to grow tuberous begonias under lights in the cellar, twelve or more. That meant going down cellar to water them every few days from March till June, and when I did not have the strength to bring them in last autumn I had about decided to give them up. These fat fellows have led me into trying again—and in a far easier way than before.

I got into ancient battered sneakers and work pants before my rest to be sure I would go out and get them safely planted. My heart was so light and carefree suddenly as I imagined I would have the strength this time and turn over a summer leaf. But people are coming to lunch today, and I felt I must first rearrange the flowers, and then, walking across the lawn to a massive white peony all in flower, I felt so shaky I thought I might fall. On such occasions it is a comfort to put on the Lifeline so if I did fall I could get help. But after the flowers were done and I had trimmed the artichokes and put them to soak in salt water, I was feeling very ill with cramps and had to give up any idea of gardening. There I was in my old sneakers crying with frustration.

All is not lost. Nancy had offered to plant the begonias for me when she helped me unload the car yesterday. She will do it later this morning—what a blessing! But I am still feeling frail and ill and must now go and lie down for a half hour. Rosemary Rawcliffe, who is hoping to make a film of *A Reckoning*, is coming for lunch with Honor Moore, a poet I did not know till now but whose book I have enjoyed these last weeks. I dread meeting a new person, but at least there is sun and a blue sea to make a welcome. On such occasions I miss Tamas terribly.

Monday, July 2

I HAVE BEEN to Captain Simeon's almost every day for lunch. Inviting a friend gives me some sense of having a life, that I am not entirely useless. In going over the June encounters I find more people than I would have guessed connected with writing or with my own life as a writer. On the 2nd, Julie and Stephen Robitaille were here from Gainesville, Florida, where I took part in a short series on creativity and old age. Dick Eberhart was to have read but was not well enough, so I

never even saw him. Too bad, as we have been friends for so
many years and he is such a generous man and poet. I loved
having Julie and Stephen here, as I had fallen in love with
their old log house in Gainesville. On the 16th was the memo-
rial gathering in memory of Lotte Jacobi. Earlier that week I
had lunch with Mary-Leigh and Beverly to hear about Beverly's triumphant show and tour in Indiana. We meet rarely
but I always enjoy those rare meetings very much.

Thursday, July 5

WE HAVE HAD so much cold weather that it was staggering to
live through a July Fourth when the temperature went over
ninety and was eighty when I got up at six. I am watering for
the first time this summer, and when I set the hoses in the
annual bed late yesterday afternoon and watched the foun-
tain spring up and shed its welcome freight, I thought, as I so
often have before, that watering a thirsty plant is one of the
greatest joys life has to offer, surpassed only, no doubt, by
feeding a starving baby.

Maggie Vaughan celebrated the Fourth by bringing a delicious lunch of cold salmon (how good it was) with a dill and
mayonnaise dressing, tiny lettuce leaves from her garden, and
fresh peas, plus a nameless dessert with tiny cakes and a deep
purple sauce. It was a lovely intimate day of good talk and no
hurry, but it was over ninety when I went up to lie down—an
altogether spoiled old woman, as Maggie insisted on washing
up and making order in the chaos of the kitchen. Today is a
fraction cooler and more bearable, and we are promised
cooler, drier air by afternoon.

Later that evening Fred Rogers called me to hear how Chris and I had fared, and that set a seal on the day. With all he has to do and be for millions of people, Fred manages the human and intimate with such grace. He has been like a spiritual father for Chris and a constant, loving support to an old lady in Oregon who attached herself to him years ago. This is a bond I share to some extent with Fred, the remorseless pull of the admirers and friends whom one does not know, but who need caring and attention.

The end of the week was strangely a mixture of people working on filming one book or another of mine. Martha Wheelock is on the way to making *As We Are Now* into an hour-long television play and has a producer to go in with her. She and her friend Kay Weaver came Monday. On Thursday, Rosemary Rawcliffe and Honor Moore came to take me out to lunch. At noon on Monday, Doris Grumbach and Sybil Pike came in the afternoon, so I could catch up with their adventure of moving to Sargentville, Maine, and opening Sybil's bookstore there. I had seen now and then how exhausted Sybil had been by keeping her job at the Library of Congress going as well as the bookstore. Now at last she is free to enjoy what she loves best. It is a fairly sumptuous life, as they will be back in Washington, where they have a small apartment, for the winter months, a little city life, concerts, opera, which Doris loves, in contrast with rural Sargentville and the canoe our dismal spring and summer have not yet permitted them to use.

I can't complain of loneliness these days.

Friday, July 6

YESTERDAY IN MY summing-up of a full week I forgot to mention Ellen LeConte. She is a new friend and has been very attentive these past months of depression and illness. Recently she let me see two short stories, carved out of her first novel, for which she now has an agent who is enthusiastic about a very "literary" writer, and that is rare. Ellen's style is charming and exact. I found myself laughing sometimes at the precise charm of a descriptive phrase. She is best at that sort of thing, but has not yet, I think, come to grips with the short story as a form—"punch and poetry" was O'Faoláin's description, as I remember it. Ellen is very good at the poetry, less good at the punch. For the punch has to do with situation, with putting convincing characters in a situation where something is going to happen, if only a change of mind.

Thinking about this took me back to Breadloaf (where, curiously enough, Ellen goes to the writers' conference in August). I taught short story in that horrendously competitive conference, and one year, the novel, when I was expected to read and criticize six novels! Ellen says the students are now required to show only forty pages. I found it a painfully chauvinistic atmosphere which became impossible for me when John Ciardi followed Ted Morrison as director. I thought the other night with some satisfaction that I have no enemies (the reward for being in no position of power), but John Ciardi was, I believe, an enemy—an enemy who did me harm in both obvious ways (a cruel review of my poems in the *New*

Republic) and more subtle ways, as I am convinced he managed to keep me out of being elected to the Academy of Arts and Letters. The worst came in his essay as foreword to a book on writing poetry in which he simply denied my existence altogether, although for one winter in Cambridge we met four or five times with Richard Wilbur, Richard Eberhart, and John Holmes! I was not there!

Tuesday, July 10

FOR THE PAST four days, no journal. I have again been ill with bad intestinal pain, lying around waiting for it to pass. It did not help that suddenly we had twenty-four hours of humid heat. Last night I could not sleep at all. Fan, no fan, nothing worked. But this morning the air is clear—what a difference! I even walked down to the annual bed and picked two sprays of delphinium, and from the terrace perennial border two magnificent Japanese iris of a dark blue-purple. The deep and light blue of the delphinium spires against the flat Japanese iris makes a spectular bunch. Yesterday I would not have had the strength to walk and pick flowers. So I am better but still rather shaky, with no marrow in my bones. I talked to Dr. Petrovich about how frail I am these days when I saw him on Friday, so he has asked for some blood tests to see if there is need for a booster.

I had a good talk on the telephone with Tim Seldes about Susan's plans to work at two books stemming from the four years' reading she has done at the Berg with my archive there. These books will use my letters. She plans one which

will be a biography in letters, since I wrote my parents twice a
week after I went to New York to join Eva Le Gallienne's
Civic Repertory as an apprentice, and wrote twice a week
through the next twenty years or more until they died. Tim
will negotiate with Eric as to how this can be financed, and I
am suddenly happy to think that two interesting books will
still come out before I die. Long ago I determined that no
biography should be written till after my death, but these
Susan-books would be possible. There will be no "interpreta-
tion," which is what I fear, only connecting material to join
the pieces together.

When I began this journal I felt finished. The past
usurped the present and there appeared to be no future. But
lately I have been slowly re-creating a person, the person I am
now, and so begin to live again.

Monday, July 23

ALMOST TWO WEEKS of exhaustion and misery during the heat
wave. I decided I must see a specialist and try once more to
get some help. I did finally see Dr. Flavin, highly recommended, whom I have seen before as a consultant with Dr.
Gilroy, and like very much. I went with a brief summary of
the hell I have been in for a year, what medicines I am taking,
etc. Dr. Flavin did not examine me and asked no questions.
He simply prescribed amitriptyline, which I did not recognize
until I had had the prescription filled. Then I realized that this
is the drug that makes me feel like a drunken sailor, blotto for
days. It affects my head and I stagger around. I have left a

message for Dr. Flavin to call me back, but in the last few days
I have come to see and to believe that there is no medicine
that can help, that I simply must learn to live with it and
forget about imagining that some doctor might find a solution.
Hundreds of people have my problem. One remembers hearing of the agonies of Harry Hopkins when he worked with
FDR on the New Deal.

It has been hard to give up even writing this page-a-day of
journal, so I hope I can get back to it, and that this morning,
humid, foggy and hot, will mark a new beginning. At least I
have been seeing for lunch a person every day—and for those
two hours life is worth living. It was a great joy to have Ted
Adams drop in to take me to lunch. He was driven by a former
Yale classmate who has returned to upstate New York to end
his days in his grandfather's house, after living in Paris for
thirty-five years!

Ted, who has had open-heart surgery and various other
operations, and is home after ten weeks at the New York
Psychiatric Hospital, was far from depressed or sorry for himself. He bubbles with energy and love of life, full of laughter
and amusing gossip, and his unfailing joyful appreciation of
his many friends. We have not been in touch for years. Ted
was business manager of my Apprentice Theatre when he
was just out of Yale, and I paid him fifteen dollars a week. He
loved the whole experience.

What is it that makes Ted so lovable and life-enhancing? I
think it may be because he is filled with love and curiosity
about people of all kinds and with an interest that spills over
into all sorts of stories *and* that he is not ambitious for himself,
not in the way so many of his theater and musical friends were
bound to be. He asks for nothing except to be accepted as
himself. That in itself is rare.

Thursday, July 26

AGAIN DAYS GO BY and I don't write even a paragraph. We are
living in a strange tropical forest atmosphere of continual rain,
thunderstorms, and relentless damp heat. It saps what little
energy I can muster simply to keep going. Today for the first
time in two weeks I woke to what looked for a half hour like
clear sky with a dash of sun thrown in just after sunrise, but by
seven it had clouded over, of course, and here we are again in
our tropical limbo. When I went out with the bird feeder I
saw that a tall, rosy lily with seven flowers on its stem had
been beaten down by the rain, so I put on rubber shoes and
went out to rescue it. That gave me courage to pick a few
daylilies from the back of the house, and suddenly in all the
blank space where there have been no flowers because of the
heat a few pale yellow lilies make the house alive again and
"lived in" as it has not been for days.

I am amazed at the difference they make, for I have felt
that it was simply too hot for flowers. Partly, of course, I do
not have the energy to go out and pick. Down in the annual
bed there are flowers, I imagine, but up here in the big perennial border below the terrace the phlox, which is just opening,
has been torn and battered. There is one new glory I can be
happy about, and that is the blue hydrangea from Winterthur.
The remarkable thing about it is that the flower is flat, not a
huge pompadour, and so, elegant. Then it is the most extraordinary brilliant blue, rarely seen in any flower. I asked Huldah to give it to me to remember our wonderful week on the

island of Sark, where there are blue hydrangeas everywhere
against the whitewashed stone cottages. When I am trying to
get to sleep and remember landscapes I often go back to Sark,
the magic island where I went first alone, after dreaming of
doing so for years. It is only three miles long, and all of it high
up in the air, buttressed by tall cliffs. No cars allowed. You
walk everywhere and picnic in fields of primroses and bluebells.

Sunday, July 29

IN SPITE of the downpours and the constant muggy heat I have
seen a lot of people lately, and as a result achieved almost
nothing at this disorderly desk, but life after all does come first
now, before the very little "art" that exists in my impover-
ished life. It is always a special day in the year when my friend
Phil Palmer, a Methodist minister, comes for a good long talk
and we catch up on the world and on ourselves. Phil, rare
among ministers, is outspoken in his defense of the homosexual. Unlike so many others he is never belligerent but simply
states the case in such a benign and loving way he would be
hard to withstand. It is the more touching that he was born in
rural Maine, had no immediate contact with a homosexual
group, but has simply been motivated by intelligent compassion. He too has recovered from serious illness, a heart attack
two years ago, that forced him to retire from the job he held,
which had been his dream for years. Such a hard bit of bad
luck that it was snatched from him so soon after his appointment.

He spoke of the danger that illness may make one turn inward at too great an expense of care for others. I took this idea to heart, but what he does not know, of course, is how many letters I do still write, because although I have changed and am often at a loss for energy, my books still inspire people to trust me as a friend. They haven't changed, so the letters are written to a person who no longer exists and put me in the dilemma of how to answer. But hardly a day passes without some irresistible demand which I do answer willy-nilly. For example, I am asked to write a letter to a dying woman whom I met briefly years ago. I did write that letter this past week after two or three sleepless nights.

After Phil, Angela Elliott came for lunch and we had a fine time. I was carried along by her exuberant happiness that the connection has at last been made, for I had to put her off earlier on. I had been terrified that I would not feel well enough this week, but all went well, and ever since I have enjoyed five marvelous huge blue scabiosa Angela brought me.

The next day was a real celebration with Peter Pease, a young lawyer who dropped into my life a year or so ago, and simply delights me with his passionate nature, romantic and analytic at the same time (so like my own). He brought me a delightful small carved bear made by the Zuni Indians—a bear with bright turquoise eyes. And he, Peter not the bear, hugged me and sparkled happily at me all through lunch. A treasure of a day which I shall unravel in memory and knit up again when I cannot sleep. That time I spent in New Mexico remains a touchstone. How rich and haunting it is in my memory. I met Judy there—it happened we were each paying guests at Edith Ricketson's along the Acequia Madre.

Last night I had dinner with Frances Whitney and Royce Roth, who are spending their yearly two weeks at Dockside.

Friday, August 3

MOTHER'S BIRTHDAY and a perfect summer day, so a hose is on
in the picking garden, which is now yielding wonderful nasturtiums. They have to be picked in clouds of small, vicious
mosquitoes, but worth the bites for the delicious smell when I
bring home a small bunch after only a few minutes under fire.
Both my parents, lovers of the sea, lovers of silence, would
have been entranced by Wild Knoll.

There has been a long gap in this journal because I have
again been too ill to climb up to my study. But this time I get
the sense that the doctors are trying to get me well, and dear
generous Janice Oberacker took a whole day out of her grueling job as president of the Portland Community Health Ser-
vices Group to come here and help me. Dr. Gilroy had to put
off a three-o'clock appointment to six-thirty at the hospital, so
it was a long day. Janice was an angel about it. I may have a
low-grade infection which was causing the queasiness and
nausea I imagined was due to the new drug Dr. Flavin is
trying. I'm allowed a rest from the drug until Monday and
then must try it again. Let us hope!

Susan Sherman is the only friend who could do what she
did for me to celebrate Mother's birthday, a small collection
of quotes from letters, read early this morning in the brilliant,
peaceful morning light, read with tears of joy to find my
mother so triumphantly herself and given to me this morning.
Here is one small excerpt from a letter where she speaks of
Dos Passos, not uncritically: "Heavens what a boon to have

wanted something in life, however humble, and to have found a way of trying to do that thing even *unsuccessfully*—to have kept on wanting what one lives for—right inside in the core of one's life is the one thing that matters—there in that core where one is strictly alone and not a soul can enter nor help nor deter."

It spoke to me freshly, as now in these pathetically dimmed days the "one thing" for me is to manage a page a day of this journal, and when I am unable to write that page I slide back into a sense of uselessness. It is here and now, of course, that the letters to me from readers have become life-restoring in a way they never have been until now. When I was well, to answer them took strength from me, but now that I am ill and cannot answer they give me small shots of courage. They keep me going on these last laps of the long-distance runner.

Saturday, August 4

WE ARE HAVING a real heat wave. It was seventy at eight this morning and poor Pierrot got locked in the garage so I called at eleven and at two in the morning in vain. He was happy to be released at five this morning and I went happily back to bed for two hours.

An exquisite bunch of pale pink roses was delivered yesterday by Foster's. The card sent me love and the name of a stranger in Danville, Virginia. Lovely to have these dewy fresh flowers on Mother's birthday.

After that, I began to ruminate on ordering bulbs. It is

high time, because I order direct from a Dutch firm and they are after me to get going. I have something of a block about bulbs this year. As always the very few tulips I planted were eaten underground by mice or chipmunks, or later, when they were three feet tall and full of buds, by deer. It is hard to have deer enter the picture. They do not eat iris, thank goodness, but daylilies yes, and now marvelous Asian and other true lilies. Luckily they have not been tempted by the giant allium I have planted lately in the front border.

When I watered yesterday I was confronted like a slap in the face by hosts of Japanese beetles eating the climbing white hydrangea that covers a part of the terrace wall. It's the weekend, so there is no one to help me place the beetle traps that are ready to hang. How frustrating that is.

Now I must go out and fetch the mail and do a few errands before the heat takes over. But this is real summer weather, and I have only to remember the bitter cold of December to be glad of the sun, and, last night, an almost full moon.

After bulbs, then Connie Hunting's poems. I have promised to write a word about them. What a joy to be asked to do so for such a fine and original poet!

August 10

THIS IS AN experiment to see whether I can manage a simple Sony recorder and in this way do the equivalent of a written journal, since I have so little ability now to write. We'll see what happens.

One of the strange things my state of extreme weakness

has created is to tear away any protective wall between me and suffering in the world. This is neurotic, because what I do over and over again in the night is to be overwhelmed by vivid images of the Holocaust. Or recently, what I've just seen on television: the starving children in the Sudan. Forty-five thousand a day die of hunger. Or, nearer home, images of parents who have abused a child. All this I live with in the night, knowing that I can do nothing, knowing that it's neurotic to waste the energy when it could be used for something positive instead of for something negative. It's a real problem, not something I'm making up. I think it has to do with the incapacity to use what little energy I have for something positive.

The household—it's ridiculous to say so, because I do so little—eats up energy. For instance, taking down the bird feeder, although it's wonderful to go out and see the dusk when I put it in the garage. Then it's wonderful to bring it back in the early-morning light at half-past six or seven when the grass shines under the rising sun and everything is new-born.

Harwich, Massachusetts

Saturday, August 18

I'M NOW AT Rene Morgan's, which is a wonderful haven. I've known Rene now, I think, for fifty years. She will be eighty in January, and we've become what I might call root-friends. There are flowering friends, and every year one or two come into my life, but there are not as many root-friends. A root-friend goes back a long way and therefore a great many things never have to be explained because they are already known.

I do think keeping a journal, even if it has to be spoken instead of written, is good medicine. It makes me sort out what's important in my life now. Speaking of friends, certainly they are enormously important. Without them, I probably would have suffered some kind of breakdown.

It's marvelous here, where Rene helps to draw my bath, makes my breakfast—oh, what heaven!—and is there, to put it in its most simple terms, to manage. In York there's no one right there to manage—that moment when suddenly it seems impossible to open a package and you can say to somebody, "Come and help me." I can do this rarely in York. But of course, living alone in York has its advantages. It keeps me independent. If I didn't have to go out and fill the feeder I might just sit in the chaise longue with my feet up and never do anything again.

Deborah Pease, that good friend, has managed to break the spell which made me feel that I would *never* be able to use a small recorder like this and that it would just get in the way of my being able to say anything for a journal—for a prospective journal. She sent me a recorder and cassettes to make the experiment and offered to transcribe whatever I do while Nancy is away. What an adventure—a door opening to work again. It is proving to be much easier than I thought, though I realize more and more that I must think ahead, plan what I want to say.

Today is muggy, and last night was really hell because there isn't a draft in this room. Even with the little fan on I couldn't breathe, so I did not get to sleep until after seven. Meanwhile, I was reading Peter Matthiessen's *Killing Mister Watson*, a historical novel about the Everglades in the eighteenth century—and into the nineteenth, I suppose—when it was the province of various entrepreneurs and crooks. It's wonderfully well-written but somehow it isn't the book I need at this moment.

I also brought John Updike's autobiographical essays, and I find them, much to my astonishment, quite dull. I think he wasn't in the mood, perhaps, to do what he thought he was going to do, which was to replace the biography that some-body wanted to write with an autobiography which would be unlike most autobiographies—chiefly long essays. Well, we'll see. I've only read one so far. It gave me a rather mean plea-sure, because I felt that what I've written in books like *Plant Dreaming Deep* is a good deal more interesting!

I find that I wake up every morning depressed. Here it's wonderful to know that Rene is there to get my breakfast, that there's somebody to help me with a button I can't manage to get buttoned. At these times the presence of someone I care about and who cares about me is infinitely precious. I'm en-joying every moment of it. Except, alas, that I'm homesick for Pierrot and also a little worried about him. Susan reports that he did come in yesterday and she fed him. He ate a lot, she said. Then she brushed him all over and he purred. So at least he has been in the house once since I left. But of course dear Susan has her little dog with her—this angelic little tiny fluffy poodle who couldn't be sweeter. But the fact is that for the cat a stranger has come to stay, and he's jolly well going to keep his distance. Well, it will only be a few days. Nancy is coming tomorrow to catch him again and feed him, as Susan has to go to Connecticut to hear her father give a speech.

It astounds me when I realize how many of my friends still have living parents, because for me it has been forty years since my mother died. I've been without parents for a very long time, and it seems extraordinary for Susan to be able to go to hear her father speak. But then one also has to remember that family life is not only love and safety. When I think back to the families I knew fairly intimately as a child—the Limbosches, the Greenes, the Hockings—I have to remember that a child in one of these families had to endure tension and quite a lot of unhappiness.

Still, I'm lonely for that feeling of belonging, and it's really that, isn't it? It is that as a member of a family one belongs. And there are very many people around us now who don't have that possibility. Few people now live in houses where they have lived for more than a few years—houses which therefore seem home to the children brought up in them. A lot of us are looking all the time for family—for what can be family—and what I suggested about root-friends is, of course, that they are family. They are those who can be counted on in times of trouble and perhaps even more important rejoice with us in times of triumph or success.

I did think some years ago that it was sad there was really nobody to whom I could send a new book with the feeling that it would be a family event—that no one would read me as my mother did ever again. But I have to remember that there are a great many people who do read me—who read me with devotion, pay attention, and feel comforted and sustained by what I've written. So when I am depressed, as I am this morning, it is good to think of that, to remember that.

Depression comes from impotence. It's irritating not to be able to walk a straight line, but to fumble, as I walk, to stumble is what I mean, to almost fall so often, and to feel extremely tired and begin to pant if I walk even twenty yards. It's a strange transformation of a person who used to be quick and volatile and who has now had to become slow and careful—careful not even to feel too much because then I start to cough and feel dizzy.

Sunday, August 19

IT'S BEEN NEARLY four days of this wonderful transplanting into Rene's world, where I have no responsibilities—where I simply breathe in and out. The peaceful wind in the trees—the beautiful Japanese pines, of which Rene has two, remarkably outlined, formed, if you will, against the sky. It is exactly what I knew it would be, what I dreamed it would be—this perfect peace. I'm reading a little, I rest a great deal. I look forward to delicious little meals created by Rene—last night, a wonderful shrimp salad. Today we may go for a drive, as I stayed home all day yesterday with an attack of cramps.

John Updike's second essay in the book I am reading, *Self-Consciousness*, speaks of his psoriasis. It interested me, for Judy had psoriasis but never mentioned it. We had been living together for several years before I knew it.

I've been thinking so much of our life—Judy's and mine—in Cambridge, those fifteen years, the last five or so at 14 Wright Street. It was a simple old house—one hundred years old—that had been a harness factory, so Judy called it Harness House. I was in Europe when we were turned out of a rented house on Maynard Place and she found this house and bought it. The wonderful thing was that the minute she described it and where it was I remembered it distinctly and remembered thinking when I'd seen it some years before that it was a delightful little house. Little indeed—one bathroom on the second floor, two studies on that floor and a tiny guest room which I used as my bedroom, a parlor downstairs, and a

CREDIT: INGRAM, RETTIG & BEATY, REAL ESTATE

14 Wright Street, Cambridge, where Judy and I lived

living room behind that and a rather primitive kitchen.

I'm saying all this simply to gloat a little, as Judy bought this house for eleven thousand dollars, which for her at that time was a considerable sum. It sold the other day for three hundred and fifty thousand dollars! Of course, since then the market has dropped, but it obviously sold because of the location, not really because of the house. It had two garages but no garden. So there it is now, flying up into high society.

I think back on those Cambridge years as the happiest of my life and the only ones in which I had a home—a real home. Of course, Nelson was a home, but that was a home for a solitary, and the lovely thing about the house on Wright Street was what we shared there—our little walks in the evening to get food for Fuzz Buzz and Scrabble, our two cats, walking around the neighborhood looking up, especially at the attics lit up at night, wondering what student was writing a paper on, say, Virginia Woolf, up there. Compared to our life in Cambridge, mine in York is silent and solitary. I almost never hear another human voice, and that has its own extraordinary value.

Monday, August 20

NOW IT IS MONDAY. How great to begin a new week with a beautiful, almost autumnal, day—lovely clouds with sunlight through them. I've been wondering why it is that I feel bored, in spite of all Rene's welcome loving care. She's amazing. She keeps everything so in order without appearing to do anything. And all these dear little meals of which I can eat so very little. Why am I bored? I think I made a mistake in not having mail forwarded, because I suddenly realize that those letters are the only roots left of my professional life. And every day some letter brings news from a friend or also, very welcome, news from someone who has just discovered my work and wants to tell me what it means to him or her. So, cut off from mail, and also I must say from the small chores which I so often complain about, such as taking out the bird feeder, it is as if I'd stripped myself of everything that keeps me more or less alive. I realize more and more that doing these little chores is very important for the sense of myself. And I, in some ways, long to be home again, though I also bask in the "life of Riley" here.

Today we are going to see if we can find a place that serves oysters, because I know Rene loves them, and I'm hoping to take her to lunch.

We get the *New York Times,* which is depressing these days. It is frightening to think that there are that many Americans in the frightful heat and so at risk that one can only pray, pray that it will not end in war and not end in tragedy for the hostages. For the weapon of hostages seems to be the only defense Hussein has.

This morning there were fewer birds. I wasn't woken up as I usually am by bird song.

The news of Pierrot is very good. He's really been tamed by Susan, who can pet him for half an hour and he purrs. He comes in to be fed. This has taken quite a burden of anxiety from me, for I'd become stupidly concerned about his staying away, although I knew he would not starve to death, but I thought of his blue eyes at night looking up at the lighted windows. He actually meowed when a high wind blew up, meowed to be let in, and this was the best news of all. Actually it's taken him two years to meow to be let in. He never used to do that. He would just wait and know or hope that someone would come and let him in. In fact, he has in the last six months become a much tamer cat than I ever thought he could be. When we have a rest together in the afternoon or sometimes in the middle of the night he suddenly meows as if to say, "Where are you? I thought you'd gone," and comes up and rubs against me and then goes back to curl up at the end of the bed. Being away from him like this has made me realize how fond I am of him.

Tuesday, August 21

A GRAY, COLD DAY, but it's wonderful to be cool. Wonderful luck that the last days here have been so comfortable. I sleep very well. I don't dream, don't have any of those frightening dreams that I have been having at home. There's no doubt that old age is a journey into a foreign country, so that one is constantly being astonished by what is not possible, or by what is different from anything that has gone before. For me at present, which is of course partly due to illness, it is the astonishment of not being able to move fast or walk steadily, to be this fragile, clumsy person who is constantly stopped by her own fumbles. And it's extremely comforting to be with Rene, who is remarkably well, but is a little older than I and is also entering this foreign country. There is a certain pleasure in being with somebody who is also discovering it and discovering herself within it.

It's too bad that the two books I've been reading have not been really more nourishing. Strange man, Updike, extremely aware, as I guess all Americans are, of class differences, of the fact that in Ipswich he was moving into the squirearchy, if you will—old New England and all that that means. And the things that one takes for granted, which I was on the edge of at the Shady Hill School, and with Anne Thorp and the Copley Greenes especially, the clubs, the Somerset Club and the Tavern Club. When old Mr. DeWolfe Howe had to have blood transfusions the entire club walked up the hill to the hospital, only to find that they were all too old to give blood!

So somehow or other I got news of this or somebody asked me. Anyway, I gave blood. And old Mr. Howe never ceased to rejoice at getting this poet's blood, and I think he wrote a little rhyme about it. He certainly mentioned it to me in many short notes that he sent. He was such a dear, gentle person, with his tribe of children, Helen and Mark and Quincy, who all made their mark and were all short in height and somehow very conscious of this. Their mother was an Adams and, I think, called them "my tribe of dwarfs."

But the thing about a club is that it's part of your whole identity. It's something you take for granted, and it gives you a shine, or whatever you want to call it, a glimmer that other people less fortunate do not have. I've never been a member of a club. I think I've never wanted to be. It's not exactly the famous Groucho Marx statement: I wouldn't want to be a member of any club that would have me. But there are times when I miss the sense of belonging to a privileged group. I think of this when I realize freshly that not having been to college means that I don't have a reservoir of people from my class who go on through life, as Huldah Sharp and many other friends of mine have. Notable among them, of course, is dear Eleanor Blair, although now she is ninety-six most of her classmates are dead. It's this slipping under, this falling over the cliff that begins to take place when one is about seventy-five. I only began to be acutely aware of it then.

Friday, August 24

I AM HOME NOW. It's always a confrontation when I come home after a time away, because all I see at first is what needs to be done, and what is piled on my back: a week's mail this time, for instance, and I feel as if something is closing down on me instead of something opening up. But it was a real holiday, which taught me several things—among them the kindness and the imaginative way in which Rene Morgan treats a guest, so one feels totally cherished and at home. She said that it was not exhausting, but to me it would have been—to produce three meals a day alone amongst other things.

The bad revelation it gave me was that apparently my attacks of diverticulitis, or whatever it is, have nothing to do with stress, because there I was, without even mail, with no magazines—though Rene did get me the *New York Times*—with very little stimulation, the kind of stimulation that is really part of my identity. I was therefore completely passive, and yet on Monday I had one of the worst attacks I've ever had—with very bad pain. The problem with the very bad pain is that the medicine I take for pain is constipating! But for the moment *now* I'm really better and hoping that the good effect of a week of total rest will be seen *now*.

It was wonderful to have the pussycat so affectionate last night. He kept looking at me out of his half-closed eyes and then reaching out with his two big paws for my hand, which he really clasps. He is adorable, but although he came in at midnight, he wanted to go out at four. I did not want to get up and stagger downstairs. This morning, getting up at seven instead of six, seven seemed terribly early, and I do feel tired today.

I'm going now to give this first try at dictating a journal to Nancy to type so we can send it to Deborah Pease, who gave the recorder to me and who is, I think very anxious to hear how it sounds. I think my voice comes out all right. I hope so. And maybe this long rest has made my voice a little clearer than it was.

Monday, August 27

YESTERDAY WAS a marvelous day, the proof that a week's rest and Rene's tender ministrations have helped me over the hump and I have almost resumed my real life. The first sign was Saturday evening, when I roasted a leg of lamb for Janice, parboiled potatoes and onions to roast with it, and enjoyed the preparations and the good smells mightily. The kitchen has been a barren place these past months. Janice rejoiced with me, and it was like the old times when she came to dinner once a week.

But yesterday was the real proof of a renascence at last. I had been haunted by a line that might be the key to the Christmas poem, which I thought about a lot at Rene's, but which did not jell there. But yesterday morning I suddenly was empowered, and sailed into the poem as though this were a common occurrence, whereas it was actually the first really creative time in months. When I was revising for the fifth or sixth time the phone rang and it was Bill Ewert, the angel who prints my Christmas poem for me. Serendipity!

Meanwhile the heavy air had cleared and the ocean was that Fra Angelico blue we have not seen often this disappointing summer. It was the dream of summer at last after so many heavy, damp days.

I have been browsing happily through the pile of magazines accumulated while I was away and got an electric shock of joyful recognition when I saw a painting by Emily Carr reproduced in *Newsweek* and the notice of a retrospective show in the National Gallery of Canada at Ottawa. The painting is of a cedar. Has there ever been a painter who loved trees as much? She is quoted as saying, "Everything is green. Everything is waiting and still. Slowly things begin to move, to slip into their place. Groups and masses and lines tie themselves together. Colors you had not noticed come out, timidly, boldly. In and out, in and out, your eye passes." This is a quote from her remarkable journal, which has long been by my bed and which I must reread.

Emily Carr is a hero as a painter who was unable to paint for fourteen years (as Rilke was unable to write for twelve) and then found her palette and her brushstroke and did such remarkable work. She is a different hero in the journal, the woman alone, fashioning a strong inner life in spite of depression and the hard struggle to make her work known and accepted. It was a special grace that I came on her yesterday again.

Tuesday, August 28

THERE IS a slight edge at last to my mind, that extra-sharp impact of things that I have seen for months in a kind of passive acceptance, without excitement. This morning I am excited by ideas I have about how to clear the counters in the kitchen, which have been a jumble of cookie tins and boxes for years.

It helped yesterday to look out on a blue sea—to look at it, dazzled, as I used to be, and dazzled not only by what is outside in this beautiful place but also by what my life has given me over seventy-eight years. It seemed to have come to a dead stop, and that was the most frightening thing. Not only was I miserable and often hopeless, but even work had come to a standstill. But yesterday at long last Eric Swenson wrote that Brad Daziel's selection from my books, both poetry and prose, will come out for my seventy-ninth birthday. Hallelujah! It has had an extraordinary effect to know there will be a book next spring. And if all goes well this journal should go to Eric on my seventy-ninth birthday to be published for my eightieth. I had planned this long ago, so it was awfully frustrating when I was too ill to keep it on a regular basis. In a way that has not changed, as I have had two attacks of cramping since I got home. But I have come to see that any pill that stops the cramps affects my mind and explains the lack of edge, the blur in which I have been living. Better three days a week with a clear mind than seven feeling drugged and fuzzy-minded.

Last night I found again, in the turntable bookcase by my bed, a book I bought years ago about old age, *The Moon Is Up: An Anthology for Older People,* edited by Dorothy Saunders. In a chapter on memory, most of the selections emphasize that, as Walter Savage Landor is quoted as saying, "The recollection of a thing is frequently more pleasing than the actuality; what is harsh is dropped into the space between." For me this is simply not true. In these months of illness where I live on memory, what came back was unfortunately mostly disasters of one kind or another, remorse, a harsh judgment of myself. Especially where love affairs were concerned, pain was always there, a leitmotif.

Wednesday, August 29

IT IS NOT that I did anything wrong and not again the hot temper that led me into foolish overreacting that creates remorse now, but more a kind of clumsiness, especially where intense feeling was concerned. I am more aware than ever that loving is far more rewarding than being loved. The lover has all the imaginative reward, the long drive by moonlight to see a lover while she is silently waiting and not especially on the *qui vive*.

Yeats haunts me when he writes:

> O heart we are old;
> The living beauty is for younger men:
> We cannot pay its tribute of wild tears.

I suppose I miss that intensity of feeling more than I can say, so it has been like a miracle to feel the sharp edge come back in these last days. To write a poem! I had thought that door was closed forever.

Dr. Flavin just called. I told him that I had about decided that pain was better endured than no pain and a blurred mind, so I have decided not to take a pill for the cramps, only simple medicine like Kaopectate and Tylenol with codeine. He agreed with me and said, "When the medicine creates a worse illness than that it is meant to cure, better give it up."

Last night I slept badly and spent hours trying to imagine what it is like for our men in Saudi Arabia, somehow surviving in 115-degree heat with no letup, no air conditioning, heavy packs, nor the shade of a single tree—a sojourn in hell. What courage it must take simply to walk a mile, or oil an engine— the everlasting thirst. My heart aches for them. Like every other war in the end, it seems so useless, "stupid," as General Eisenhower called it when he was president.

Thursday, August 30

TOMORROW IS my father's birthday, and I realize once again how complex memory is. The only memories which stay fixed like images in a painting are ones where there is no emotional trauma, such as for instance my vivid memory of sitting on the porch in Yonkers with Bon Bon shelling peas, Teddy the St. Bernard and Buster the red setter lying at our feet. The warmth of the sun and Bon Bon's sunny good humor stay with me as a moment of perfect happiness and safety.

But when it comes to such a complex relation as that with my father, I see how memory has changed with every passing

Tea in the garden—Mabel and George Sarton at 5 Channing Place in Cambridge

year. It took many years for me to begin to accept his lack of understanding where my mother was concerned, to accept his attitude toward me, his inability ever to discuss anything rationally where money was involved, big wounds like his suddenly shouting at me, "Why don't you get married?" when I was deeply involved with a woman with whom I could not live.

But as I grew up, well past the age of fifty, I began to be able to see him as himself, not only as my loving but hurtful father. At that point I began to miss him, his humor, his passionate belief in the history of science. I began to feel an affinity with his courage, the long, incredibly hard work, and the passion that drove him toward accomplishing what he dreamed. I began to realize what it had been to carry on that

struggle alone, often jeered at in the academic world as senti-
mental. I began to evoke his beaming smile and to remember
with poignant nostalgia tea in the garden at Channing Place
when Mother lay on the chaise longue with a Chinese shawl
around her shoulders and Cloudy on her lap, my father in a
battered straw hat smoking a cigar. How hard they both
worked, and how well they knew how to rest in each other at
that daily intimate pause! I knew that bliss again when I was
living with Judy at Wright Street and we had tea and often
took a little walk around the neighborhood when she came
home from Simmons. That ritual of tea with a loved one and
of course a cat—in our case Tom Jones, who later appeared as
the hero of my book *The Fur Person*. That ritual meant family
life to me. And I can see how different it was from most people's idea of it.

Neither of my parents lived to be as old as I am now,
which makes me feel like a pioneer.

Yesterday after taking Nancy out to lunch at Piper's I suddenly fell, dragging one chair into another in some inexplica-
ble clumsy misstep, and sprained my ankle. I have been so
afraid of falling that maybe it is a good thing I had the experience with only minor injury to show for it. Last night when I
went down at eleven to let Pierrot in I thought I might have to
sleep downstairs, it was so painful, but I managed to get back
to bed, and this morning it is not excruciating and I have been
able to put on a sneaker.

Saturday, September 1

ANOTHER LUMINOUS MORNING—the ocean like blue satin—and
as I woke up a wonderful sound of waves breaking, although
it is so silent and windless. The tide is rising and perhaps
bringing in waves from far off to break against our rocks.

Yesterday was my father's birthday, but I hardly had time
to think of him, as Steve Robitaille was here from Gainesville
with a colleague, a wonderfully sensitive technician, to catch
some of the atmosphere of the house and surroundings for a
videotape they are making on the "Old Age and Creativity"
seminar in which Dick Eberhart and I were the chief propo-
nents. Since I am seen only on a stage reading poems, it was a
good idea to move into the way I live as well. They were here
for hours, and then we had lunch, so it was rather an exhausting day, all told.

It was hard to say goodbye to Nancy, off on the *QE 2* on
Monday for eight weeks' holiday. I did feel a curious empty
feeling after I was alone here after Steve and company had
left. It's going to be a long haul but a good test of what resilience I still can muster, and I am comforted by the knowledge
that Nancy has earned this holiday after eleven years working
for me. And also I am much better these days and so should be
able to cope. That would not have been true two months ago.

Very rarely these days does a book come into the house
that beguiles me so that I have to stay with it for hours, bliss-
fully concentrated, whatever else I should have been doing.
This happened early this week when Susan Sherman, the

most imaginative of givers, sent me a copy of the Metropolitan Museum's entrancing book of poems and paintings called *Art and Love*. It is stuffed with treasures, among them two Vuillard interiors I have never seen reproduced, and poems, too—many I did not know, although I was gratified to find my own "A Celebration for George Sarton" among them. For an hour I was "carried away," and that happens rarely these days.

I do feel better and have at least a little more vital energy. I had felt in limbo, forgotten already because I was ill and thus of no account—finished as far as publications go. So what a lift I got when Eric wrote again to tell me the book would come out for my seventy-ninth birthday! They had chosen a rather full title, so I suggested *Sarton Selected*, and I hope they will use that.

Sunday, September 2

LAST EVENING at the time when I usually climb the stairs to bed, after taking in the bird feeder and clearing up the supper dishes, I felt so tired I found myself lying on the chaise longue in the dark. There in the dark the proportions of the enclosed porch where I sit and beyond it the small room which the flower window dominates were beautiful, airy, and open. There seemed to be no wall between me and the house, between its inside quality and my own, alone there, being myself.

Labor Day, September 3

I WENT DOWN at half-past twelve last night, sure that Pierrot would be ready to come in. He did run toward me, then changed his mind, gave one of his strange wild guttural meows, and tore off! I did go to sleep almost at once, only to be woken at four by a heavy rain, so of course I went down then and let him in. He can be infuriating, but being attached like a kite to something on earth keeps me tied down, I suppose, a little short of madness!

Eleanor is here, helping me tidy the kitchen today, to get rid of most of the open boxes of crackers and such, and to fill the electric bread box, which will keep them crisp. At last one part of the counter is cleared. But idiotically enough, showing her all this and helping her make decisions has worn me out.

Yesterday there was a good review of Nancy Mairs's new book, *Carnal Acts*, in which she faces the deteriorating, excruciating taking over of her being by multiple sclerosis. Ever since she told me that she had had to give up driving—and one can imagine what that last door into independence and power to move cost her—I have thought of her almost every day. Her courage alone is genius, but when I read that what she had sent me some time ago, the journal of her African journey to visit her daughter, who is with the Peace Corps, is included in this book, I know already how remarkable it is.

There seemed to be no wall between me and the house

Holidays are depressing for those who live alone. I had lunch with Edythe yesterday, and on Saturday had a good long talk with Jean Anderson from Seattle, but have made no plan for today under a gray sky, a low-key day.

Tuesday, September 4

YESTERDAY DEBORAH PEASE called twice to tell me how good she thought what I'd recorded on tape sounds. I'd sent her Nancy's transcription.

It's now September 4, an autumnish day with a rough,

dark-blue sea, very clear air. The autumn air at once gives one extra energy. It's like a *piqûre,* that is, an injection. I can hear Edith Kennedy using that word *piqûre* but I have forgotten what about. Perhaps simply a cup of coffee. How often I think of her and the rarity of that household, where there was always marvelous conversation because she gathered around her people who could make it. I can't remember all their names now, but they were musicians and scientists, poets and novelists, and her young sons, who were full of ideas. Paul Child was a frequent visitor and at one time lived in the house. He was then associated with the Avon School near Hartford.

My world is depeopled. Every person seventy-eight years old lives in a somewhat depeopled world. The trouble for me is that I often loved people much older and wiser than I. So I'm left now in the lurch, being, trying to be, the old wise one and feeling like a great goose. Which reminds me that Dorothy Wallace, who is in Provence and is sending me delightful cards, sent me the other day a card of a troop of geese "living in liberty." That's what it says in French: *"Troupeau d'oies vivant en liberté."* So here they come looking like an army of geese. One almost expects the goosestep, and in fact one of them is doing it—one of the leaders of the troop. It is a hilarious sight.

I've always loved geese, partly because of Céline Limbosch, my mother's dear friend in Belgium, where I spent so much time. Céline had a pet goose called Franz, a male with two wives, one of whom he treated badly. She was to keep her distance, whereas his favorite was allowed to stay about a foot behind him. What nobody had realized until a very hot summer when I was there is how much they needed water. I knew it when I saw they were panting, so I asked Céline if I could get a pail of water for them. Everybody thought I was crazy, but the minute they saw this pail of water they were in heaven. They put their long necks down in it, they lifted them

Celine Limbosch ("Mamie") with Franz the goose

up and shook them, then went at it again. It was so convincing that Céline decided they must have a little pond. So a tiny pond of cement was laid down in the lawn, and every morning began with Franz let out from his pen and striding to this, by then, very dirty pool, drinking and performing his morning ablutions. I have celebrated him in a poem, "Franz, a Goose."

Dorothy's card has brought me more than the pleasure of itself. It has also brought me a delightful memory of Céline's garden, the tea table with the white cloth on it out under the apple tree, and our sitting there, laughing and talking.

Nancy called last night, and it was so good to hear her

voice. It cheered me up right away. Nevertheless, getting up this morning has not been easy. For some reason it just feels very empty here, although Nancy, after all, was never here when I got up. She came at half-past eight and she was never here in the afternoon or night. Something has gone out of the house, and one of the things is purely materialistic: someone to help me get the rubbish ready on Monday morning. The rubbish men come at about eight o'clock on Tuesday morning—not until tomorrow this week because yesterday was a holiday. I had hoped that Eleanor Perkins, who cleans for me, could come on Monday and Thursday so she could help me with the rubbish. But she can't come on Monday, so I'm left high and dry with rather heavy weights for me to drag out on Mondays as well as filling the garbage bags, and I don't look forward to it. In fact, I dread this kind of effort very much. It's just bad luck that Eleanor can't come on Mondays. It's already adding quite a large sum to my expenses to have her for two days instead of one. But this I'm giving myself as a present. I think I should be giving myself a few extravagances! It's important to think of oneself, sometimes, as a needy child, and to be kind to it.

So this morning I'm off to get another bottle of Scotch and also my tickets for Las Cruces, where I'm going to see Lee in November—my old friend Lee Blair, who for years has had frightful arthritis as well as a great deal of pain from a replaced knee. She finally moved to New Mexico, and the climate there has been like a miracle, because for the first time in years she's not in acute pain. She was to have come here last week, but it did not work out because she slipped and tore a ligament. So I decided to go and see her!

I think the fact that I did make that decision shows that I must be better. Maybe next year I might be able to go back to England. I'd almost given up any idea that I could go to Europe, which makes me think of what Oscar Wilde said so wisely: "The tragedy of old age is not that one is old but that one is young." My extreme youth will be shown when an enormous package of bulbs comes from Holland and I shall try to put at least some of them in and hope that Diane will be able to do the rest.

Wednesday, September 5

I WENT OUT at half-past six and saw a great golden flush in the sky to the left, as the sun had not yet risen, but the sea was already a marvelous blue, and everything so still and shining. I was glad to be out.

I've been wanting for some time to remember poems that have lasted for me all these years, some of them since I was a child at the Shady Hill School and Agnes Hocking made us learn them by heart. How well I remember learning poems by Kipling, such as "The Seals." Shady Hill was an open-air school, so we sat at our desks in sleeping bags from Sears Roebuck which contained our legs and which folded over our backs. On the floor of the big room where we met Agnes Hocking to recite poetry we could scramble around in these sacklike sleeping bags being *seals*. What a wonderful school it was! Should I ever have been a poet without that inflammatory teacher, Agnes Hocking?

In this context I must also remember my mother. Every night she came to sit by my bed and read me poems in her beautiful voice, so that I went to sleep with the rhythm of poetry, its sound, deep in my subconscious. It was mostly, as I remember, from an anthology called *The Tripled Crown*, rather a chauvinistic British selection. I remember the first line of one poem: "Eleven men of England lie torn and gashed and slain . . ." [Eleven men of England . . . lie stripped, and gashed, and slain," from "The Red Thread of Honour" by Sir Francis Hastings Doyle.] It was full of poems of that sort, but they were exciting to me at seven or eight years old. As I go through this year of getting well, and thinking about old age, I want to remember some of the poems that have come with me all this way.

Here is one I go back to often, by Frances Cornford, that rare lyric poet. I pick up her book and open it, and although I know the poems almost by heart, I'm struck alive again:

On Reading the Greek Anthology

This people with unchanging vision sees
    The silent-footed hours,
That love as simply as the almond trees
    In his season flowers,
That certain as the winter to the wood
Is sorrow for the beautiful and good.

[From *On a Calm Shore*. London: Cresset Press, 1960]

I must not forget to put in a poem every few days.

I've been in a very unholy mood for the last forty-eight hours. Resentful of being alone here and feeling the pinch of having to do so much that is heavy for me, so I get overtired very quickly. Yesterday, for instance, I dreaded bringing in large loads of food and liquor. But blessed Pat Chasse called and asked if there was anything she could do, so I said she could bring in one package of food. She was in York, so she could come quickly, and then when she got here and found that one of the hoses had broken she even fixed that. Luckily the hardware store was open on Labor Day. But if one does have these destructive moods or when it is hard to think of one's blessings, one is apt to think only of the infinite frustrations which beset every human being at certain times. One example was the hose suddenly showing a leak when it was high time to water the garden.

Today the man employed by Mary-Leigh to come once a year to do an extensive pruning is here. He prunes the fruit trees and the ornamental cherries and keeps the garden, which is a formal one, in shape—accomplishing an incredible amount in one day. He not only cuts down lots of branches, but makes everything look one hundred percent more loved and cherished.

The amazing thing is how many pages my talking for about five minutes will turn into when Deborah Pease transcribes it for me, as she will do until Nancy comes back.

Thursday, September 6

A DOWN DAY, with a sky so hazy that the ocean blends in with the sky and haze so the field seems to drop off into nowhere. It's interesting that I've never seen the field green after it was cut. It's a delight to have it green rather than the usual desolate brown.

It has been a year in which many of my friends have had hard times for one reason or another. It's a tremendous lift to talk on the phone, which I do about every other day, to Lee Blair in New Mexico. I hear a strong, happy voice saying, "I love it here." She got a kitten from the Animal Rescue League, but I'm afraid she should have gotten a cat. The kitten is too wild and tears up the curtains. An old purrful cat sitting for hours with its paws tucked in would have been a better idea. It's a little bit like Grizzle with me, because I was too old to bring up a four-month-old puppy and had to find it out the hard way. It's not easy bringing up Pierrot, because of his erratic behavior at night. Sometimes he wants to come in at eleven, often it's at one-thirty in the morning. Last night I decided, well, I'll let him be out all night. Then, at about eleven, I opened the door and there he was, waiting to come in! How was I to know?

The wonderful thing with Bramble was that she climbed up to my bedroom window and sat on the windowsill there until I let her in by moving the screen. Of course Pierrot, this dear, magnificent Himalayan, is much too clumsy to climb up on the roof. I'm sure he'd fall off, so I have to go down over and over again. Many people feel that the stairs are lethal for my heart, but I have the opposite view. I take very little exercise. I'm extremely shaky, so that walking even four or five minutes is not possible. I just manage to get out to the car and back.

Where I miss Nancy is especially helping me lift heavy things, which I can't do now. Sometimes I leave them in the car until someone comes to help. This happened in a lovely way when Bill Ewert and his wife, Mary, came around at four to see me and talk about the Christmas poem. The Christmas poem has to be written in August. Bill will get an illustrator for it, as he always does, and all this takes time. It's wonderful for me that I was able to write it and that he likes it and that this has happened once more. It makes me think that I should give myself a deadline and force myself to write a poem now and then for an occasion. Some of the poems I've written as Christmas poems are among my best.

The strange problem is where time goes when, after all, I'm not writing a book—only these short journal entries. I'm not writing poems. I'm only at the moment trying to improve an interview I had with the *New England Quarterly* because I felt that I was too negative and that it was showing the psychological effects of this long bout with frustrating illness. I must try to bring it back, to be more cheerful, and more what I think I truly am.

Bill Ewert and Mary and I had a lovely talk about everything. Then I remembered that there was liquor out in the car that I hadn't been able to get in. I asked Bill, and he happily lugged it in.

Where does time go? At present, my new method requires doing two hours of housework before I go to my study. I make my bed, have my breakfast, tidy up downstairs. It always takes two hours. By nine o'clock at the latest, I should be up here at my desk, and I often am. But then there is yesterday's mail to sort and answer. I read it before lunch, but rarely these days do I get upstairs in the afternoon, so it's lying in wait. Today there were bills to pay—ten or fifteen minutes gone right there. Then I dictate the journal and, this week at least, try to improve that interview. That is all I have strength for before half-past ten, when I go out and get the mail and do errands. That is my whole day's work. It's hardly what most people would call work, but for me, saying these few words into a cassette is a tremendous effort, because my mind is still far from able to move at full speed. It's like lugging something very heavy onto a track before it can move.

I'm happy—very happy—about remembering those old poems that have lasted for me through the years. I suddenly thought about G. K. Chesterton's "The Donkey," which I learned to recite when I was nine or ten and have never forgotten. I suppose donkeys have been on my mind ever since I borrowed one for a summer to let it recover from being shut up all winter, not able to run, and to get myself well from a depression. At the end of the summer

May with Esmeralda, the donkey she borrowed from the Warners in the summer of 1968

the donkey could run and I was over my depression.
   So here is Chesterton's "The Donkey":

> When fishes flew and forests walked
>   And figs grew upon thorn,
> Some moment when the moon was blood,
>   Then surely I was born.
>
> With monstrous head and sickening cry
>   And ears like errant wings,
> The devil's walking parody
>   Of all four-footed things.
>
> The tattered outlaw of the earth,
>   Of ancient crooked will;

> Starve, scourge, deride me! I am dumb,
> I keep my secret still.
>
> Fools! For I also had my hour;
> One far fierce hour and sweet:
> There was a shout about my ears,
> And palms before my feet.

Saturday, September 8

TODAY FOR the first time we have the wine-dark sea and the autumn air. The high wind in the night came and blew all that heavy, fetid air away. Pierrot, whom I went down to get at half-past twelve and then again at half-past one when he finally did come in, was so excited by the wind that he rushed off into the night making loud, feral meows. I'd never heard a cat make this kind of sound before. I had to go back to bed for an hour. The result is that I'm tired today.

I did, however, have lunch with Roger Finch, his sister, and his friend Lewis. Roger and Lewis have been living in Japan. Roger is a scholar of Japanese and Chinese. He got his Ph.D. in Japanese at Harvard. I think of him always as a very young man, so I was startled when I asked him how old he was and he said fifty-four! It's terrible how time eats us up. But Roger is a very good poet, and his first book is being published—I envy him—by the Carcanet Press in London, one of the best presses for poetry.

I am not published as a poet in England—not since before World War II, when the Cresset Press, because of S. S. Koteliansky's admiration (he was a reader for them), published my first novel and my first book of poems. It's the old story. I haven't had the critical response that would interest an English publisher.

Roger and his friend have opened an antique shop in Portsmouth, because the friend has had serious heart trouble and can't go on living away from home. He is living in Roger's old house in Cape Neddick and will be running the shop. After lunch they drove me to see it and I fell in love with a small fourteenth-century elephant there whom I think I may have to have. Roger has marvelous taste, so it is not surprising that the shop is distinguished and inviting.

Roger's poetry is baroque, full of images. He uses intricate forms, so he should come into his own now that minimalist poetry is no longer in vogue. At any rate, he has had a fascinating life. The son of a steelworker, he has sometimes invented a life of his own, full of creation and never-ceasing work. He must have a rare gift for languages, because learning both Japanese and Chinese requires an extraordinary memory.

Years ago, when I was a child, my father had illusions about what I might become. His dream was for me to be a museum curator. At the time, it seemed to me the last thing I would want to be, but actually it could be a fascinating life. When I was even younger, perhaps nine, Daddy decided that this was a good time to learn languages because your memory is better. He offered me ten cents for every Chinese character that I learned. Innocent that I was, I didn't realize that the first three or four or five might be quite easy but it would get harder as it went on. After a very short time I gave up.

Sunday, September 9

TODAY I'M HAVING LUNCH with an old friend who lives in Camp Hill, Pennsylvania: Mary Tozer. It's always nice to catch up with someone I have not seen for a long time. Mary has two delightful granddaughters who really care, and look after her. This rejoices my heart.

As for the nonwar in the Middle East, I think it is very hard for us to realize that it's going on. It all seems so preposterous in a way and so hard to get a hold on. I do very often think of what it must be to combat that heat day after day and night after night. And we hear now that mail isn't getting through, that they are still on those awful rations and don't have real food. I still think it was grotesque to see our president rushing about hitting golf balls with fury just to prove that he was *playing* on holiday while Rome burned. For some reason he believed it was important that he be seen playing while we were on the brink of what could be a really frightful war.

Monday, September 10

THE DAY BEGAN with rain, but a gentle rain, and we do need it; now the sun is out. I'm lying on my chaise longue downstairs and have just read Susan Sherman's marvelous compilation of letters to and from Judy Matlack and me. This is something Susan does for birthdays. She recently did one for my father's birthday, the 31st of August. This last collection is extremely moving to me, because both in letters to Judy and to other people, I make it clear what a beautiful relationship it was, although there were hard times because Judy was, I believe, permanently melancholy; also she never accepted her relationship with me and certainly did not want the passionate side of it. So there was a great deal of what I suppose one calls "adjusting" to do on both sides. But there was also deep caring and understanding. One of the most interesting things about the letters Susan selected is that several are from our best friend, Ruth Harnden, who alas now has Alzheimer's. But they are such kind letters to me, so understanding, comforting me because she knows that it is not easy to live with Judy. On the other hand, I know it is not easy to live with me, because of my tempestuous heart.

Judy did accept that there would be strong attachments all my life even when I was living with her, and some of these letters were written in the period of Juliette Huxley. It's curious that I should have been reading these letters just now, because last night I had a really terrible night in which I couldn't stop a memory which pursued me like a devil. It recalled much that had been extremely painful and difficult in various love affairs and other aspects of my life. I couldn't get away from it. I kept saying to myself, it doesn't matter, it's all past now, but it still kept pouring in, first one whole period of my life, then another. I slept not more than two hours. Pierrot, for once, came in quite early, at eleven o'clock. It was a kind of torture. Nothing can be done with these memories. They have to be laid aside. What could be done *has* been done.

Now it is very peaceful and I can begin to absorb the day. Judy Burrowes and her friend Chris took me out to lunch, and we had a good time, except that Captain Simeon's is so noisy that we didn't have a chance to talk as we wanted to. I like Chris very much and felt at ease with her, so that was good. Then I came home and had a rest on my bed with Pierrot for about an hour and then began to think of household things that must be done. I did have very bad cramps this morning and was unable to do anything at my desk, so I'm even more behind than I was, and this makes a kind of chaos in my center, hard for me to handle when I don't feel well.

Dorothy Wallace, the most imaginative present-giver I've ever known, sent me five French novels, because she remembered that in one of the journals I said that I no longer see any modern French novels and wish I did. Isn't that marvelous? I can hardly wait. Besides that, of course, there's the *Times*, which I haven't started. A queer sort of upside-down day because I felt so ill.

Wednesday, September 12

I HAVE TO REMIND myself of what day it is, because I was knocked out completely for Monday and Tuesday, especially yesterday. I didn't sleep Monday night, because of atrocious pain. At such times I get a little panicky and wonder if I should go to the emergency room at the hospital, but there's little they can do. So I take paregoric and Tylenol and my regular diarrhea medicine and in three or four hours it usually subsides. The trouble this time was that it did not subside, so I got extremely tired, and that's why I couldn't do anything yesterday.

However, great news. That wonderful woman Karen K. brought me something called brown rice cream, which is supposed to be very good for smoothing out irritable intestines. I took it last night and I think it is wonderful. Now I'm going to have it for lunch today. Luckily, Eleanor Perkins was here cleaning, so she could go out and get the mail. There are these big lacunae now in my life without Nancy. I usually call if I'm ill and ask her to get the mail on her way here. But I'm learning, and I am triumphant because this morning, although I feel extremely shaky, I got up, changed the bed, washed the sheets, adding a small laundry to that load, dried them, folded them, and also did my regular routine: had a bath, dressed, went down and made my breakfast, this time a croissant, which seems to have worked all right, coffee, and orange juice. Now, of course, I'm beginning to feel like someone who's climbed Mount Everest. I think the rest of the day I shall have to rest up and rejoice that I feel so much better.

The problem with being knocked out for two days is that so much has to be done that haunts me and simply makes the tension worse. In this case, it was a note from a friend who had sent me flowers for my birthday months ago and was never thanked and finally decided that I must have been ill. That came about ten days ago and has haunted me. I *must* write her and explain. So, in the middle of the afternoon yesterday, I managed to creep up here, find her telephone number—she lives in Albuquerque—and call her and explain. That was a tremendous relief. But the problem remains that there are perhaps five hundred of such queries in the boxes of letters unanswered, strewn about this room, and there's no doubt that it creates tension. It's all very well to say "Just don't answer," but when it's something like somebody having sent flowers and getting no answer, becoming anxious, what do you do? Especially now that Nancy's not here, I can't pass it on to her. I have to do it myself.

Last night Pierrot came in at eleven. It was foggy, and his coming in early was a real boon, because the night before when I felt desperately ill I had to go down three times for him—at eleven, at midnight, and finally at one, when he deigned to come in. Of course, it was the end of the full moon, and that's what held him outdoors like a magnet. As there are twelve steps up from the second floor where my bedroom is to downstairs—twelve stairs up, twelve steps down—if I have to do it three times a night, each time waking up from a deep sleep, it is costly. Often I don't get to sleep again. However, he's worth it! Without some living thing in the house it would become too lonely, too lonely for words, too lonely for silence. I would just, I'm afraid, cry. So he is a delight in spite of what he costs me.

Yesterday it was quite fitting that the poem that came to mind was Edward Rowland Sill's poem called "Peace." It is an example of Agnes Hocking's genius at teaching. Here we were, a noisy, excited fourth grade, or maybe even third grade, I'm not quite sure, and what she did was to suggest that we be absolutely still and listen, listen to the sounds beyond the cars going by, a fire engine, or the noon whistle and get to the silence which is above all that. It meant keeping absolutely still for quite a while, maybe for as long as five minutes, almost like a gymnastic exercise for the soul, for these restless little children, of which I was one. But we began to love it, so that we were always asking to say that poem, and when I was feeling so very miserable yesterday and in such pain, it came back to me like a blessing.

Peace

'Tis not in seeking,
'Tis not in endless striving
Thy quest is found.

Be still and listen.
Be still, and drink the silence
Of all around.

Not for thy crying,
Not for thy loud beseeching
Will peace draw near.

Rest, with palms folded,
Rest with thine eyelids fallen—
Lo, peace is here.

It was not always a blessing to have to know so many poems by heart when I was a child. Once, when my parents and I were crossing on the *Mauretania,* a very narrow vessel which held the prize for speed across the Atlantic at that time, it happened that we were in the tail of a hurricane and we were all three of us very sick. When the propeller came out of the water on a big wave and then bumped itself down jaggedly, one felt nauseated. So I decided that I would *comfort* my parents by reciting all the poems that I knew. I was in the top bunk, of course, and so I went on and on, enjoying every moment of it, until finally after about an hour Mother suggested that perhaps they needed a little time to be quiet.

I wish I could remember all of those poems—forty or fifty—that were my daily companions, including "The Hound of Heaven" by Francis Thompson, which my school friend Jean Tatlock and I used to recite in the streets of Cambridge at night. These memories are precious. I've dwelt on the painful memories, but I'm now swimming along on those memories of my life as it was before puberty, when all was passionate but clear.

Now it occurs to me that one of the strange things about the night before last (the night I couldn't sleep at all and was in such pain) was that for once the sound of the sea was not at all peaceful. It was very loud. Loud waves breaking against the rocks. There was a full moon, which means a very high tide. It was a restless, noisy ocean. That is very rare. Last night it came back to its soothing sound and I was grateful.

Friday, September 14

Now NANCY has been gone for two weeks, so that's a fourth of her time away. I must say it was hard not to have her when I was feeling so very ill. But I'm better now, and Maggie Vaughan comes this afternoon with all the food for the weekend. We might even get out to do a little cutting down of "deadheads," especially of the phlox in the terrace garden. I've come to a real impasse with Diane, who I thought was going to be a gardener and would take care of the garden, but she only comes when I ask her for a specific purpose and then feels that she's done her duty and after perhaps a day of work doesn't come back for weeks.

Yesterday, for the first time in months, I had the strength to go down to the picking garden and see what was there. Very little. It's mostly a carpet of weeds and grass. But the triumph was that I did pick a little bunch of flowers all from my garden for Maggie, and then came back and picked some big bunches of phlox, which is still glorious, for the library and the flower room. I realized once more how it's not the picking that's so tiring; it's the arranging. When one is not well, making choices is one of the most tiring things. When I had my tonsils out—it was done very late in my life, when I was fifty—and came home after two days (as a matter of fact I didn't go home but went to Cora DuBois's, because Judy was away). Cora was by nature a stoic and also perhaps a little unimaginative about pain and other people's physical problems, and decided that what I needed was something to do. So she presented me with a plan, or not a plan—with a great many bags of bulbs—and asked me to make a plan for planting them in the garden. This was extremely difficult for me to do. I did do it, more or less, and then had a drink. Then she had made—I think it was ham, I'm not sure what—but something I couldn't swallow, for supper. When I said, "I can't swallow it," she said, "You swallowed the *drink* all right." In some circumstances it's better not to be a guest.

I'm reading with enormous interest and admiration Nancy Mairs's new book of essays, *Carnal Acts*. In this book she comes very close to the marrow as far as talking about what it is to have MS (multiple sclerosis), and also one gets the sense of being given as much as possible of the person Nancy is, an extraordinary woman if only in how she deals with MS.

It's not only a full-time job but also an extremely discouraging one. One thing that impressed me comes rather late in the book when she talks about one of the difficulties being that the symptoms change so often and so fast—that just when you've got adjusted to a routine which contains perhaps driving a car, you suddenly can't do that anymore and have to redesign your whole life around one more thing that has been taken from you.

Another thing that interests me enormously is that she said she'd grown a sense of humor through having this frightful illness to cope with all the time. Sometimes she falls, and says in the book it's a *pratfall,* and pratfalls make people laugh. "So sometimes I just lie there and giggle." This is extraordinary. But all the time, woven through it, are concerns which have nothing to do with illness, such as her and George, her husband, going to one of the sites for atomic missiles and being arrested. Going deliberately to *be* arrested. What that means for somebody who can't walk without a wheelchair and faces the fact that the wheelchair will be taken from her makes one look at her with great admiration. Wound through the whole book like threads in a tapestry is her feminism. And here she's just as honest as she is about everything else.

It makes me . . . (I made a "pause" then to try to find a quote from one of Susan Sherman's wonderful compendiums that she sends me for anniversaries.) There was one remarkable one about my father in which there is a quote where I talk about what happens when Mother is ill and he goes completely crazy. He's never in the least sympathetic about her being ill, and I remember very well when, very rarely, a doctor was called if she had a high fever. My father then behaved as though this were a social visit, and went out of his way to tell humorous jokes to the doctor standing at the end of the bed so that the examination in a way could never take place, and Mother was never left alone with the doctor to tell her own story. I know she minded. But that's just one example of the various rules that have to do with the relationship between men and women and which haven't changed very much. Nancy Mairs sets down a sort of series of rules, of which rule number one is: "Keep quiet. If at all possible, a woman should remain perfectly mute. She should, however, communicate agreement with the men around her, eloquently, through gestures and demeanor."

Well, this explains something of why I've remained such an isolated person. I do like to talk, though I hope not too much. But I certainly like there to be a conversation, and I don't like to have to always assent, possibly because I had a position where I had to dominate, where I had to exercise power, when I founded the Associated Actors Theatre. I became used, before I was twenty-five, to people listening to me. Maybe this is not all good, but at least it has given me the sense of myself as not merely someone who must please men. And it's amazing how all women have this rooted in them even if they are unable to believe in it.

At the Notre Dame Poetry Week—I was so thrilled to be asked, by the way—there had been an open discussion scheduled after breakfast. When I arrived, thirty or forty people were already there, but the other participants had not arrived. I started in asking and answering questions and talking. There was quite a lively discussion by the time the two men panelists arrived, and immediately, unconsciously, my whole tone changed and I, who had been fairly authoritative and definite, became meek and mild. After the hour was over, one of the women came up to me and said, "What happened to you?" It really shook me, because she was absolutely right. What happened to me was that I became what is expected of women, not what I have fashioned of myself all these years.

Nancy Mairs's book is full of wisdom and never hortatory,

always able to extrapolate what seems to be in some ways a very special set of troubles that she has to overcome, physical problems that have to be met. She's almost always able to transcend them, or at least to see them as symptomatic of human life in general. The book has enormous appeal to any woman.

Besides Nancy's book, I'm having a kind of orgy of reading French. I used to be much more *au courant* with what's being written. I subscribe to the *Manchester Guardian* which has excerpts from *Le Monde*, but I almost never read French anymore, now that most of my European correspondents are dead. The only remaining one is Solange Sarton, a distant cousin of mine who lives in Brittany. Her letters are precious because they bring me French again. I seized upon the five French novels Dorothy Wallace sent me like a cat who hasn't had catnip for years. Had I been a cat, I'd have been rolling over on the floor and purring with pleasure for hours, the pleasure of simply reading the language again and feeling completely at home in it. I was so afraid I would not, but I think that a language learned before one is fifteen probably does stay with one. I still have my Belgian accent; I never did have a very pure French accent.

When I go to bed now I have a delight before me. A single French sentence, not even the content, but just the sound of it, is wonderful. I might add that I lost French, which was my first language—spoken until I was two—when we had to leave Belgium. I re-learned it when I was seven and we returned to Belgium for a year in 1919. We didn't speak French at home in America, because my father had to learn English and Mother *was* English, so we always spoke English for his sake. In a way I'm sorry, because in that way I lost French, but it did help him to become a wonderful stylist in English. It was a feat to have learned the language as well as he did.

When he was a young man he took Berlitz lessons in English.
When he wanted to buy a second strip of tickets the professor
said, "There's no point in your doing that, Sarton. You'll never
learn English." Sometimes we can surprise even ourselves.

Monday, September 17

I HAD LOOKED FORWARD to the weekend, because Maggie
Vaughan was coming, bringing all the food, and we were
going to have a lovely time to talk and be together and not
worry about anything.

We had, I'm glad to say, good talks and on the whole a
good time, although it rained all day Saturday—wouldn't you
know it!—and all that day I was simply ill and had to lie on my
bed. This I do resent, since I had had such a terrible attack on
Monday and Tuesday that I felt I've *had* it now and surely I
shall have recovered and be in splendid shape for the weekend.

Maggie is wonderfully understanding—a most imaginative person when it comes to bringing food she knows I can
eat, because I can only eat two or three mouthfuls of anything. She had made delicious tiny cold hamburgers, and we
had mussels, that was the great thing—mussels with a wonderful cream sauce for dinner on Friday, the night she arrived.
It was just right for me. She had made an angel food cake,
so we had some of that, and delicious little cookies. And we
caught up on everything—her extremely occupied life with
all the very good deeds and organizing she does on Hospice
and Family Planning and many other things in Maine. She
is a true Mainer who cares and is willing to give time. I have

CREDIT: ROD KESSLER

May at her desk on the third floor, 1975

great respect for this and love to hear about it, even though I myself am such an indolent dog these days. Still, it's a great pleasure to have money to give away, and I do have that now.

I find that writing a check is a lot easier than writing a letter, so sometimes I spend time writing checks and feel very virtuous. Writing a letter is still the hardest thing of all. I come up here to my study on the third floor and I want *so much* to communicate with a good friend who maybe I haven't written to for months, like Jean Alice Crosby, the prioress of that wonderful Carmelite monastery in Indianapolis where I stayed two or three years ago when I was giving a reading, and of which I have the happiest memories possible.

Jean Alice's letter for my birthday was one of the truly

May in Grundlsee, Austria, 1934

real presents, partly because I did get a lot of letters but so
many of them from people who, for one reason or another,
were not happy, were in crisis, in depression, having a hard
time. At my age that is bound to be true. Many people are ill.
I hear suddenly that someone has Alzheimer's and it's hard to
believe. But Jean Alice's letter was very much like her singing
voice, which is the most spontaneous soprano I've ever heard.
It's like a *bird*. She hasn't been highly trained, because she
entered the convent as a very young girl and has been there

ever since. Her letter has the lilt of happiness. She's no longer the prioress, since in their organization a prioress has only six years in office. Now she's through with that responsibility and a free woman, more or less. Her passion is the garden. I read this letter with great joy and have meant to answer it since my birthday all those months ago. Now I suppose it will never be answered, and I have to accept that she gave me a wonderful present and that's what she wanted to do. But I would like her to know that the reason I haven't answered is not laziness but illness. They are very different. *How* different I learn every day when it seems impossible, for instance, to get up. Today was particularly hard, because I'd been so ill while Maggie was here and in so much pain. The third day I usually feel a lot better but also very tired and shaky. This time when going down to get the cat at eleven last night I didn't exactly curse him, because I love him very much—but I've now made the decision that I'd better get a cat door even if an occasional raccoon manages to get in. We'll see.

Today is beautiful, of course, now that my guest has gone—a dark blue ocean with a shining band of sunlight at the horizon. Maggie even did a little gardening, cutting off deadheads for me, and I went out for a minute to show her what I wanted. She cut down a few tradescantia, which have become very melancholy, and a few other things. It was sheer bliss to be in the garden and to be using my hands, to be dealing with growing things again. I suppose I stayed about five minutes and then felt terribly shaky and had to go in. But it was worth it, and it's now a wonderful recompense to see the garden looking a little tidier than it has for a long time.

One of my problems—I'm sure it's that of everyone in these United States—is that I wake up at night and can't go to sleep again, thinking about the men in the desert in the terrible heat and the word for holy war [jihad] which escapes me at the moment. It is very frightening, and it is very sad to see the human world once more cracking—*cracking*—about religious belief or taking refuge in fanaticism as a way of justifying hatred. There's no point in talking a great deal about this now, but I certainly didn't sleep a wink two nights ago. I kept trying to invent ways of getting off the subject. I would try to remember every great beach where I'd ever walked or remember everything I could about Grundlsee, a lovely Austrian town where I spent two or three summers. I could evoke all this, but then behind it there was always this shadow. And the shadow would gradually take over.

I don't feel well today so it's hard to say even these few words. It is worth doing, I'm sure, if only to give me a chance to see what's really going on here.

Thursday, September 20

How FAST the month has gone! I simply can't believe it. But of course I lost four days in the last ten being ill. Then after the weekend, after Maggie had gone, it took me a few days to get things organized here, for I must soon get back to rewriting that interview for the *New England Quarterly*.

It is again an absolutely beautiful autumn day—a marvelous shine on everything.

I did get a note from Nancy yesterday on the *QE 2*, agreeing with me that it's not as it used to be. She was on the original *Queen Elizabeth* years ago, but she said she was enjoying her deck chair and a good book. Of course that is the best part of the whole trip—peace and quiet, lifting one's head to the horizon as it dips and rises in front of one, being restored by a cup of bouillon. What memories rise up when I think of those ships! Of course my favorite luxury ship was the *Normandie*. I came back on that just before the last trip, before war was declared. We came back blacked out, so we didn't even get news on radios. On that trip, which was very significant for that reason, I met Bill Brown with a group of Yale men of his class bringing back drawings by Picasso and intoxicated by their first explorations of Paris and the arts there. But within a few months, or less, Bill was drafted and from then on I had a GI Joe friend and our long forty-year correspondence began. Then when Bill had leave now and then, before he was sent overseas, he'd come in to New York with his pay and take me out to a grand dinner.

I must admit that my favorite ships were not the luxury liners *Normandie* and the *Queen Elizabeth*, but much smaller ships of the Bernstein Line, which took ten days and sometimes landed at Antwerp, sometimes at Bordeaux. The point was, with an allowance of one hundred dollars a month, ten days where I didn't have to buy meals or pay for a hotel were a tremendous boon. So I arrived with a little money. Not only that, I could work. I used to go into the bar and type on a book from nine to eleven, when the bar was opened to the public and I put my typewriter away. Dutch gin was ten cents for a small glass, so I would have a Dutch gin at eleven. The people who took the Bernstein Line were of course never very well off, often intellectuals, and I made some good friends among them. One was Evelyn Pember, with whom I later stayed in Rodmell and with whom I saw Leonard Woolf more than once for dinner.

There was something very good about that *long* trip—ten days, as I said. You could really settle in to the ship. I did some good writing on those Bernstein liners. But it's all so long ago, because once there were jet airplanes the temptation to fly became irresistible because of time saved. But what I miss, I still miss, when I fly is that transition. From the slow ship you are first still saying goodbye to Europe—if I was on my way home—stretched between two continents, and only after about four days did you begin to look the other way, begin to turn toward home. As the transitions were always painful for me—from both sides I was leaving beloved friends and was torn by goodbyes—it made a wonderful balance to have time, time to think about what had happened, prepare for what was ahead, which was—when I was on my way home—teaching or poetry readings.

Thursday, September 20

I FINALLY DECIDED a couple of days ago that I could not stand my voice any longer. So I found a nose and throat man right here in York. His name is Dr. Chassé. I'm to see him this afternoon, because Dr. Petrovich did suggest that there might be the possibility that this strange voice I have now is caused by polyps on the vocal cords. If this is true and they could be removed—I don't think it would be a major operation even— one of the reasons why I am so depressed would be taken care of. It has been hard never to sound like myself, to have a strange, subdued, cranky voice. So I pray it will work. Though I feel very tired I'll try to have an early lunch and then I'll go to the doctor at three-fifteen. My spirits soar at the thought of something in all this going downhill that would be a respite, would arrest the descent, and give me a little help.

We've been having extremely cold weather—thirty degrees at night—so the garden is really practically finished. I am saddled with a big joke, of course—an enormous box of bulbs from Holland. But I shall have no difficulty giving them away. Diane comes tomorrow and perhaps we can take a look at what there is that she can put in for me. I'm going to try tulips again. One set of purple tulips lived through the Maine winter intact, not eaten in bud by the deer. The deer have been terribly destructive. They ate almost all the lilies. One of the things I must discover when I open the box from Holland is whether I *did* order lilies, because I should put some in, hoping the deer won't be around *quite* as much next summer. Who knows?

Friday, September 21

IT'S NOW SEPTEMBER 21. I think that means the last day of summer and the first day of autumn. It is a perfect first day of autumn, and we're getting a dark blue ocean and brilliant sunshine.

Yesterday I called Dr. Chassé's secretary in the middle of the morning, and much to my amazement she told me that he could see me in the afternoon. So off I went wondering what he would find, how I would like him, whether this was possible at all. He did various tests, including anesthetizing my throat. Then he said, "I think I know what's wrong. I think I knew as soon as I heard you speak." What is wrong, it seems, is that one side of the little door that opens and closes when one eats or speaks has atrophied. Well, this is extraordinary news and I don't know whether anything can be done about it, but he is going to look at X-rays of my heart and all the things they have at the hospital. I'm to see him again next week. So for just twenty-four hours anyway I've had a wild hope that perhaps this most humiliating of my ailments might be helped. I liked Dr. Chassé very much.

I came back very tired and unable to sleep. However, this morning I've at last gotten the social security mess cleared up. This had to do with Eleanor Perkins's social security. It meant getting a check Xeroxed—a check I did find which proves that I did pay, although they accused me of not having paid the first quarter. So we'll see. There's some comfort at least in the fact that it takes them months to answer any communication. So I shall be left in peace for a while.

Diane is supposed to be coming to do some gardening for me but she isn't here yet. She's apt to be late in the morning. She said she could give me a full day, so we should get quite a lot done.

Sunday, September 23

A MOST BEAUTIFUL autumn day after a gloomy, rainy night, but I'm so glad for Susan, who left to get back to New York around lunchtime and had a really wonderful sort of light to go in—that shining autumn light. I don't suppose she's home yet—it's a long trek. But it has been a very good weekend. She arrived late Friday night and has been working on papers here—papers of mine that Nancy got ready for her—so it was very homey and peaceful. She was hard at work in the guest room while I was hard at work trying to feel better in my bedroom with Pierrot, happy that he's sleeping with me *all day*. And that is more or less what I've done.

CREDIT: MONROE SHERMAN

Susan Sherman with Cybèle

It's discouraging not to feel better. I have not had cramps but I feel extremely tired so that all I want to do is to lie down. And I decided that that was the thing to do for the weekend and maybe tomorrow I'll feel better.

It is amazing that already autumn is here. It seems that every season has ripped off before one had time to know it had arrived. As we drove out to the Cape Neddick Inn for dinner last night Susan and I saw two beautiful deer—a doe with a fairly grown-up fawn. Their ears looked enormous against the light. They stood there on a little hillock in the field, didn't move, were not afraid, so we glided past and left them standing there, very much at home against the ocean. It is, of course, a magic place when things like this can happen as they do nearly every day. The deer are after the apples now, so they come a lot.

As always, the Cape Neddick Inn provided very good food. Unfortunately I'm not well so it wasn't exactly what I needed, but it was lovely to be with Susan, looking very beautiful—starting the school year and having learned—I want to say Bravo!—to use a computer this summer. She had one of the students—a brilliant boy and apparently a marvelous instructor—teach her to use it. So she is now buying one and it's going to make her work on the Sarton papers infinitely easier. Anyway, she's very clever and for the first time I realize what this means to her, to have the power that this extraordinary machine provides if you know how to use it. If I were twenty years younger I'd have one, but as it is I'm happy with this little Sony recorder.

Inevitably the situation in the Middle East is always there. I have strange dreams about it almost every night. I dreamed the other night that we had defended Tibet in the way we're defending Kuwait—if only that could be true! The truth is we do not defend small, valuable countries but only countries which have something we need and can't bear to lose. It's a cynical time. I think that the American people who are accepting rather well that we're almost engaged in a war *are* accepting it because they're not being told what it is going to cost—what taxes we inevitably shall have to pay.

Monday, September 24

ANOTHER GLORIOUS autumn day. There was a little crimson streak in the sunrise when I went down at six to take the rubbish out and fill the bird feeder—which the squirrels have practically destroyed, so pretty soon I'll have to use the new

CREDIT: ANNE C. TREMEARNE

one. As they cost twenty-seven dollars and last about three months it's no joke. The squirrels are intolerable. The worst thing about them is that they are so old. I shouldn't say that, because I'm old myself, but some of these squirrels must be fifteen years old, because I recognize them. They've been coming to the feeder since I arrived here!

Anyway, last night I stayed up until nine-thirty in order to see two-thirds of the first part of the much-touted documentary film *Civil War*. A great many of us, myself included, really have not put our minds on the Civil War, at least not for a long time. Of course I never went to college, instead went into the theater as an apprentice at Eva Le Gallienne's Civic Repertory in New York. I'm glad I didn't go to college except for one reason, and that is, of course, that there are great areas of my knowledge of history which are very weak. I never took a course in American history in high school or at Shady Hill, which has now become famous for its excellent inaugurative year on the Civil War. It was extremely moving to watch what I saw of the documentary last night. I learned a little about the Civil War by going south in 1940 when we were still in World War II and I could not go to Europe as I had been used to doing. I decided it was time to go on a journey to discover America and to read my poems at various colleges. Anyone who wanted me for twenty-five dollars could have me, if they put me up for a night or two. So I wrote to two hundred colleges, and much to my surprise, and, I may say, to everyone else's, fifty accepted my invitation to come. They were scattered all over the country, so I spent a whole winter exploring. These colleges were often in small towns— I'm thinking, for instance, of Sterling College in Sterling, Kansas. It seemed that a good way to find out something about the United States was to travel to fifty colleges.

The big emotional experience was going south. For a Northerner this had to be a major shock. From my car I saw children who looked not more than seven dragging tow sacks and picking cotton. They were poor whites, sharecroppers, not blacks. But there was also the shock of entering any town and seeing the signs "White Only" or "No Colored," of knowing that going into a restaurant you wouldn't be turned aside unless you were black. Everything was painfully vivid as I traveled. I also—and that's the other side of it—was tremendously moved as for the first time—and here I was in my twenties—I began to realize how horrendous the Civil War had been and was haunted by ghosts wherever I went, and haunted by memories I did not have, but *should* have had, of first meetings with such heroic figures as Robert E. Lee. Lee was a nonexistent figure to most North American girls in high

school. He was simply mentioned as the general-in-chief of
the Gray Army. It was Lincoln who was emphasized, and only
as I went south and read and heard more did I begin to see
what an extraordinary *mentor* Robert E. Lee was and how
magnificently he handled failure. In fact, we could go back to
Lee and learn something new every day. All this was coming
back into my mind as I watched the film.

I think I became American—wholly American—on that
trip, and again ten or more years later when I bought thirty-
six acres of woodland and an old farm in New Hampshire,
about which I've written a great deal. But until those two
experiences I was really *tethered* to Europe.

One of the most memorable of the experiences I had in
that autumn was the ten-day visit to Black Mountain College,
then at the height of its experimental life. They were building—all the faculty and students gathered together every afternoon to build the main building. I became convinced that
this shared manual work was an extremely important part of
the spirit of the college, and I wondered what would happen
when there was no longer that bond between faculty and
students. As it turned out, the college did have an extraordinary life and an extraordinary influence, but it did not last.

Of course, the greatest adventure of that trip was discovering Santa Fe and the Sangre de Cristo Mountains. The landscapes and the colleges there were in a different category
from my *collision*—I can only describe it that way—with the
South when I first came to it. One of the things that amazed
me was the conversation, wherever one was, wherever one
might be, in a restaurant, or among friends, in a city like
Savannah, or Charleston (I fell in love with Charleston—who
doesn't?). *Always* the Civil War or the War Between the
States, as it is called in the South, came up and very often
dominated the conversation, perhaps partly because I was a
Northerner. But I got tired of hearing always of something

that happened one hundred years ago, and finally the Belgian immigrant in me revolted. I said to them, "You know, in Belgium they've had the Germans three times since 1870. It is not the only subject of conversation." Southerners are polite and I was not attacked, but I felt this deeply. The trouble is, I suppose, that such a brutal defeat and the brutal way the North handled the victory has left a permanent clot, really, in the bloodstream of Americans. It's interesting to think that now there is beginning to be a new topic of conversation, and the reason for guilt is the miserable way we treated Native Americans.

In the Civil War documentary film there are wonderful photographs of black families, slaves, working in the fields. I hadn't realized that they worked from dawn to dusk, which meant that in summer that might be a sixteen-hour day. It's so close to us in time. A little more than a hundred years and hard to imagine.

Wednesday, September 26

I AM GOING to see Dr. Petrovich at noon. I'm really glad I can, because I seem to be more tired than I've ever been. It's as if my heart weighed more. Walking a few steps exhausts me. It is scary, and I wonder if I'm on the brink of a heart attack. Thank goodness, dear Karen K. called yesterday to see if there was anything she could do. I have two packages in the back of the car that I had to leave there until someone came along. She came and saved me.

I had acute pain for four or five hours after lunch, and I

couldn't watch all of the Civil War film by any means. It's a remarkable job but it's so painful, so painful to think, for instance, that nobody believed in Abraham Lincoln, that he was surrounded by ambitious men who thought he was some kind of gorilla and should be pushed aside so that one of them could take over. I wonder how often that happens, when a very remarkable leader is simply not recognized by those who should be his followers? Of course, Lincoln had incredibly bad luck in his generals, and this is one of the things that makes watching *Civil War* so painful.

This morning I came up here to my study determined to finish the blurb for Larry LeShan's book *The Dilemma of Psychology*. It's a very good book, but it's way off my beat, so I've worked very hard on it. In fact, it has cost me three days and two nights. I could not sleep at all the night before last, worrying about it.

Duffy Schade is a photographer who has done some very sensitive photographing of the moods, the images of nature, in my poems especially, and has been reading them and showing them in churches and to groups here and there. She was very insistent yesterday that she would like to do something to help me—and to drive up from Connecticut. So it occurred to me that there is that huge box of bulbs in the garage. I suggested that she might come in early October and do a few hours of gardening for me.

Last year I was able at least to put in twenty-four hyacinths. They're always very effective in the bed that I see from my chaise longue. They are mixed colors and really very charming, with two rows of daffodils at the back. Last year I was able to plant the twenty-four lying down—that's my new way of planting bulbs—but it makes me realize that I'm worse rather than better, because I don't think I could possibly do that this year. I'm terribly shaky this year.

Sunday, September 30

THIS IS THE LAST DAY of September. Tomorrow we'll be in autumn. Today it's rainy and gloomy, and I am trying to come to terms with a very knotted object, to put it mildly, every day since Friday, so I haven't been able to think about the journal. It's interesting how when everyone plans to have a quietly planned time, everything explodes and it's quite impossible. Deborah Straw and Bruce Conklin had been due to come here for a long time to do a two-part interview, one hour a day for two days. I didn't know that Bruce was bringing his camera and planned to photograph me constantly. I knew it would be a strain, but I decided to be sensible and rest. Everything will work out all right.

The first thing that happened was that Dr. Chassé, who is really, I think, going to try to help me with my voice, changed the appointment instead of seeing me on Friday, which would have been fairly easy. I have two CAT scans and an X-ray at the hospital at one-thirty, so that took my rest time. Janice Oberacker's dear dog, Fonzie, is very sick, and she herself has a bad cold. I couldn't call on her. Karen K. is away for the weekend. I can drive all right, but parking the car and then having to walk to the hospital from the parking place and then driving myself home would leave me very tired. I went into a tailspin of fear. I called Anne and Barbara and they suggested that I talk to Priscilla Powers, Janice's friend. Although she had a crowded day at home and outside appointments, she managed to come for me at one-thirty. It was marvelous to see that car drive up and to know that I was going to be taken care of. It's absurd, but at present walking is such a problem—I'm so afraid of falling—that to just be in somebody's care is a blessing.

I spent half of Friday at the hospital having the CAT scans and other tests. I was so tired when I came home I couldn't think about supper. I made myself an eggnog and went to bed.

I was fast asleep at one-thirty on Thursday afternoon when the phone rang. It was a friend who shall be nameless, but a dear friend, who had epilepsy, whose profession is taking care of retarded people, especially adults, and who is now on a job where she is up all night from nine to nine in a kind of nursing home for crippled people. She is never very well, but she has a strong character, full of compassion and love. She's been living for the last three years with a woman who is in the nursing profession and who has apparently loved her and they seem to be able to make a go of it. Unfortunately, however, this woman has what amounts to seizures of rage. She called me on Thursday at one-thirty to say that her friend had bitten her leg very badly, had tried to strangle her, and the marks were very clear on her neck. I said, of course, that she must go at once to the emergency room at the hospital to see what was what. Her brutal friend had also put her out and she didn't have any money except what she earns on the night job, which pays very little. I said I would get her a cashier's check right away and send her five hundred dollars by air express. I was so blotto, being asleep and exhausted, that it seemed to me impossible to get up, pull myself together, drive to town, and do this little bit of business before the bank closed. Luckily I made it and then I went back and tried to rest.

Meanwhile every night the extraordinary PBS film on the Civil War goes on. It's made from contemporary photographs.

It comes as a traumatic experience, because so much of it has
been shut out. I mean, when you see and are told that eleven
thousand men died in *one* of the battles, it's very hard to take
in. And when you hear that at the start of the war one in seven
Americans was a slave, it's hard to take in. It was especially
hard to take in what Sherman's march to the sea really did.
The brutality of it makes one cry aloud with shame and rage if
one is a Northerner. At the same time the horrors of the
Southern prisons, of Andersonville, are borne in. Certainly
this film makes you think that war is not only hell but should
be abolished, that it's something so bad that people should be
allowed to let rage take them over to this extent, that one
would wish that we were never to have anything to do with
war. I suppose the film had added impact because of the present situation in the Near East, where after all we now have
two hundred thousand men ready to fight, and all the
matériel. If you have that many people, ready to fight, won't
they fight? Doesn't the time come when it's the only thing to
do? Because it's too humiliating to call them home when nothing has happened?

So all together these four or five days when I was very
concerned about a dear friend, and was suffering through the
Civil War on PBS, and at the same time being given a little
hope by Dr. Chassé about my throat but also making more
visits to doctors, keeping more appointments at the hospital, I
feel I've been running, all the time running, sleeping very
little, unable to eat because by the time I got to a meal I was
too tired to eat it. What I am hoping, assuming our friends will
be here to finish the interview, is that I shall be able to have
lunch with Edythe Haddaway, who is coming to fetch me.
With something hot in my stomach perhaps I won't feel quite
so frail. It's ridiculous to feel as frail as I do, really ridiculous.
Meanwhile the gray skies and rain don't help.

Thursday, October 11

IT'S BEEN A LONG TIME—perhaps as much as two weeks—since
I've been able to get back to thinking about this journal. I've
been through a long ordeal—of feeling a great deal worse,
being unable to breathe very well, and dragged down in every
way. Talking the journal didn't seem the thing to do. Then on
the holiday weekend, October 6, I began to feel really very ill
and worried. I called Pat Chasse, my dear visiting-nurse
friend, and asked her to come over and give me advice. I said I
thought the lung needed draining and I can't breathe because
of accumulated liquid in the lining of the left lung. She said
we'll go to the hospital and they'll operate tonight. I thought
they would never operate on a weekend, that was not *possible*. She assured me that they would, and to call Dr. Petrovich
at once.

So I did and he was responsive, suggesting I meet him at
the emergency entrance right away. So off we went—extraordinary Pat and I—what would I have done without her? Right
there in the hospital bed the X-ray machine was wheeled into
the emergency room and they took an X-ray of the chest and
found that indeed there was a great deal of liquid that should
be removed. I asked about being able to get a surgeon on the
weekend. Dr. Petrovich said, "We'll get somebody." If you
can believe it, by nine o'clock that night the doctor had oper-
ated and taken six hundred cc's of liquid out.

I can breathe again. Dr. Petrovich thought I had better

stay two or three days. Actually I've had this small operation before—it's done under local anesthetic and it's never worried me—but this time the surgeon was not quite as adept as the former ones and I have had a good deal of pain and find it difficult to stoop.

But the main thing is that I had a talk with Dr. Petrovich the next day. Because he's so busy, a chance to sit down and talk is rare. We did talk, maybe five minutes, sitting side by side in my hospital room. I said to him that I feel somehow off my track and I don't sense the direction I'm going in. He said, "You'll never be well, you know." That was followed by a rather loud silence as after a clash of cymbals. *You'll never be well.*

For so long I had imagined that I could get well, that it was very much up to me, therefore, not to overdo, to treat myself as a good patient, ever hopeful. When people asked if I was feeling any better I answered, "Yes, I do seem to be feeling better," but not lately. Now I think it will be a relief to be able to say, "No, I don't feel any better."

What Dr. Petrovich added was that he could, perhaps, improve things slightly, and that of course is what I'm hoping. At first, under this shock—which was quite a shock—I felt that I couldn't even make the effort of the journal, that I must consider my life as finished. Then I began to think about it and how much one needs a reason for living. Without grandchildren, for instance, there is nobody really whom I live for, although I have many dear friends. But what I should live for is to continue my work till the very end. There are, after all, numbers of people who face chronic illness, illness which can't be cured, and perhaps they will be glad to find somebody who can talk a little about it. There is also Dr. Chassé, who is fervently trying to find out the cause of the crack in my voice. I also wondered if it was worth going on with that, and then I thought, well, it would be marvelous to be able to speak on the telephone without this scratchy sound. So why not go ahead? I have time, after all.

During this difficult weekend and this time in general, friends have never been more helpful, more life-giving. Dorothy Molnar, little Sarton's mother (Sarton is named for me and is now eleven), who had called several times earlier, told me they were coming for the weekend to a banquet and asked what could she bring me to eat. I suggested lamb stew, so she brought wonderful packages of lamb stew which could be defrosted, and delicious chicken vegetable soup. These good meals have sustained me wonderfully until this weekend. The other heroic thing she did was to empty the old Frigidaire, because Mary-Leigh Smart, who owns this house is giving me a new refrigerator. It is coming in the next few days and I was dreading emptying the old one, dreading it terribly because I really don't have the strength for anything like that. Dorothy did it, bless her heart.

Meanwhile Pat Chasse, who was responsible for my getting myself together and asking for help, came in with her friend Dale. They took care of the house, house-sat, and fed the cat, who only came in to eat and stayed out all night—he is a curious character. They like it here and had perfect weather, whereas now, ever since I've been home, it has poured morning, noon and night. To take the bird feeder in at dusk and out at sunrise I have to get dressed in a raincoat and heavy shoes. I dread it, dread the effort. And also it is frightfully gloomy. After all, this is the great month in Maine— October. It should be brilliant, the leaves golden and crimson. They are beginning to turn, but they're falling in the rain, and there's no shine on them. It's very gloomy indeed.

Other friends are helping. Judy Burrowes comes in a few minutes to do some writing for me—to answer some of the fan letters which I have felt bad not to recognize in any way. She will be here very soon.

So this is the beginning of a new journal—the journal of a woman who now knows she will never get well.

Friday, October 12

QUITE UNBELIEVABLE, but it's still raining. The gloom—one week without a shred, a touch, of sunlight—has been pretty depressing. How strange life is! When I was giving up all hope of ever getting well, I saw Dr. Petrovich yesterday and he suggested that we might try a medicine which would prove that the liquid they take out of the lining of the left lung to help me breathe better might have some negative elements in it, which could be helped by a new drug which contains hormones. If we could get rid of whatever is building up there I would have more energy. For the first time he admitted that the very small amount of energy I have is not explainable only by the fibrillating heart, which is now old and very tired. I had been begging him to consider that something besides the heart might be involved for more than a year—maybe two or three years, actually—but I had given up because nobody believed me. He had even said that at my age, with the heart I have, I could be as short of energy as I am.

Maggie is coming for the weekend. Although rain is predicted for the whole weekend, it will be wonderfully cozy to sit and talk and catch up on everything as we have not done for quite a while.

Carolyn Heilbrun sent me her new Amanda Cross, which

has a marvelous title, *The Players Come Again.* I've been reading it during most of every night for two nights! I read *much* more thoroughly now, but also it brings all kinds of ideas into my head, and unfortunately being wide awake most of the time it's not only ideas about Carolyn's excellent invention in this book but also about all the things I haven't done. I remembered with horror that I had never answered Bill Heyen, who sent me a whole group of poems on the Holocaust a month ago—poems he's written alongside others by a Jewish poet friend of his. Years ago I was tremendously moved to find that a poet of German descent—as Heyen is—had been so possessed by the need to write about the Holocaust that he did so when very few poets had attempted anything of the sort. He is a remarkable poet—a remarkable man, one to take comfort in, one to go back to and be nourished by.

Sunday, October 14

JUST A MINUTE AGO the sun came out—out of the fog and the drizzle, the rain, and the thunder and lightning. We've suffered for, I think, nine days without a break. It's been the worst episode of weather I've ever been through here—so *terribly* depressing. This morning I didn't even want to get up, to plunge again through the wet grass, fill the bird feeder and drag it back. Of course, it's been a blessing to have Maggie here, because alone I should have been close to despair. But she has always—life-enhancing person that she is—brought delicious food and every possible thoughtful thing to make life more bearable.

A good example was our dinner the Friday night she arrived. She brought two dozen oysters and cracked them on the terrace wall with a hammer, although it was pouring rain. The task was much harder than the first time she'd done it several weeks ago—as if she could never get them open. But finally there they were: twenty-four delicious oysters on a bed of ice as our main course. Then a little casserole of creamed corn— corn from her garden—and another dish full of peas—frozen, but originally from her garden. Dessert came in tiny demitasse cups, which made me think of Greenings Island and our demitasse of coffee after lunch, when there was always animated talk before we went off to have our naps. Here was the same idea: that is, variegated demitasse cups, each filled with chocolate mousse and decorated with a cookie in the shape of a heart. It was an elegant luncheon, including a glass of some white wine I had stowed away in the refrigerator. Imagine inventing a meal like that—exquisite, not too much of anything—such variety of tastes and colors.

Yesterday—again one of these awful days—we went to the liquor outlet and I was able to refill my rather empty liquor cupboard as far as Scotch goes. Of course, we talk a great deal, although I have to climb the stairs and lie down rather often. I certainly don't feel less frail. That's why I'm so eager to be allowed to try this new medicine that might possibly help me.

I've now finished Amanda Cross's new book, *The Players Come Again*. It's a very fascinating one of this series. I'm not absolutely convinced—that is, I want more—and I think a lot of readers will. She seems to me to have neatly escaped a very hard thing that she suggested in the book itself was going to be done, was going to happen. At any rate, for the last two or three days Kate Fansler has provided me with food for thought and delight in a charming, personal style, as Carolyn is meticulous in her scholarly work and in her literary work about not talking about herself, and it's amusing to find Kate surely the projection of someone she would like to be and *is* to a very large extent. At any rate I enjoyed it immensely. I think I'll call her sometime today.

The nights and this strange weather have been very bad. I've simply kept quiet and tried to rest and not let my mind go wildly off on escapades into the past as it has been doing lately. But the nights have not been easy, and last night was particularly difficult because of the large flashes of lightning—silent—not the thunder, which was only a low rumble, but always there for twelve hours. A breathless night, not in any way appealing to the senses. I felt irritable and put upon.

Monday, October 15

AT LAST THE LONG rainy spell is over and we are having a real autumn day—sun, light through the leaves, and the ocean blue. I've been trying all day to get to this machine. I spent half an hour replacing the batteries, thinking that was the trouble. It turned out that I simply had it stuck on the pause button and couldn't make it go. So I wasted the morning and it's now late in the afternoon.

I want to be sure to talk a little about what a miracle the telephone is for me now. It's what I live on. Sometimes it gets to be too much when many people call between five and six and I get tired. But yesterday after Maggie left I was resting, in fact, may have been asleep, with Pierrot at the foot of the bed, purring, when the phone rang. I heard a voice say, "May, this is Joy." Joy Greene is the only one still alive of the

four Copley Greene sisters, who were as close to an adopted
family as I have had in America. Katrine was my age and died
of cancer.

Joy must now be well into her eighties—a most extraordinary person. Curiously enough I've thought of her a great
deal in these last difficult months. I've wanted to say something, but I didn't want to press my illness on her or anyone
else. In fact, I've hesitated quite a lot about calling people,
because what do you say? "I'm sick." What do they say? But
here was Joy. She'd been thinking of me and wondered how I
was. So the whole story poured out—poured out in a way that
I've held back, and suddenly as we talked I was crying. I
haven't cried for months. One of the strange things about this
long illness and depression is that I have not had that relief—
and it is a relief. I felt it as tears poured down my cheeks and
Joy said, "Of course we'll cry together, we always have."

It was wonderful. She thinks she might be able to come
and see me for an hour or two. This is where I *am* in a very
strange state these days, because I'm not sure that I can handle it. We left it that she would call me again. I lay back on the
pillows and let the tears come and felt a sort of deep joy that I
haven't felt for a long time. I think it's partly the sense that I
was with family, because the Greene's really were family. I
adored their mother, Rosalind, wrote a poem to her on her
seventy-fifth birthday, and I was intimate with the daughters,
each in a very different way—all except Ernesta, the youngest
and the most beautiful young woman I think I've ever seen,
who shot herself when she was twenty-five. Joy's call was an
extraordinary experience.

Then the phone rang again and it was a friend of mine
from Victoria, British Columbia—in fact, she arranged a lecture for me some years ago. She was the muse of the *Letters
from Maine*. I hadn't heard from her for a long time, so it was
wonderful to hear her voice, to hear all is well and that she is

teaching many patients as a gerontologist. She had suddenly felt that she needed to know what was happening to me.

I'm not feeling well. Of course, it's been an exhausting afternoon, because they brought the new refrigerator and Mary-Leigh came with the men, and she could not have been kinder. She didn't want me to get overtired, and she had arranged everything and helped the men. And now there it is. At last there will not be water on top of every dish; every dish will not have to be covered very carefully. And it looks awfully nice. It has been quite a day!

There is a great charm of flowers because Maryann Parnell sent me a bunch of pale blue scabiosa, and they are magical, such a delicate, summery flower. After all the rain and misery of last week, when they came they were like a blessing, they came in so airily and settled so happily into the room. There are still wonderful flowers from Phyllis Chiemingo and part of a bunch which came simply from a fan with a rather curious note saying: Now you really must get well, and you will. Of course, that came right after I had been told by the doctor that I would never get well! However, the flowers, yellow freesia and dark blue delphinium, with, strewn among them, a very delicate pale yellow orchid that looks like a whole lot of spring butterflies floating through the air, are exquisite. I took the orchids out, and they're in a vase by themselves right here where I can see them. Some of the roses, the marvelous roses that Susan Sherman brings—for she's found a place in New York where she can buy these by the dozen—became, when I was in the hospital, a wonderful, rather brilliant pink, and they are still not faded. It's amazing.

Duffy is coming on Wednesday to plant bulbs. I had meant this afternoon to open the Dutch bulbs that have come. I thought there were lilies among them, but now by looking at the catalog it seems to me that there are not.

Friday, October 19

I'M WAITING for Karen K., my kind driver, who is coming to drive me to Dr. Gilroy's office, hoping that he will be willing to prescribe the new drug which Dr. Petrovich, the heart man, seems to think might possibly give me a shot in the arm and a little more energy. That would be marvelous, as I'm now on the fourth day of a really bad attack of diverticulitis, or whatever it is, very bad cramps, and in fact it's an ordeal to go to the doctor under these circumstances, but I'm anxious to get a prescription for this new drug.

So much has been happening, so much that I wanted to put into the journal but have not felt well enough. One of the things is that my old friend Karen Saum is coming this afternoon for the weekend, bringing dinner, and it will be wonderful to see her and catch up on her marvelously giving life. Karen is a grandmother. She has three grown sons. She's now on her way, when she leaves me, to see, I think, her second granddaughter.

Of course, on a less personal level, it has been a great shock to have Leonard Bernstein drop off the earth as he did the other day. He'd had trouble with lung cancer, I guess, and it was a fairly easy death. But what a tremendous mourning all over the world, for here was a man with such dedicated exuberance—a genius as a conductor and also as a composer.

Sunday, October 21

AT LAST I'M BACK. I've neglected this little machine for days, because a great deal has been happening and I've simply had to think a lot and I haven't had time to get through the underbrush yet. The main thing is that I saw Dr. Gilroy last Friday, hoping that he would prescribe the drug that Dr. Petrovich had talked to me about, which might make me more comfortable. I went to see Dr. Gilroy determined to state my case once more. Amongst other things why it is that for eight months I have spoken to doctors about losing fifty pounds in a year and nobody said, well, there must be some reason for that. In fact, Dr. Petrovich went so far as to say that my fibrillating heart plus my age were enough to explain my extreme weakness. Lately it has been harder and harder to walk, even a few steps, even from here to the garage. So I've become rather ruffled, I should say.

I talked about this to Dr. Gilroy and ended my little speech with: "So what now?" There was a slight pause and then he said, "May, we have not been able to diagnose what is wrong with you, but now we think we can." It looks as if it is cancer, which has spread from the area of the mastectomy to the lining of the left lung and showed itself by the fluid which has accumulated every three months or so and has had to be removed and for which I was in the hospital ten days ago. Of course, cancer explains the loss of weight, fifty pounds, I realized at once. He also said that it was very likely the reason for my voice having been so affected. That was the shock, but it was not nearly as bad as it might have been, because he immediately said that they were going to try the new drug, Nolvadex, that it had had amazingly good results, that if it works for me I'll have a very much more comfortable time. I won't be as frail and it might add two or three years to my life. So this is really exciting, and I've already started taking the drug. Dear Karen K. drove me there.

The other Karen, Karen Saum, arrived at about five o'clock to spend the weekend. This has been a remarkable weekend. Before she came I was thinking so much about her. For one whole year she lived here on the weekends. She worked in Augusta and came back here, often on Thursday night, and only went back early Monday morning. She had work to do here, loved Tamas, went for long walks with him, and did all the cooking on the weekend. The marvelous thing was that we had shared a true communion of the spirit for three days but then I resumed my solitude for four days from Monday through Thursday or Friday.

Thinking it over, I decided it was the best living relationship I probably have ever had. Of course, Judy—Judy Matlack was the best—but after Judy then this was the most remarkable. Of course, it was much later in my life—I was sixty-five and more.

It was an event to see Karen, looking wonderfully hale and full of everything that she is, because this is a woman who is now *here*. One could say she has reached a time of great fulfillment in her life, which has not been easy. She had three sons when she was very young and first married. Then her husband divorced her and she was left with the three sons to support. She has worked for H.O.M.E. now for quite some time, and is one of the people responsible for getting a high school degree for the people of H.O.M.E., so that these women who used to be trapped in mobile homes can now go to school and get their final degree. What Karen has done, the spectacular thing, is to see that those who are equipped for it, and who want it, can go to college and graduate. I think four or five have already graduated from Union College up there. It's just a miracle. But adding to that, when she was living with me here she was writing. She wrote autobiographical essays about her childhood in Panama which I thought were excellent. In fact, I thought *The New Yorker* should take them, but they rejected them and she was never able to get them published. Then she began, after she left here, to write whodunits. This is about the fourth one, I think—but the first one to come out. The others will come out one by one. This one is very amusing for me, because it's full of things that have really happened to Karen, particularly at H.O.M.E.

All Karen did for me was incredible. This morning she changed both our beds, putting on clean sheets. Before that she had done another laundry for me. She cooked delicious meals for us while she was here. She also did work of her own, and she did many odd jobs. There were quite a few, because this kind of help is what I lack most. It was a spectacular, unforgettable joy to have Karen in the house again. She says she'll come during the winter now and then.

In fact, my little plan to manage without Nancy while she was away by having friends come for the weekends has worked very well. Susan Sherman will be here this coming weekend. It has been a series of great adventures, but it does prevent me, unfortunately, from doing this journal as often as I should. I was very depressed when Karen arrived, and she noticed it. I couldn't hide it. But by the time she left I was immensely cheered, having had a loving companion beside me with whom I could talk things over.

Nancy is back and will be coming tomorrow morning. I've managed without her, but of course I've missed her very much and it seemed as if the heart had gone out of things in lots of ways while she was gone.

Unfortunately the lights went out at about four this morning. Karen was asleep, and I went around trying to get things organized in case we had to make breakfast without any heat or light. I found out, among other things, that both the flashlights which plug in and are wonderfully bright were not plugged in, so there was no way to get them to help. I stumbled around, finally lit one candle, had a terrible time getting Central Maine Power on the phone, because their number had changed and with one candle it was almost impossible to read the new number in the book. I did finally get it, and was cheered by their saying that they thought the outage would be over at five.

Meanwhile I began to feel very tired, which was natural enough, and went back to bed. I woke at half-past six—late for me—very agitated because there were lots of things Karen and I had planned to do, including ordering and getting into her car a great box of sweaters that I was sending over to H.O.M.E. Also a couple of persimmons from two dear fan-friends who, knowing I love persimmons, each had sent me a box, which arrived, I think, on Friday or maybe Saturday. They had to be unpacked and arranged.

Lovely blue asters from Susan Sherman also came just as the only bunch of flowers in the house was fading.

Wednesday, October 24

THE RAIN HAS STOPPED after the most depressing day yesterday of rain, and all night the plopping of heavy raindrops against the windows and the roof. It was a *heavy* twenty-four hours in which I didn't feel very well. The thing that's depressing now, I must admit, is that I have very bad cramps again, have had since Sunday afternoon when Karen left. I wonder whether it could possibly be the new drug. Maybe—I seem to be supersensitive to any drug, and here I am again. I've now taken a large dose of paregoric, Kaopectate three times, and two Tylenol Extra Strength for pain. It's now four, or quarter of five—and I took these things between half-past one and three this afternoon. I must say that I do not feel acute pain, but the trouble is that I also feel completely exhausted. As I said to Edythe when we talked at three on the telephone, I feel terribly lonely. It's not a loneliness for a single person; it's not wanting somebody to come and see me; it's loneliness from a feeling of helplessness—that I can't handle so much pain. Yet it goes on and there is apparently no answer, because when I did go to a specialist, Dr. Flavin, and he prescribed drugs for the pain, I had a very groggy head and simply didn't feel like myself. I told him finally that I thought I had to stand the pain and forget about trying to stop it. I think this is the truth, but the trouble is it takes hours and hours of my life and leaves me exhausted. It is just a tough knot to untie and I don't know what will happen, so I'll keep on taking the new medicine, and hope.

It is now a beautiful autumn afternoon—a quarter of five—the light going over the swamp that I look at through the window by my chaise longue. The ocean is behind me—a wonderful dark blue. But what is most beautiful now is the light through the leaves, although this has not been a great autumn from that point of view. Right now, in the last two days, there is more color. Beyond the high trunks of the Japanese pines there is a great tapestry of orange and yellow and lime green in the trees in the woods and beyond the swamp below the house.

What's fascinating here is that there are so many kinds of

CREDIT: SUSAN SHERMAN

landscape. I have almost everything. There are freshwater ponds. There is, of course, the great ocean itself. There is the swamp, which is entirely different from the ponds. It's a great place for deer, but I haven't seen a deer since the big rain we had two weeks ago—when it rained for a whole week. The deer disappeared; perhaps they found it better to be somewhere all curled up to wait for it to end.

It's amazing how Pierrot loves the rain, or at least he wants to go out so much that he will go out finally in a deluge and stay out for an hour or two. The trouble is that there comes a moment when I call him, when I know that he wants to come but is afraid. He's hiding under a bush, doesn't want to come out, and that's the bad moment. Last night about eight I finally got dressed over my pajamas, in a raincoat and scarf, put on real shoes, put on the lights at the garage, and stumbled out through horrifyingly heavy rain. There he was, against the garage door where it was a little bit shielded by the overhang. I picked him up, he mewed at me, and he then hung limp in my arms. But I don't have much strength, and before we got to the door he had escaped, much to my despair. I called and called. No sign. Then I had the wit to look at the front door, and there he was waiting to come in, meowing to be fed. One very satisfactory thing about Pierrot is that he has a huge appetite, so that he almost never refuses his food. So many cats are difficult about food, but he is not. The thing he loves best, I'm afraid, is lobster. I always give him a claw when I have a lobster, but I don't have them very often, so he's had maybe only two this whole summer.

And isn't it incredible to think the summer is over, and we are in the middle of fall. This morning I paid November bills, including the rent on the house, and thought, I can't believe the year is nearly over. And where has it gone? And where have I gone in it? Well, I've gone toward a great deal of acceptance of difficult things to accept. I've gone to no longer minding so terribly that I can't answer people. I look at the letters, I reread them, I think, Oh, how marvelous that somebody could say that, but I don't lie awake at night because it doesn't get answered. And this is simply a matter of reality. I can't. I do manage to pay bills, and I love giving money away. So when I go up to my study with the idea that I am going to write a letter, it very often ends simply in my sending a check to New Forests, or H.O.M.E., or one of the many things that I love supporting and want to support.

I shall miss terribly Frances Partridge's last journal, which I ordered from England. All through this rather difficult two weeks it has been the saving grace to go back into—that so *human* journal. This journal she began the day after her hus-

"My desk"

band died. It's the journal of somebody wandering around trying to live through total grief and sense of abandonment. She does succeed amazingly, of course, sees a great many people, always describing them marvelously well, so that at the end of the description of a dinner party you feel that you have been there. Of all the Bloomsburyites she seems to be what one might call the best *person*—a very honest, warm, loving person, with no illusions about herself, no false ambitions—a remarkable person of goodness.

Nancy has put up the new feeder. Right now there is a hairy woodpecker at it. It's quite amazing to see what putting up the new one has done, because the birds only eat about three-quarters of it every day, whereas the old one, which the squirrels had gnawed their way into, poured out seed. It was absolutely empty by about five. I wonder how long the new one will last, because of course the squirrels are already lying upside down on it, gnawing away and trying to make bigger holes.

There are far fewer finches. Of course, many of them have left now, but chickadees are there, and the nuthatches, whose voices I really love, are there. There have been no grosbeaks here at Wild Knoll, except, alas, once, a rose-breasted one who became very tame. I found it extremely hard to forgive Bramble, who caught him. Luckily I didn't see it. I found dark blue feathers—not the rose breast, but the very dark blue feathers—and knew what had happened. In fact, I think I wrote a poem about it which is in one of the books. I miss the twenty or thirty goldfinches who used to come, swooping around, singing, and sometimes twenty sitting on the wire that holds up the bird feeder. The air was always full of wings. That's changed now. We're going into winter.

Twice I've heard skeins of geese go by but didn't catch them in time, so I haven't seen one yet. But of course they are on their way now—south—and soon the monarch butterflies will be gone. In fact, I haven't seen one since this terrible rain, so they may have already left. I'm hoping a titmouse will turn up, maybe this evening, but right now there's nothing there but chickadees and the woodpecker.

How marvelous to have Nancy back! This morning I felt rather shaky, and there was a good reason for it, so I asked her to drive me to town. We did a few errands and quickly came home. The reason I was shaky at half-past nine was that while Nancy has been away I have asked Eleanor Perkins to come twice a week instead of once—she cleans wonderfully for me—to tidy up drawers and cupboards on those extra days. She has been absolutely magnificent. What a present it is to be given a tidy drawer or closet where all was chaos. The last time she was here—on Tuesday—she didn't ask me but she started on the sweaters. There was a sort of glory hole where the sweaters were folded and put on top of each other. I've tidied that up about once every six weeks, but it was always in disorder again very shortly—the trouble being that there were too many sweaters. Many of them had a spot or a moth hole right in the middle of the chest. Disorder that needed desperately to be cleaned up. So Eleanor went at it last Tuesday, and I dreaded this day—Thursday—because I realized that she would want me to make decisions and help her get it finally in order. The trouble is that if I do anything in the morning, anything, a little work at my desk, *all* my energy is used up. That, of course, is what happened this morning. By nine-thirty I was a total wreck and wanted only to go back to bed. But at least there is order where there was only chaos. The house will feel better when Susan Sherman comes tomorrow night. It has a new spirit because it's so tidy and so proud of itself.

At three this morning I woke in a sweat, remembering that I had never answered Pat Carroll's dear letter saying that she would come and take me out to lunch if I could set a date on a Monday when she had a free day from her performance in *Nunsense,* at the Charles Street Playhouse. That was in answer to my letter telling her how sad I was not to be able to see the show, which everyone said was hilarious. But of course I couldn't. It's so typical of Pat to offer to come all this way, rent a car, and take me out to lunch. I was very touched, but somehow her letter never got answered. Fortunately I woke up at three this morning with it in my head, and I did manage to do that—the only good thing I did this morning before I went out.

The Charles Street Playhouse is very dear to me—or was, a little bit the way Ellery Sedgwick was about his arthritis. He used to say, "Sister pain is very near and dear to me." Well, the Charles Street Playhouse was very dear to me, because it was there that my Associated Actors Theatre closed after three weeks and after Richard Cabot had given me five thousand dollars as a last hurrah. I certainly thought that would carry us through the winter. He was so generous, dear man, and wrote my father this wonderful letter:

September 10, 1935

Dear Professor Sarton,

I am much moved by your letter. That motto of yours is one of the most satisfying that I have ever heard. [*Je n'ai pas besoin d'espérer pour entreprendre, ni de réussir pour perséverer.*] I should like to enroll myself also behind that noble idea. I have for many years held your life and your work in high honor because of the greatness and austerity of your aim. You have the same *feu sacré* which I felt in your daughter when she spoke to us here in Northeast Harbor.

The only permanent monument of dramatic art is in dramas which it stimulates into existence—dramas that would not be written save for the favoring atmosphere furnished by an attempt like your daughter's. Noble and

vivid acting and the interest aroused by it does I think
help to inspire dramatic writers. It had its effect on
Shakespeare and more recently on the Irish playwrights
like Lady Gregory, Yeats and Synge.

But even if your daughter's attempt fails, I believe it
will have by-products of great value. At any rate I feel
honoured and warmed to be associated even in a slight
external way with such a noble attempt. I am proud to be
living in the same epoch with your daughter. How proud
you must be to be her father! I am sure her spirit and
yours are deeply joined at the root. With many thanks
for your letter.

Yours, with profound admiration,
Richard C. Cabot

My father, I think, must have written him to apologize for this
outrageous daughter who had somehow allowed five thousand dollars to leak away in three weeks.

We did three plays. Actually they were not too bad. *Dr.
Knocke,* Jules Romains's play, with Norman Lloyd marvelous
in the lead; Maxwell Anderson's *Gods of the Lightning*—
about the Sacco-Vanzetti case—which was directed by Jo
Losey, who later became famous as a movie director in England; and *Gallery Gods* by Rich Duschinsky, adapted by
John Housman. It was nothing to be ashamed of, but the thing
is that the theater was empty and for once Boston was full of
good shows. Both Katherine Cornell and Eva Le Gallienne
were in Boston during that time. So the competition was
something. Anyway, the Charles Street Playhouse is semi-
redeemed now by Pat Carroll's triumph there. It's a small
theater, but it has a lot of charm. Over the years it has devel-
oped, I think, faithful audiences who know that there will
often be something interesting to see there.

I do rejoice and thank God that my theater failed, because
the theater *is* an angel with its feet tied to a bag of gold. For

the four years in which I directed that little company, I spent
most of my energy and many sleepless nights raising money.
The marvelous thing about being a writer is that you don't
have to raise money, you have to *live*, but it's probably easier
to get a job—I did it by teaching and lecturing—than it is by
doing anything in the theater. Of course, it's much worse now.
When I think that the Civic Repertory, which employed
eighty people and had a repertory of twenty-six plays at the
end, could have survived the depression with one hundred
thousand dollars a year! It now costs over a million to raise the
curtain on a one-set show on Broadway.

Thursday, October 25

TODAY, which began at around six-thirty with streams of crimson light through rather black horizontal clouds, has now
darkened altogether. Apparently we're going to have rain
again. I can hardly bear it. The day has lost the magic which
was there yesterday afternoon when I sat here in my chaise,
looking out at the light through the leaves.

Monday, August 26, 1991

I DISCOVERED when going over the copy editor's queries on the manuscript that there was a gap between October 28 and November 10. There was a time when I dictated as usual but the cassette did not "take." It may be that some days were lost as a result and they contained very important news. I feel this must be filled in, late though it is.

Sometime between those dates an event took place that radically changed my life here and set me on the path to getting well.

Susan Sherman had been here for a weekend and was so appalled to find how ill I had become that she decided she must somehow come here and take care of me. Since she teaches full time in the English department at the Riverdale Country School in the Bronx, this concern involved complex decisions and planning in the middle of a semester. She conferred with her brother-in-law, Dr. Lawrence Rosenberg, about the medical aspects of my illness and his response was immediate: "Go right away." He agreed to go with her to have a talk about the plan with John Gulla, head of the upper school. One of the problems in her asking for a leave of absence was that Susan and I are not related. Ours has been for years a loving friendship, and because of her work for the past five years on my archive at the Berg Collection in the New York Public Library, she knows more about me than anyone on earth now, and far more than I myself remember! Susan has taught various books of mine at the school and I was in-

vited to read poems there a few years ago, so I was not unknown to the administration.

I still find it hard to believe that this extraordinary
woman's plea to come here and take care of me for the rest of
the semester was granted, but it was. So on November 4 she
drove up from New York

While Susan was negotiating I had had to go into hospital
again, finding it hard to breathe and in pain. When she found
me there I told her that I had had a talk with Dr. Petrovich
and said to him, "I think I am dying." He said I probably was,
so I met Susan with that hard news and she reminds me that I
told her we would go it alone together or words to that effect.

I now understand H.O.M.E.'s motto, "Expect a miracle!"
for I have seen a miracle happen. The time Susan and I spent
together through Thanksgiving and Christmas and into late
January knitted us into the most subtle, loving friendship I
have ever experienced; the substance of that is recorded in
the pages that follow. What is not recorded, although I had
dictated a passage about it that never "took," is how Susan
took hold, as cook, nurse, driver, arranger of flowers, and ima-
giner of every sort of fun and good time.

Almost the first thing she accomplished was to find out
about and arrange for me to have oxygen available at night.
My bedroom is on the second floor. How to get it upstairs?
Here Nancy and Susan worked together, an excellent team, as
Nancy's expertise about such things matches Susan's exuberant faith that the impossible is possible. They managed to run
the transparent tubing that carries the oxygen along the ceiling and up the stairs somehow. It took some pretty hard work
for Nancy who is tall and could thus cope with the height. It
was a great success, and is paid for by Medicare, a further
miracle.

Saturday, November 10

A GRAY DAY—for the ovations of sun are gone that have filled the house and made every flower transparent. The roses have been just incredible these last days. But that light is gone and I'm in electric light if I'm in light at all. But it's restful—a gray day.

The only trouble is that I'm trying a new system for the medication: to have food with the most difficult drug so that maybe I won't have such bad cramps. Yesterday I didn't get to talk at all to the machine, which is, in a way, an alter ego. So when I haven't talked to it, I miss it. I miss the other part of myself which is only functioning intermittently these days.

I had so hoped to get up to the third floor today and send English calendars to the friends I've always sent them to at Christmas. They should go now—I mean the order should go now. But I must not let these things get in the way of what really is my work, which is to try and get well. It's a full-time job and quite discouraging at times.

But what a rest when sumptuous white Pierrot, the Himalayan, with his blue face, sleeps on my bed! I don't move. I even go to sleep because I don't want to disturb him. The giver of rest, that's what he is these days.

And Susan, so discreet and so sensitive to all possible needs, wafts in and out like a—I don't know what to say—a sort of fairy presence—making good things happen. Like exquisite small meals. She is very aware of the value of a Japanese meal, of very little food on a beautiful plate. So the meals have been festive even though I can eat often almost nothing.

I'm waiting now for Maggie Vaughan, who is coming at eleven for a little talk and to see me. The house is full of thoughtful presents she has brought here over the years. I'm looking now at a wonderful electric lamp which you can put on when the lights go off and which is so powerful that it will last four hours. I could even work, therefore, when it's on.

I've started to read George F. Kennan's *Sketches from a Life*—an enormous pleasure to come into contact with this very subtle mind. I also have a biography of Sylvia Townsend Warner. But I've given up on Osbert Sitwell's *Queen Mary and Others*, although it had its fine moments, like everything in life, and like everything she was.

Sunday, November 11

A BRILLIANT SUN and wind are with us after a wild night of rain and wind. The house seems a fortress against the high tides of water and movement in the skies. In a way it's very cozy to be indoors with only dear Maggie, who came for an hour in the middle of all that wet, bringing two dozen eggs from her hens and as always some extra treats, in this case the very thin liver from her own farm, which I only see otherwise in France. What a treat it is, and we shall have some tonight.

Susan is now out getting the Sunday *Times* and some oysters so we can have oyster stew, which is a real holiday treat, I think. I have been trying on denim pants which Edythe shortened for me. Oh the good offices of my friends! What would I do without them? Anyway, these pants look great now that they've been shortened, and I put them on with a sweater—a jerkin, I should say—made for me by Judy Burrowes, for Judy is coming tomorrow and I want her to see me in it. Edythe is coming this afternoon, so she can admire her handiwork. She is a marvelous tailor and knitter.

This morning I managed to pay the bills and order three cases of wine for Juliette Huxley from an English wine place which offers cases of just one bottle of various kinds. So it's rather fun to open them. Juliette's birthday happens to be on Saint Nicholas, so this is both a Saint Nicholas and a birthday present. I think it's her ninety-fourth birthday, but it may be the ninety-third, I'm not quite sure. It makes me heartsick that I'm incapable of communicating on a less mundane level than the wine for Saint Nicholas, for Juliette. Now I can't write letters. It's partly, I suppose, because she can't. She doesn't write letters anymore and neither do I. There are only those letters from the past which will come out after her death—and perhaps after mine. It is a great joy for me to think about—a great giving of joy to the world—women's friendship.

I was afraid that Pierrot in a catlike way was beginning to fall in love with Susan, because, after all, it is she who feeds him. But I'm glad to say that he follows me around. He came all the way up to the third floor, to my study, meowing, this morning and said, Where are you? He's now asleep on my bed and presumably will be while I have my rest. So that is good news.

Deborah Straw and Bruce Conklin sent me a copy of Galway Kinnell's *When One Has Lived a Long Time Alone*, a marvelous title because it's one of those titles that make you dream.

When one has lived a long time alone it's a kind of special bliss to have a dear companion suddenly part of the household as Susan is. Impossible to describe how precious that moment when I wake from my nap and we have a cup of tea has become because she makes the house home. It hasn't been home since I came here, in some ways. It has been a place of great fertility in which I've written some of my best work, but it has also been a very lonely place. Now, for a little while, it is not.

Monday, November 12

WE ARE REMEMBERING the millions of deaths as a war with Iraq draws frighteningly closer every day. But here what we have is wild November wind. It was a clear sky but very restless, a pounding, constant atmosphere of innocuous tempest. So it's been a rather restless day, although a good one in many ways. I decided to do a laundry, also had a bath for the first time in several days and really outdid myself physically. The trouble was that I was extremely tired as a result.

Dear Judy Burrowes and her friend Chris, whom I had expected at three, had misunderstood and came at eleven. Fortunately I was dressed, so I could sit here on my chaise and enjoy them. We did have a very good talk. Judy had sent me the most magnificent anemones. I'm so glad that she came while they were still in their glory. They are the most incredible flower. As I sit here I'm looking at them, wide open, with their purple hearts and their still very crisp petals. They've lasted for five days. They close at night, and then in the morning when I wake up, there they are, like small gods by my bed.

I must add while speaking of flowers that there are still roses from the one hundred and eight that Susan brought from

CREDIT: SUSAN SHERMAN

A Roman emperor in cat form

New York last week. So it is just a week since Susan came and since I came home from the hospital. In a week we've achieved a wonderful rhythm of our life together, a great sense, I think, of companionship at a very deep and still level. It's an absolutely wonderful time for me. I've realized how lonely I've been for that kind of exchange which doesn't need any words—which is simply Susan's watering the plants, or asking me how I nourish them, or presenting me with an elegant tray. She is very inventive about food, delightfully so. So I'm spoiled. Besides Susan, other friends, of course, spoil me all the time. Tonight we're having cooked lobsters that Margaret Whalen and Barbara Martin brought, a tremendous treat.

I've now started on the Sylvia Townsend Warner biography. I think at last I've found the book that I can immerse myself in and long to go back to bed to read every evening. I have various other books, but none has seized me as that has.

Of course, there is the *Times* every day with its load of horrendous news.

Now Pierrot, who looks like a Roman emperor in cat form, has walked across the room to have a little drink of water. Susan has tamed him. He does not go out after six, so that means that she doesn't have to call him in at midnight or at one in the morning. He comes docilely up to my bed and goes to sleep at the end of it and sleeps all night until four, when Susan, who I must say is a saint in this respect, gets up and lets him out when I ring my little bell.

Wednesday, November 14

I DIDN'T RECORD anything yesterday, because it was a very busy, decision-making day. The first decision, the hardest, was whether to go to the dentist to try to find out why one side of my mouth is so sore—the gum is sore. Fortunately I made the right decision, and Dr. Dinnerman, that marvelous dentist, was able to see me yesterday. So we drove in—my first time in Portsmouth for nearly a year. He was able to find right away what was wrong—my losing so much weight has made the pressure greater on the lower partial, and a little piece of what anchors the partial to the two remaining teeth that are mine had been twisted so it was digging into my gum. No wonder it hurt. The minute he fixed it I felt better. Now I've been able to chew without constantly moving from one side of my mouth to the other.

Before that I had left a message on an answering machine for a caterer in Kittery because I suddenly decided that the answer to Thanksgiving was to have a chicken cooked for us, vegetables and everything, and brought the night before. I found in the yellow pages what looked like rather a grand caterer, and I thought he would never answer, but he did and was delighted to do it. We're going to have a roast chicken stuffed with mushrooms and oysters, and marshmallow and sweet potatoes and vegetables. Edythe is so happy, and Susan, who hasn't been happy about Thanksgiving, suddenly said she couldn't resist, so she will join us. Of course, I wanted her to. So now Edythe will make her wonderful lemon pie. We're all set, and peace has descended. I'd been really worried about Thanksgiving.

Finally, I got someone to put on the storm windows. We've been having tremendous winds, and the wind comes through the cracks around the windows, of course—there are forty windows. Chris Cote, who has been doing this for me, is very ill in the hospital, so I had to find somebody else—not easily done. I called Raymond Philbrook, and he couldn't do it, but he had an idea—a young man who remembered me from the days when the Lesswings ran the hardware store is coming on the weekend to do it. A relief. It's one of those things that has to be done, and where do you find the workmen?

A day of mighty decisions. I didn't write here, and also I must admit I got extremely tired. Somehow making decisions is the hardest thing I have to do. I feel very passive and not, so to speak, in charge, but then it comes to the fact that I *am* in charge and had better get on with the business.

Susan has persuaded me to get a VCR. Nancy will go with her tomorrow and help her buy one. We think this will be great fun. I've never had one, because I don't like looking at things without people. I don't like going to the movies alone, so to speak, but now Susan and I will have this resource, since I certainly will not soon be going out for meals or able to go to a movie as Nancy and I used to do ages ago.

I'm lost now in the biography of Sylvia Townsend Warner. It's interesting, because this is a first book by a young woman, and it's extremely good. Of course I have only read one hundred and fifty pages but I'm very impressed. At last I've found a book which I want to go back to, which, at night, I can pick up after the oxygen tube has been arranged around my neck. It is not any trouble, just a sort of nuisance, so I read for half an hour and then go to sleep, and sleep wonderfully because I can breathe.

Yesterday, I might add also, one of those wonderful visiting nurses, this one called Brock, came to help me with the digestive problem which has been so difficult. Milk of magnesia seems to be helping some, but today I don't feel at all well—I again have cramps, and am very tired. It may be a result of all those decisions. This reminds me of the old story of the man who was sorting potatoes and found it exhausting. They said, Why? All you are doing is throwing away. He said, Making up my mind—or something to that effect—is what is killing me. That's what I felt yesterday. Today there are no great decisions to be made. I'm taking it rather easy. I have to because of cramps.

Friday, November 16

I DIDN'T DO anything yesterday, if I remember. The days go terribly fast. It's strange, because I'm not doing very much but there are constant interruptions of household things. Yesterday was wonderful. The electrician, Bruce Woods, came to fix the garage door, which was sticking and wouldn't rise beyond about three feet. Then he did a little work in Susan's room—the guest room—where two of the lamps needed looking to. Wonderful Bruce was willing to take them home and work on them there, which very few electricians will do. He is just a darling man. I realize more and more how lucky I am here to have the help I have.

And *big* news! Bill Ewert is bringing the Christmas poem, which means signing fifty for him to give away. He does this as a present to me every year—a generous man. The trouble is that signing fifty is an ordeal for me right now and I'm not sure I'll be able to do it. But I can always do half and mail him the other half if necessary.

At last the wind has died down and we have a beautiful, warm autumn day. The big news yesterday was that Susan and Nancy went and got a VCR so over the weekend we can look at movies. Susan had to take it back for a little defect, but it will be home for lunch. So many people have told me I should do it. Of course, with my fear and hatred of machines I was sure I could not run it. But Susan is intrepid, and Nancy is a genius at mechanical things and put it together, discovering the one little wire that was wrong in the package from the firm that makes them. So we're lucky to be able to get that fixed today.

The holiday looms. In a minute I'll go up and send out some notes for Thanksgiving. What's on my mind is partly Christmas things for England—straw baskets filled with goodies. I try to do this for some of my relatives in Suffolk and also, of course, send them to friends. So there's lots on my plate right now.

The biography of Sylvia Townsend Warner is proving to be a great joy. It really is beautifully put together—complicated woman as Sylvia Townsend Warner was. Complicated and fascinating—a true original. So now I am going upstairs to struggle up there at my desk.

Sunday, November 18

WELL, it's Sunday evening and we are celebrating the new VCR. Today the second movie we've seen was Cher in *Moonstruck*—a beautiful movie which uses the music from *La Bohème* all the way through. A lovely romantic movie in which all the actors do extremely well. I enjoyed every moment of it. Especially perhaps the moment when Pierrot was on my lap and Cybèle was on Susan's lap and there we were all four of us watching the VCR. No growls, no roars—perfect peace—but then, of course, Pierrot wanted to get down and the moment was gone. But it's been a good day.

The weather has been good, a bit of cloudy, gray weather, not dazzling. All the leaves are gone, so there is no leaf shine anymore, but there is the surf and moving, in the sense of motion, gray ocean breaking in very large—I was going to say contemplative—waves, but it doesn't sound quite right!

The big event yesterday was that Bill and Mary Ewert brought the new Christmas poem. The setting is beautiful. Mary Azarian has done a superb job of making a poetic vision of goldfinches on a branch. I think the poem does what I wanted to do. So it's a happy time for me to think of sending this out. It will tell many of my friends that I have been ill, which will save a lot of explaining at Christmas. It really gives me the great joy of speaking to each one as I sign the envelopes.

Friendship & Illness
Christmas, 1990

Through the silences
The long empty days
You have sat beside me
Watching the finches feed,
The tremor in the leaves.
You have not left my mind.

Friendship supplied the root—
It was planted years ago—
To bring me flowers and seed
Through the long drought.

Far-flung as you are
You have seemed to sit beside me.
You have not left my mind.

Will you come in the new year?
To share the wind in the leaves
And the finches lacing the air
To savor the silence with me?
It's been a long time.

Unfortunately I spent one hour this morning going through piles and piles of letters to try to find Peter Pease's two wonderful letters that he must have written me in late July or August and which never got answered. He also brought me a Pueblo bear with turquoise eyes. This darling bear has accompanied me through the last month in a companionable way. I wanted to thank Peter now, but unfortunately I can't find his address. I'm so good on the whole at keeping addresses that this is sad. I hope and pray he won't have given me up for lost—that he will write again if only at Christmas. When he was here I was ill, although not as ill as I have been since then, so he

FRIENDSHIP & ILLNESS

Christmas, 1990

Through the silences,
The long empty days
You have sat beside me
Watching the finches feed,
The tremor in the leaves.
You have not left my mind.

Friendship supplied the root–
It was planted years ago–
To bring me flowers and seed
Through the long drought.

Far-flung as you are
You have seemed to sit beside me.
You have not left my mind.

Will you come in the new year?
To share the wind in the leaves
And the finches lacing the air
To savor the silence with me?
It's been a long time.

— *May Sarton*

WILLIAM B. EWERT, PUBLISHER · CONCORD, NEW HAMPSHIRE

*Text copyright 1990 by May Sarton. Original woodcut copyright 1990 by
Mary Azarian. 536 copies of this first edition were printed at Firefly Press
in December, 1990, for private distribution. Of these, 36 copies, on special
paper, are signed by the author and the artist.*

really didn't know that I couldn't answer, couldn't write, and he may have been a little peeved that I didn't.

So—yesterday the arrival of the Christmas cards, and a movie, which was great fun. Today I managed to write one page in praise of Dorothy Healy, who founded the Maine Women Writers Library at Westbrook College, where there is also the May Sarton Room. I wanted so much to do something worthy of Dorothy but I dreaded the effort, so it seemed quite wonderful that I was able to write it this morning after looking for Peter Pease's letters for nearly an hour.

Tuesday, November 20

THANKSGIVING is nearly upon us. Already flowers have arrived. I suddenly remembered it was Beverly Hallam's birthday tomorrow. Foster's managed to get twenty anemones, the big ones that florists can order. I hope she will watch them opening. It would be wonderful to have a movie that showed anemones opening to that marvelous dark eye at the center.

I'm sorry to say that I've not been feeling well at all. Susan is so imaginative she realized that I probably didn't want the wonderful meal she was planning and said, "Let's just have bouillon and Jell-O for dinner." It was like a reprieve, because I simply didn't feel like eating.

However, the nurse came today and said that things are going well and gave me good advice about how to manage this troubling digestive system. It's a great support to have the visiting nurses come, for they take time and talk things over with one so wisely.

I also saw Dr. Petrovich at two-fifteen. Susan had never been to that office with me. He was delighted and said I looked different, that I looked wonderful. That is because of Susan and not being so isolated and being so beautifully and sensitively taken care of. But much to my surprise, because I've not been feeling well the last two days, he was also pleased because there is very little liquid in the lining of the lung where they drained so much out a month ago. If that is true and therefore the new medicine is working and keeping the liquid from increasing, I'm on the way to being well. It's almost incredible. I haven't taken it in yet, because it hasn't reached my physical being yet. But that was all so life-enhancing, seeing Dr. Petrovich, getting the anemones for Beverly, that I suggested that Susan drive me around Long Sands—which she hadn't seen yet—to the best fish place around here, the York Beach Fish Market, where we could buy lox for Serena Sue Hilsinger and Lois Brynes, who are coming the day after Thanksgiving to share a bottle of champagne. They are the editors of *Selected Poems of May Sarton,* which goes on bearing fruit. I have not seen them for a long time.

We drove along that beautiful beach, unfortunately almost at high tide, so I didn't see the lovely flat wet sand where people walk their dogs. It looks like a modest European watering place with Victorian houses all along the edge. People don't realize how varied York, York Beach, and York Harbor are. They are three different worlds. York itself is a kind of middle-class, very attractive town with lots of old houses—really old, eighteenth-century—within it. Then York Beach, which is, as I said, Victorian; its architecture is not distinguished, but it's a marvelous beach. Then York Harbor, which used to be a fashionable summer place, and there are still grand houses there and an entirely different atmosphere from either York or York Beach—the atmosphere created years ago by the very rich.

Susan was fascinated, and we came back along that lovely beach with the sea a Fra Angelico blue. She reminded me that I've used that phrase a great many times, but it is an extraordinary, serene, and moving shade of blue—one which always makes me think of Angelico.

Friday, November 23

MY CHIEF REASON for Thanksgiving is, of course, my friends. From there I went to looking around the room and celebrating a few of them. There is a constant flow of love coming toward me like a daily tide which lifts me up after the difficulties of the morning, always hard these days because of cramps. I begin by midmorning to emerge into the kindly light of love.

Such a peaceful day after Thanksgiving. In spite of the dreary rain outside a lovely day here inside. Serena Sue and Lois came for a glass of Mumm's champagne and lox at eleven-thirty this morning. I haven't seen them for maybe two years, so it was really an event. We had a wonderful talk about everything. Nancy came down—she had never met them—and Susan was here—whom they were anxious to see, of course—and it was a beautiful scene. There were lovely roses opening—small roses that Susan had given me for Thanksgiving. They were on the table—the grand bottle by our glasses—and it all looked so festive and felt so festive that it was delicious.

Tonight Susan and I had the second meal of our Thanksgiving feast, as I imagine most families are doing tonight. The stuffing with oysters and mushrooms was especially good—

very good heated up—as were the mashed sweet potatoes.

But I did not accomplish—and that is not strange—much at my desk today. Maybe tomorrow when for once we have no guests to receive we may have a good, peaceful, workful day. I might get a couple of hours at my desk. I do begin to feel better, there is no doubt. One way I can measure is that I look forward to meals, even think about food, whereas for months the very thought of food made me feel ill. Now I often have hot cereal for breakfast, and that goes down very well.

I miss Sylvia Townsend Warner, but I'm now reading Jean Medawar's book [*A Very Decided Preference: Life with Peter Medawar*] about her extraordinary life with her husband, who was of course one of the geniuses of the era, won the Nobel Prize when he was under forty, one of the inventors of penicillin. This is a charming book.

Here comes Susan to put me to bed, so I'll stop.

Tuesday, November 27

ANOTHER WONDERFUL clear sunrise, a great expanse of sky, and one takes a deep breath looking out on it.

Yesterday we went to the hospital, for me to have a chest X-ray and blood work done and then to have a talk with Dr. Gilroy. I was hoping for a big hurrah and that they would feel that I am making progress. Dr. Gilroy is cautious, and he's right, of course. He thinks that there may be less fluid, and they're going to wait another three weeks before deciding whether to drain again. They might decide *not* to drain, because if the medicine is working it might be that this amount

CREDIT: SUSAN SHERMAN

Sunrise

of liquid would be steady and would never need to be
drained. This would be extremely good news. When I asked
him why when things were going on the whole very well I still
feel terribly tired and so lacking in energy he couldn't answer
me. I think I should be walking a little every day, which I've
not been doing, although I do go up and down the stairs many
times.

Friday, November 30

IT SEEMS UNBELIEVABLE that Christmas is already in the air. The big box from H.O.M.E. arrived yesterday with the wreath in it. I'm always so touched by this wreath. It brings back the many images of H.O.M.E. itself and the people working there, building houses for the homeless, the women finding a chance to get an education. It's so marvelous to think that it exists and that there are—unfortunately it was Bush who said it—such points of light.

In the magazine section of the *Times* on Sunday there was an article on the black principal of a school in a deprived district of the Bronx. She has insisted that the children be clean. It is almost unimaginable. Many of these children have never had a bath and their clothes have never been clean. She brought a secondhand washer and dryer, and when a child arrives at school dirty she washes the child's clothes. These are first and second grade—I think up to fourth grade. She washes and dries the clothes and has spare clothes for the child while he or she waits for fresh ones. Think of the pleasure it must be to have a clean dress when you've never had one!

It takes me right back to a summer when my mother had had to go to England because her mother was ill. I was left with my father, and various arrangements had been made for me to stay with friends who kindly took me in. Amongst them were two women, Miss King and Miss Coit, who ran a summer school as well as a winter school where children learned to act in extraordinary plays that they put on in New York City. The one that I was in that summer, which was then given in Portsmouth, was Indian—a Hindu myth [*Nala and Damayanti,* August 11, 1922]. They taught me never to stand up straight. One always held oneself in a slightly curving stance like a dancer, as seen in the Rajput paintings.

I was given a makeshift cabin in the woods in Ogunquit, near their house. I was sent without any change of clothes. My father had no housekeeping skill at all. I suppose I was about nine years old, maybe a little older than that, but I was miserable because my dress was dirty, my underwear was dirty, and nothing got washed. That summer is one of my few memories of real misery. The other nightmare was that Mother had left an Irish girl to come in and clean for my father. She reneged and sent her younger sister, who reneged and sent an even younger one. So it was a little girl of about seven who came in to clean the house!

There were two cats, and one of them used the kitchen sink as its pan. So when I got back from a visit, not only was I in dirty clothes which I didn't know how to get clean but also I had to clean up after the cat. My father wrote to Mother, "It's *hell* with three cats!" It wasn't Mother's fault. She was called away suddenly to her mother in England. She did everything she could, but it was, I must say, an extraordinarily grim summer for both Daddy and me. Where all this began was in reading about the wonderful black woman in the Bronx who washes the children's clothes! I understand the bliss it is to find yourself in a clean dress.

I have again been having a hard time of digestive problems. They cause a lot of pain and also anxiety. I wonder why I don't feel better when, on the whole, the doctors think I am doing pretty well as far as my fibrillating heart goes, but I don't have any sense of not being ill. I don't have any memory of a day when I could say that I certainly feel better than I did yesterday. Every day I feel more weak and shaky, often sick, often with bad cramps. It seems the best time of day when Susan hooks up the oxygen and I read for a little while before I go to sleep. Pierrot is a great comfort. The sight of his soft, glossy coat as he lies on the end of the bed is somehow health-giving.

Saturday, December 1

AN ABSOLUTELY PURE blue sky. The leafless branches outside my window look gold against it. We are having some magnificent days. But today I'm discouraged. I am eating more and doing about an hour at my desk every day. Susan's wonderful care should make me feel better, but it doesn't. I am down to ninety-four pounds and very shaky.

I was determined to go to the bookstore, so Susan drove me there, for I've run out of reading matter. I did get four books—a tremendous treat to look forward to. One of them is a biography of Rachel Carson and one is an older book of Rosamunde Pilcher, who wrote *The Shell Seekers*, which I greatly enjoyed.

The reason I'm talking about going to the bookstore (incidentally, they have a very good collection of my books) is that making choices is an extremely difficult thing, for my old head balks at this sort of demand. I was glad to get home and read the mail in peace and eat some of Susan's delicious mushroom soup. Now I'm lying on my bed thinking I'm only happy when I'm horizontal and happiest when Pierrot is lying beside me. He's not at the moment.

I talked to Blue Jenkins, my old friend who lives in Greenfield, yesterday. She's back from the hospital after an attack of phlebitis, and I'm delighted to discover that she's getting the help that she needs and it isn't very expensive. A young woman comes in the morning and gives her her breakfast and helps her have a shower and get dressed. Another person comes in the evening and helps her get her supper. This is ideal, it seems to me, and I have been, in the last few days, considering that I must put my mind on finding out about help after Susan goes. So I called the hospital and they will send me a list of people who do part-time work.

Yesterday we had a real treat on the VCR—the first half of *Babette's Feast*. It's a Danish movie laid in a small desolate village in Jutland. I can't wait for this afternoon when we'll see the end. It's exciting—the VCR. It certainly lights up the day and takes us right out into other worlds. It's something I need, although all I really need is to feel better. A little better would make an enormous difference.

Monday, December 3

WE'RE HAVING WILD wind and rain with big surf at the end of the field. Thank goodness it isn't snow, because it would be drifting under the high wind. But it's very exciting to see the surf now.

Something I wanted to add yesterday was that since this is the season when we think of friends, a great many people call me. Yesterday between four and five I had calls from friends in Montana, Connecticut, Palo Alto and Santa Barbara in California, and Wisconsin.

Surf at the end of the field

Thursday, December 6

JULIETTE'S BIRTHDAY. I think she must be ninety-three. Oh, how I wish I could run in and embrace her, and see whether she has adopted one of the stray cats who were trying to become members of the household when I was there two years ago.

Yesterday was a great day in that the cable people came and fixed the television Edythe gave me for my bedroom. It's now on cable and I can look at it from my bed—even shut off the ads when I don't want them. A marvelous present.

Now there is sunlight pouring in—another of these brilliant winter days. At this moment and for about a half hour—from about eight-fifteen to nine—the sun spotlights flowers on the table by my bed, this time two white freesias. What white is white as that?

The bright pink roses are still beautiful although they've been here a week. They go on singing their happy song for such a long time. In winter they are one of the best of flowers.

We have now found a place for the huge red poinsettia that Phyllis Chiemingo sent out of the generosity of her heart. She had sent a white one, knowing I love white and thinking perhaps that it would go in the flower window, but it was much too big. I changed it for a red one and found a place in the library where its opulence and its deep redness make a kind of ovation in one corner. I must send Phyllis the poem today.

Yesterday I sent it to seven people. I do almost nothing but write the address, but that means finding the address, which is sometimes quite a search. My address book is too full, and while I'm finding one address I see four or five more names of dear friends to whom I want to be sure to send the card.

I'm happy because Anne Woodson liked the poem so much. When I called them yesterday it was to find out if they had snow. We didn't. We had a wild rain- and windstorm but they had five and a half inches of hard-packed wet snow—very hard to deal with, because the snowblower was no good for that.

Every now and then—and this is new, so perhaps I am getting a little better—I have longed for the taste of burgundy, but I don't dare try it because the chemistry of the pills I have to take gives wine a bad taste.

Pierrot has not been in this morning to say good morning
to his mistress. He has not had his half-and-half cream. Apparently his mother never taught Pierrot to wash his face. So
when he has been drinking cream his whole face is covered
with white dots, under his chin and then above. He looks
quite grotesque.

We had no visitors yesterday—a good and restful thing
because we saw the last half of *Hope and Glory*—a wonderful
film about the Blitz in London in the forties with an excellent
family of actors. I can't get over the bliss it is to have movies to
look at and such good ones.

In two minutes the visiting nurse will come to draw blood
and also to cut my toenails.

Yesterday the great event was seeing *The Whales of August*—a remarkably subtle and beautiful film which stars Lillian Gish and Bette Davis. Both were surely in their eighties,
and Bette Davis has died since. It's laid in a small Maine
house on the rocks looking out to sea. One of the sisters is
blind, the other one, played by Lillian Gish, takes care of her
sister and bears with her sour temper. What makes the film
remarkable, I think, is the lighting—is the fact that everything
is filmed in an understated light, filled with nostalgia as if a
memory. It's as if you were remembering all this: the rocking
chairs, the two women making valiant efforts to get along
together although they are so different, the blind one attack-
ing the other one for being "busy, busy, busy"—"Why are
you never still?" Meanwhile her sister is trying to get the
supper, or dusting, or just doing things that have to be done. I
enjoyed it more than any film I've seen for a long time. It's a
masterpiece, and what is staggering is that the producers
somehow raised the money for something as understated as
this. There is really no plot. A neighbor is turned out of his
living space by the death of the woman who owned the house
and comes to dinner with the two sisters. He's very badly

treated by the mean one. This is hardly high drama! It's all the time like a delicate fabric of human life and of what we give up to be able to live together. What remains—and I think I'll never forget—is the beauty in Gish's face—the way feeling crosses it, like a breeze sometimes when a smile is born there or a look of pain that is quite accepting of the situation. She is aware that her sister is not going to be changed. The only thing missing, though, was an animal. That may be because they wintered in Philadelphia and only summered on the coast as so many others do.

For once the phone didn't ring quite as often just after five as it's apt to do. So we had peace and quiet. But the wonderful thing about the VCR is that you can turn it off during a phone call so you still have the whole film unspoiled.

Saturday, December 8

IT'S EIGHT ABOVE ZERO TODAY. Another of these pure brilliant winter days which often by afternoon turn into cloud and darkness. Yesterday was very dark in the dusk—a real winter dark that descends like a prison—a hard sky.

Altogether the last two days have been very hard. I was again so ill. Yesterday I couldn't eat any supper, was glad to be in bed with that delicious hot-water bottle that Maggie Vaughan gave me, one of those English ones covered with heavy plush so they're very cozy. It's almost like having a living teddy bear in bed with you.

I slept pretty well, thanks to the oxygen. Also today was not entirely lost because I did write some letters—the mail was enormous, probably twenty letters at least, the beginning of the Christmas avalanche. It's thrilling to have these letters pour in from all over the country, but it is also exhausting. And I'm not quite commensurate with it, so I think the answer is maybe today to read the letters before lunch so I can get upstairs and do a little addressing of the Christmas poem now before I get too tired as I did yesterday.

A great comfort in the last two hard days has been Noel Adams's *St. Croix Notes*. He apparently is very well-known by people who listen to the morning program—the name of which I now forget. It comes from Minnesota. In a way his is rather like my own journal. I can see why being told the temperature and some observations about the weather can be nourishing and delightful to a reader. I marked one very small passage, what he calls "The man from Louis Degouy," about soup: "It breathes reassurance, it offers confidence." It really did make me laugh. It's so true of Susan's soup. We have soup every day for lunch and every day I look forward to it.

Wonderful response has come in to the Christmas poem. I'm touched, because it was rather risky—such a personal poem—when, after all, we're on the brink of war and there are all the things which are more important than how I feel. But a lot of my friends don't even know what kind of an ordeal I'm in. Anyway, that is how I felt compelled to speak. It came quite easily after I'd spent a week with Rene Morgan on the Cape and came home rested. Now Bill Ewert, with the help of Mary Azarian, has designed a beautiful frame for it. So altogether it's a great success this year and makes me happy.

Yesterday flowers came from two people to thank me for the poem. One from Liz Evans in North Carolina and one from Colleen Grissom in San Antonio, Texas. I'm spoiled—as many creators are not. What I must do is try to remember to call Rene. She always gets there first.

Sunday, December 16

A GREAT DEAL HAPPENED yesterday, beginning with a laundry,
which has been on my mind for a long time. It's awful how
things accumulate and don't get done, but that was triumphantly done by nearly ten o'clock. Meanwhile Susan was
making elegant little open sandwiches to serve with the champagne. We were waiting for Stephen Robitaille and Julie, and
two friends of theirs, to come and show me the VCR of *May
Sarton: Writing in the Upward Years,* which was made from a
reading and interview I did in Gainesville, Florida, last
March. This was the first time—and it will certainly be the
last—that I do a performance with my voice cracked and dry,
as it is now.

They arrived on time at eleven, on this gloomy day, snow
expected. We served the champagne and put the video on. It's
a remarkable job that Stephen has done. The interview is
excellent. The trouble with the reading is the frustration for
me of having lost what was a very good voice for the reading
of poetry. Nevertheless I plunged ahead and did not too
badly. Because I was onstage and there was no proper lighting—only an overhead light right on top of my head—I looked
extremely old, whereas later, in the Robitailles' house with
proper lighting, during the interview I looked old but handsome and myself. All through the reading I kept feeling, This
is not May Sarton. Where is May Sarton? It was a semi-pleas-
ant, semi-difficult half hour to live through. But everybody
was enthusiastic. The poems, after all, are worth something

even when they're no better read than I could do. So that was a big piece of day.

Then I lay down after a delicious lunch that Susan brought me and had a sleep and took pills for the pain. At four I got up and we had our ritual tea and saw the end of *Madame Sousatska*.

It is quite a thrilling film which ends with the boy genius at fifteen playing the Schumann concerto and muffing it a little, but getting an ovation. I dislike, I find, films and books that deal with a genius discovering itself, and this one is no exception. But Shirley MacLaine, who plays the boy's teacher, does a superb job. She's usually an attractive heroine and in this case she has to be very unattractive.

Today Edythe is coming. She always is the one who fixes the little candles on the tree, then we decorate it. So Susan, the magician, is leaving us lunch and will go out. When the tree is decorated the big work of Christmas is done.

I've now started all the books. An excellent biography of Rachel Carson—not a biography as much as an analysis of how she worked, how she accomplished what she did accomplish. The tremendously hopeful thing about it is, of course, her life itself, which proved that one person *can* change the world. The whole environmental emphasis, the whole thing that's happened since *The Silent Spring,* was to a large extent brought about by Rachel Carson. It is a tremendous change and it is worldwide. So her life is a shot in the arm to those who are trying to make things better. I think of Char Radintz, who certainly is a shot in the arm with her work for Nicaragua and the farmers.

Monday, December 17

A REALLY AWFUL DAY HERE—sodden rain. I did do something
at my desk this morning, but there are so many names and
faces that swim up into my consciousness when I'm writing
addresses on Christmas cards I am pressured. But now there
is a sort of peace. I feel that I'm better for the first time in
months, for this is the third day in which I don't feel actively
in pain and troubled as a result. There is a wonderful feeling
of space. I've been crowded by the illness and the pain, by
running upstairs and trying to get ten cards done suddenly,
and then I'm so tired. But I did have a little nap and the
pussycat is asleep on the straight chair. Susan is out doing
shopping, inventing a surprise for our supper. She is wonderful at making surprises.

Every day the mail brings books: the first book of poems
by a woman with whom I've been in touch for some years,
Jane Coleman, out in Rodeo, New Mexico. This is a strong
book—a strong book full of the love of the Southwest—quite a
relief after so many "confessional" first books of poems. It
stands firm as a rock, and will last.

I'm still immersed in the Rachel Carson biography, a
model of what a book can be about a woman who is certainly
great but who would never have wanted a personal biography
to be written. Paul Brooks has found the way to do it by many
quotes from her work. When he quotes from her directly,
from letters, it's often about her work. It's always fascinating.
The thing which strikes one again and again is the struggle.

She had to work, write short pieces, for money. There was always the struggle. She was supporting her mother and two nieces, and working for the government, where there was all the—I was going to say the claptrap of the bureaucracy!— and in a way at least at times that's what it was.

We are still looking at a video now and then. We are now in the middle of Jean Renoir's *Les Règles du Jeu*. I think it was actually filmed in one of the Rothschild chateaux. We see it well, the pretty shocking life of weekends at a chateau, where shooting pheasants is the chief pleasure in the morning and flirting and changing partners in the evening. It's hard to take—the shooting—but I suppose it's part of a whole lot of rules of the game. Maggie and Bill went on a pheasant shoot in Scotland two or three years ago.

Parts of me are simply not operating. I feel about a fifth here as far as who May Sarton *was*. I think that was what upset me most about seeing the videotape. There too I wasn't the May Sarton that I recognize, but an old turtle peering out, still enjoying life, but at a very reduced level. So I read with enormous enjoyment still but it's the only thing that I do perhaps at full blast—except talk with Susan. We have wonderful talks, without doubt, reaching into our childhood, into our friends. Of course at Christmas I am super-aware of friends and how rich a store there is of them. How beautifully they keep in touch at this season. Now I'm going to go up and tell a few so.

Tuesday, December 18

THE SUN IS OUT! After a rainy day what a marvel it is to see
everything edged with light: the flowers, the little duck that
Serena Sue and Lois brought me. Oh, I do love that little duck.
Everything is alight.

Meanwhile I'm immersed in Rachel Carson and found
yesterday a passage that I'd like to put down in this journal:

> Perhaps something of the strength and serenity and en-
> durance of the sea, of this spirit beyond time and place,
> transfers itself to us, to us of the land world as we con-
> front its vast and lonely expanse from the shore—our last
> outpost. The shore might seem beyond the power of man
> to change—to corrupt—but this is not so. Unhappily
> some of the places of which I've written no longer re-
> main wild and unspoiled. Instead they have been tainted
> by the sordid transformation of development, cluttered
> with amusement concessions, refreshment stands, fish-
> ing shacks—all the untidy litter of what passes under the
> name of civilization. And so noisy are these attributes of
> man that the sea cannot be heard. On all coasts it is the
> same, the wild seacoast is vanishing.

Sometimes I wonder what it is exactly that draws people
to the sea. How many letters I get from people who say their
dream has been to live by the ocean. The minute they come
here and stand out on the terrace for a few minutes they're
not even interested in speaking to me, they're simply magne-

CREDIT: SUSAN SHERMAN

The little duck Sue and Lois brought me

tized by the marvelous expanse of blue right to the horizon. When I first came here I remember I thought anything is worth it to live and watch the sunrise every day as I do over the ocean. It seemed like an incredible present from the Fates that Mary-Leigh Smart had invested in this great estate, was going to build a house for herself and Beverly Hallam, the painter—a modern house—but meanwhile didn't know what to do with the original summer house, which is what I now inhabit. The great thing, seventeen or eighteen years later, is Mary-Leigh's decision to make of this whole area a foundation a little bit like the MacDowell Colony, but this will be for

painters. The big expanse, the great feeling of being right on
the water, will never be changed. How happy Rachel Carson
would be if she knew it! And how happy I am every time I
look out!

This is the third day in which I am able to function more or
less normally. So it is really an extraordinary day and one to be
celebrated, not complained about.

It's wonderful that Susan has been able to get the James
Mason film about an English shooting party, which is the perfect side piece or comment on the French one we've been
looking at. A great piece of luck to be able to put them together. There, too, there will be the pheasants, leaping out to
be shot.

Yesterday I had the gift of a beautiful book, Rilke's letters
to a friend, from Ilse Vogel-Knotts and Howdy, her husband,
the painter. With it came the good news that Harcourt Brace
has welcomed her autobiography, which is about the last two
years in Berlin before she escaped. I'm sure that it's a wonderful, wonderful book. I think its title is *Bad Times, Good
Friends*. Ilse is a person with a genius for friendship and has
written some very poetic, haunting children's books which are
really about her own childhood and her beloved sister.

Every day the mail brings some good news from someone
far off whom I want to hear from, whom I may not at the
moment remember. And so I walk, not run, into a new day
and feel a little better. How marvelous those words are!

Saturday, December 22

BETWEEN FOUR and seven I lay awake in a waking nightmare over the war—the war that is almost bound to happen and hasn't happened. And the strange darkness that we're in while we wait and the extraordinary flightiness of our president, who seems to have no real policy. When the war starts, what then? If we win, what then? Who knows? Who knows what's going to happen? One simply suffers heartbreak thinking about it and the four hundred thousand or more families who will have a dismal Christmas this year. One has the feeling that Hussein is simply playing for time, that he thinks that if he holds out long enough things will fall apart, that the allies will not sustain the effort. Of course, that is partly why George Bush is being so adamant and so violent. He's trying desperately to hang on to the reins. There is something upsetting and even futile about this. No American can be told that we are going to throw twenty thousand lives of Americans away for a slight reduction in the price of oil. It is a grotesque idea. As far as Kuwait goes, there are argments on both sides. It was not a democracy, that's for sure, but that they have suffered, that they have been very badly treated, there's no doubt. If, as one general said recently, we throw everything into the first few hours and win, that would be an optimum end, but if we don't and then have to go on for months it's going to be a sorry, brutal, brutalizing war.

Meanwhile here at home Susan is making a hearth and Christmas house of this house. It would be, God knows, desolate without her. Janice, who usually comes and makes fish chowder on Christmas Eve, can't come because Priscilla's friend Angela is dying of cancer in Westminster. Janice must go and be with Priscilla during these last terrible hours as Angela's life wanes.

I'm hoping that this afternoon we'll be able to see Katharine Hepburn in that poignant film *Summertime*. More than any other film in which I've seen her this brings out the tenderness and the really deep capacity for love that she proved in her long relation with Spencer Tracy, who could not divorce because he was Catholic—a long, faithful love affair. I think of her nursing him when he was so ill, bringing him soup that she made, being at the same time outside the family, which must have been hard.

Rod Kessler, when he came the other day, took a photograph of me sitting in the chaise longue where I am all day long. It was not with a flash and there I sit—a really very old lady. I'm shocked to see it. Luckily inside myself I don't see the lines, I don't see the really appallingly frail and old-looking woman that I have become. The long illness may have something to do with it. If I had not been ill I would presumably not look quite so old. Certainly I would not have lost fifty pounds of weight. But one must remember that inside, a person is still there—seeing an awful lot, being aware of an awful lot, of course most of all, these days, of Susan's imaginative devotion. She *never* makes me feel for a minute that this is a weight on her, and it is, of course. I'm glad that these days she talks about school a little more. Perhaps there are moments when she misses that wonderful school where she teaches. I often think of her schoolroom, which is hung with green plants, the walls covered with photographs of writers whom the students study, and of friends. When you walk into it it seems like some drawing room for the spirit, so different from other classrooms that it's quite amazing. But Susan brings this kind of life wherever she goes. Here she has kept flowers always, when they were not sent by friends, and I must say, people have been wildly extravagant in their giving during this hard time. It's a flowery white Christmas downstairs.

Saturday, December 23

A VERY SOMBER DAY—creeping rain. Apparently it will be very warm today, then get colder, and we might have a little snow. That would be lovely. Everybody's longing for just a touch of snow to bring us back to the spirit of Christmas.

For some reason I've been thinking this morning about the vulnerability of women, the immense vulnerability of the soft, yielding flesh of women, so often battered. I suppose what brought it to mind was Governor Clements of Ohio having granted pardons to twenty-five women—women who had been battered by their husbands—in jail for having finally reacted by murder. It was a front-page article in the *Times* about Governor Clements, and I feel warmly toward him, for surely it's high time that the records of women accused of murder, who have been battered, be carefully examined by experts: psychiatrists, psychologists, and doctors.

I have warm feelings about Governor Clements for other reasons. When I read poems for the tenth anniversary of the Women's Studies Program in Columbus I was the last speaker. It was a great honor. Afterwards I was invited to the governor's house for a party. It wasn't a planned formal party—and that was what was so nice about it. He was in the middle of elections, appeared in shirt sleeves to talk for a moment with me, his charming, intellectual wife, and a couple of other people who happened to be there. We simply sat and talked for a while and drank wine. It was lovely and informal as well as making me feel like a VIP.

Domestic violence is so prevalent and maybe in many ways worse than the terrible attacks, in the rapes of defenseless women, because, inside the house, what can a woman do? Very often the police simply turn away, saying this is a family quarrel, we can have nothing to do with it. Meanwhile the wife has been threatened with death. Under these circumstances if she pulls a gun on her mate, can it be held against her? What haunts me is the extreme exposure of women. The shocking fact is that our streets are peopled by men who enjoy shooting, who insist that they must have guns, who do not go to jail when they shoot a woman in her backyard, mistaking her for a deer because she had on white mittens. It appears that men get away quite literally with murder.

So it's not surprising that I woke up upset. A somber morning. It helped to look at the beautiful red roses a fan had sent in memory of Judy and the pale, pale pink roses that the same person sent in memory of my mother. It's touching to feel that these two remarkable women *live* for my readers, as they would not, of course, if they had not appeared in a book. What a strange and moving thing it is—to be read this way, to be felt with in this way! "In dreams begins responsibility," as Yeats quotes "from an old play" as epigraph to his book *Responsibilities*, 1914.

Wednesday, December 26

THE DAY AFTER CHRISTMAS. Boxing Day, they call it in England. It's the time when you tip your butler, I suppose. Here there is the feeling—I'm sure most people have it—of relief that Christmas is over. One has climbed that mountain and reached the peak and now it's only a gentle descent into spring.

We had a beautiful Christmas—really one of the best I've ever remembered, partly because of my illness, since limited strength means I can't overdo. The day began—it used to—with Judy and me opening our presents and having our breakfast in bed together. With Susan here the day opened after I'd had my breakfast and she came with a cup of coffee to talk with me while I had it. We then went downstairs, where I opened a few small presents. Then we put on the video that Judy Burrowes had given me of Leontyne Price singing some old carols—among them my favorite, "God Rest Ye Merry Gentlemen." "Tidings of comfort and joy" is such a beautiful, restoring phrase. Price also sings parts of Handel's *Messiah.* Oh, that marvelous, rich, deep soprano! We were talking about how different a black soprano is, as far as I'm concerned, how much more moving than, say a Lily Pons, the famous white soprano who almost never moved one to tears. But this great voice does. On this video Judy gave me there is also the adagio from the Fifth Symphony of Mahler. A real revelation. I'm sure I've heard it but I'd forgotten how tender and beautiful it is, reminding me a little of "Das Lied von der Erde."

We had a quiet time of listening to music as a start for the day and then we began to get things ready, for Edythe was coming for dinner in the middle of the day. Susan had a chicken roasting in the oven, and we had got some splendid crisp beans at the Golden Harvest the other day, and the white sweet potatoes that Edythe likes. She was bringing a delicious dessert called eggnog pie, very light. Thanks to Edythe we laughed a great deal. A Christmas full of laughter with no tears is rare indeed.

The best and most important news came on Christmas Eve—a letter from Mercure de France saying they would like to get rights to translate *As We Are Now* and publish it in France. I've never been published in France. I've always hoped I would be, because several books have been translated into Dutch and several into German, although not recently, but none has ever been translated into French. It was a great event and a wonderful end to the old year, which, on the whole, has not been a very good one, although the end of it finds me more hopeful, certainly, than I was a few months ago before Susan came.

After we had listened to the video I read Susan the Christmas poems from my earlier books. There are several. The one I'm almost fondest of is the one on Piero della Francesca's *Nativity*, which, in a way, defines what makes his impersonal abstract art so moving.

Tuesday, January 8, 1991

CHRISTMAS AND NEW YEAR'S have come and gone, and I am somewhat recovered from what has been a rather long and difficult episode with one week in the hospital, among other things. It has been quite a struggle, but I think we may be reaching a point where I can handle the digestive problem, which is the one thing in the way of my getting well. I must remember when I get discouraged that the heart is doing extremely well and so I have only one last hurdle to pass.

I don't know what I would have done without Susan. She has been absolutely wonderful through this whole difficult time. Because, of course, during the holidays it was not only the usual amounts of mail and telephone calls but *triple* the usual amounts because of its being the holidays. Sometimes the telephone rang ten or fifteen times in one day—often with people I don't hear from *except* on holidays and whom I'm *so* happy to hear from. I've thought a great deal about friends, and of course it's in the Christmas poem: how I would never have survived without my friends, how meaningful and marvelously helpful they've been.

Lovely, amusing things happened while I was in the hospital—suffering from hunger as everyone in hospital does because of the awful food, although our hospital is not as bad as many others. A woman on Long Island, a reader of mine, sent me some *speculose* made by a small pastry shop near where she lives. *Speculose* is a Belgian Christmas cookie made with a lot of cinnamon. These tasted of Belgium; they were wonder-

ful. I could get the nurses to taste them and I felt like Santa
Claus, but I also could stay the pangs of hunger with these
spicy bits of Belgium.

I am better in some ways at least. One of them is that I can
read again. During the Christmas holidays I was so weak and
frail and tired that I couldn't even read. Now I can read again,
I've been immersed in a long piece in *The New Yorker* on
Stanley and Africa which is fascinating. To find that my mind
is still there is a relief.

Yesterday I did, unfortunately, see the copy of an interview I did some time ago with Deborah Straw. This is a disappointing interview, at least in part, and I think perhaps
wholly, my fault, because I should have had the sense not to
give an interview when I was as sick as I was. Its general
atmosphere is—as I said to her on the telephone—dismal. At
the end I talk about—or she asks me—what this time of illness
has meant, whether it has been all negative. I'm sorry to say
that I answer yes, it has been. There is no point in pretending
that it has been a lesson in anything except endurance and
trying to believe that someday I can get better. But when
illness goes on so long and there is apparently no hope, it is
hard to believe. I've been a very depressed person.

The saving grace has been Susan's bringing in videotapes.
So every afternoon—almost every afternoon when I wasn't in
the hospital—we looked at a movie. Yesterday it was Julie
Andrews in *Victor/Victoria*, which I simply loved—laid in
Paris in 1934. I was actually there that spring. It is of course a
marvelously amusing and *moving* film about androgyny in
which Julie Andrews plays a man pretending to be a woman
and a woman pretending to be a man, all at once. It's extremely attractive. It brought back all the glamor of androgyny as I knew it then in Paris, when we androgynes used to go
dancing at Le Fétiche with the girls in tuxedoes. But it was a
curiously gay and innocent atmosphere, I find, although it was

a year for me—a year before that—of very great pain, but it
was somehow *exciting* to go back into that Paris.

Another thing I've gone back into—not because of the
movie, but because of the interview I mentioned earlier—is
what that extraordinary time in London meant, from 1936 on.
I had been so immersed in the responsibilities and very hard
work of directing my theater company, the Associated Actors
Theatre, that I had not had time to live as a young woman. I'd
been totally absorbed in trying to raise money to keep going,
for one thing, in translating some of the plays, in directing and
acting. So when the theater failed I had a kind of nervous
breakdown, which was blessed by Anne Thorp—who later
appeared as the magnificent spinster of my novel. She invited
me to stay at her house in Sudbury, where at that time she had
a German refugee couple housekeeping. I stayed there for
three months and slept almost all the time. I lay out on a
chaise in the garden all day. I read very little. I went to bed
very early. And after that summer I was well again.

Then I went to Europe when I was twenty-five and suddenly found that I was an attractive young woman, which I
had never realized I was. I had been the overworked head of
a theater company. Suddenly I blossomed. It was a time when
I was in love with everyone and everyone was in love with
me—both men and women. A wonderful time—I was a little
like a flower opening. Of course, by the greatest good fortune
I met there a group of people who would remain important to
me over a long period of time, including Elizabeth Bowen, the
Julian Huxleys, and Virginia Woolf, whom I did not know well
and who was certainly not a backer of mine, but who was
extremely kind to me and whom I saw every spring for a long
talk—lucky person that I was. Most of all these friends in their
importance was S. S. Koteliansky, the Russian émigré, a
reader for Cresset Press, which he persuaded to publish my
first novel and my poems, and whose faith in me, which was

ardent and demanding, did a great deal for me. I must add Basil de Selincourt, who was then the main literary critic for the *Observer* and did a *remarkable* review of my first book of poems when it came out. It is the best and most discerning review the poems have ever had. When I go back to it I'm always impressed again. Basil became a dear friend—also a savage critic, particularly as he was more interested and much better at prosody than I was. He often sent poems back with queries which did make me revise, and all to the good.

Basil was a purist and didn't drink, and the house was terribly cold—there was a one-band electric heater in my bedroom but I never dared use it because I knew it was considered an extravagance. So in the winter, visits there were somewhat painful. In the summer there was the glorious garden, where Basil, amongst other things, grew a whole bank of Shirley poppies. That began my infatuation with Shirley poppies, and I've had them in every garden of mine since then.

The question in the interview which disturbs me still as I think it over was a rather inept one: "Do you consider yourself a success?" Unfortunately, like a dog growling at a bone, I rushed off with that and turned it into a question only about success as a poet. A poet is not "successful" unless he or she is in the major anthologies. When I was young and my first books were coming out, Untermeyer's Best British Poets and Best American Poets series were used in all the schools. If a poet was not in them he was nonexistent as far as the critics and general public went. I've not had a major critic on my side in America as I did in England. Louise Bogan could have done something for me but chose not to.

If you consider the whole work, what is success? In the first place, it has to do with who reads the author, over how long a time. I'm read by people from ten years old to ninety. I get four or five letters a week from that range, from middle-aged women, old women, old men, young men, young women in college. It's a rainbow of people. At this very moment somebody is discovering me in a public library. Many of these letters say, "I've never heard of you before but I saw the title of your book"—often it's *Journal of a Solitude*—"and I took it home. I loved it and now I'm reading everything you have ever written." One proof of success is if, at nearly eighty, the author is still being discovered, as I am. Another sign is whether the books stay in print. My first novel is now just out in paperback—*The Single Hound*. It was first published in 1938. These books, which often are twenty or thirty years old, are now on the shelves of almost any bookstore.

I don't think there are many writers—serious writers— who make as much money as I do. It's been very good for me in my old age, because I didn't start making a living out of writing until I was sixty-five. But since then the royalties have amounted to more than fifty thousand dollars a year. I can never be grateful enough to Norton, believing as they did, and do, in my work—keeping me in print. If somebody asked me now if you consider yourself a success I would say: Yes, I do, although I'm not a best-seller, never have been, and never will be.

Thursday, January 10

WE DID NOT HAVE the great snow that was expected. It's thin sleeting against the windows, and now there's only an icing of white on the field and on the terrace.

I have been given by the author a book of poems I love—a new book. It is Diana Der Hovanessian's *Songs of Bread, Songs of Salt*. Diana is president of the New England Poetry

CREDIT: SUSAN SHERMAN

An icing of white on the field

Society and a very generous, warm person who has done a lot for me. When I opened this book I had no idea how moved I would be by it. Perhaps it is that being Armenian in itself is such an extraordinary thing—has so much to do with survival. Armenians have been overcome so many times, terribly treated by fate, yet have a sense of life and all it means that is staggering. Her book is published by the Ashod Press in New York.

I may copy one, not one of the Armenian ones, but I liked it. "A Coating" begins with a quotation from the French poet Jules Supervielle: "There is a certain amount of delirium in every poetic creation." The poem reads:

> And delirium
> of course comes

in a jar
which every poet
keeps in the kitchen
to stir slowly
with household herbs
to shake carefully
with household facts
to watch harden
into a certain glaze.
Some buy it.
Some grow it.
I steal it from you.

Yesterday was a hard day, because I was shaky and perhaps made a mistake in trying to go up to my study not only for an hour and a half in the morning but for an hour in the afternoon. I forced myself to thank an admirer who sends me much too much, large packages of things she has chosen with love and care. It's touching but it is hard to answer. The fact is that there is very little now that I need or want. Thanking for what does come into the house has become quite a burden.

But I also managed to write a couple of notes I wanted to write in the afternoon. One was to my cousin May, who sent me a lovely pair of pink bed socks she had knitted, which I put on immediately as soon as I opened the package on Christmas day. I'm in bed so much my feet get numb, so these lovely soft pink shoes have been a blessing.

May and her husband, Richard Pipe, have reclaimed an old cottage—Dakin Cottage—in Ipswich, Suffolk. It has enormous charm, and, of course, they are gardeners. So when I saw them two years ago in the spring, it was thrilling to see the garden and to have tea with a whole set of relatives: their children, whom I didn't really know, their two sons and their daughter Isabel, whom I did know, and another cousin called Angela, whom I didn't know. So I felt surrounded and supported by family, and that is so rare and delightful for me.

I think the most meaningful gift this Christmas was a poem by Laura Rittenhouse which uses as one image the women of Kalispell, Montana. Laura, who was a bond salesman on Wall Street, came all the way to Kalispell to meet me and to hear me read there. She is a very charming woman who was immediately treated as a friend by all my newfound friends there. We were shown the town and more than the town—a marvelous small-airplane flight over the mountains, the snow-covered mountains where bears live. Laura and I parted as friends. It was my fault, a few years ago, to break off because I felt that I didn't entirely share in what she seemed to be seeking in her life, but I feel differently now. So it was a great present from life to have the dear woman reappear. She has left the money market and is writing poems. Isn't that wonderful?

A precious Christmas present came from Deborah Pease, who gave me two scarves that had come from members of her family. One is a most wonderful apple green from a Paris shop, Bramaine in the Place Vendôme; the other one, which I opened only yesterday, had belonged to her grandmother—a soft, light brown cashmere, embroidered in deep rose with a border of flowers. So beautiful. It reminded me of the cashmere shawl Anne Thorp, the "magnificent spinster," gave to my mother. It came to Anne from her great-aunt in Portland, Miss Longfellow. I felt that I ought to give it to the Longfellow House, that it wasn't right that I keep it. So I did so last year and have missed it ever since. What a miracle that this beautiful cashmere arrived this Christmas!

The great event yesterday was getting my hair at last washed and blown. It felt good to be out, although it was sleeting and dismal. We made an appointment for a permanent next week, which will get me off to the spring.

I've been reading with enormous interest a book of family

history by Rita Van Dusen Cherington, who was a student of mine in the Radcliffe Seminars. This is a very good job indeed and an extremely *rich* family—I don't mean rich in money, although there was money too, but in its immense variety, from England to America. Rita was brought up as a child in India, dreamed actually of marrying a British officer and had grown used—as colonial English did—to a great deal of pomp and circumstance and, above all, help in the house. The work that Rita did on this book, the research and the way it's organized, is most remarkable. The reason she sent it to me is that she thought that other people who wanted to do a family history might be interested in seeing it done. The printer was Thompson Shaw. Arlington Graphics, Inc., is also named on the title page. The book will be invaluable to the generations to come. It's like having four or five Thomas Mann novels like *Buddenbrooks* bound in one book. Charming little insights! One of the children was sent to kindergarten and came home and said, "I didn't like it. I *know* how to play."

I've now started, and this is important, on a new medicine only just on the market, called Equalactin. It is a medicine designed for the irritable bowel syndrome which has been such a torment to me for so many months. I'm taking it now and I'm hoping that it will work. We shall see.

I'm shaky this morning, because Susan leaves on the 26th. I must get as well as I can as fast as I can. But I'm still extremely shaky, so that, for instance, the decision to take a cup and saucer from my chaise longue to the table at the other end of the room is difficult because it's such an effort. Yesterday the visiting nurse came an hour earlier than I expected and I had already got up to the third floor thinking that I would have an hour in my study and *then* go down and not go up again—but her early arrival forced me to do that very hard flight of stairs twice within an hour. It took its toll. I felt exhausted.

On the celebrations of Christmas I want to remember the extravagance of two friends of mine who sent Godiva chocolates! It has to be admitted that this is the best chocolate in the world. I'm glad to say that Nancy feels about it much as I do so that on her way down or up she's apt to spend a few seconds examining the possibilities and choosing one of the delectable shapes.

Friday, January 11

WE HEAR NANCY'S CAR crunching on the road. The sleet froze on the road in the night, and driving must be hazardous today. I'm glad she's safely here, bringing me the mail as she does every day.

The days are creeping up to the terrifying January 15 deadline when, if Hussein has not gotten out of Kuwait, there may well be war. It would seem as if everything I pick up has reminders of what war really means. I'm enjoying so much Rita Cherington's memories of her family, and now I've reached the point where she speaks of two of her uncles, one who was gassed in World War I and another who was at the front line all through World War I, when the American army was in it, and who never recovered. The destruction of the flesh and the spirit. It's inconceivable that we could be on the brink of such horror. The *Manchester Guardian Weekly* this week has a long editorial on the front page about how Bush is regarded in other countries in the world. He is frightening people by his making a personal vendetta against Hussein. They even mention his look—his wild look. That America should be facing this more or less alone, that Bush should be able to put one million men, Americans and others, into war, seems absolutely crazy to me and to a great many other people, I'm sure. So we live on the edge of an abyss. It goes on, there's more and more unemployment, one more factory after another closes—one here on the 28th. The fiscal situation in Massachusetts gets worse. The Bank of New England right in the center of York has been temporarily closed. It is a frightening time—and a time the more frightening because the values seem on the whole so crooked.

Meanwhile Susan and I are getting ready for her departure in various ways. One of them is that we went for a walk around the house yesterday afternoon. After my nap we set out from my chaise longue in the closed-in porch, crossed the room where the flower window is and the front hall, into and around the library, back through the kitchen, across the porch to home base, my chaise.

Saturday, January 12

THE TERRACE is again trampled by deer. Susan heard stomping around in the night. That is chiefly because of the yew. There's a yew at the left end of the terrace, and they love yew and eat it—all they can get of it. There is also a very large tall yew at the side with the big maple and other trees. The deer stand up and chew that as high as their heads can go so it looks as if it had been pruned in a circle.

I realized in the middle of the night that I'd thrown away the Burpee seed catalog, because I can't garden anymore.

How ridiculous! Diane sows the picking garden, and although it's a big job and takes hours of time which of course I have to pay for, it does give me some flowers to pick. Nasturtiums flourished last summer, the cosmos was marvelous late into the fall, and some scabiosa too. So I must try to get another catalog.

There's no doubt that I'm better. This is what I must cling to—that I *am* better. The hard thing to handle is that I'm better but I still feel excessively weak and exhausted all the time. Getting myself to record a little this morning took quite an effort, and I got Susan to come and help me make the bed so I could put it off for five minutes. Now I must get dressed and go upstairs to my study and get Maggie's care package ready and write a few notes.

Monday, January 14

SOMEHOW ONE GETS the sense that the days are longer. There's more light. What a difference that makes to one's whole being.

The video we saw yesterday is *The Baker's Wife*—a marvelous old French film. It is faded, all except the music, which sounds like a village band and is very bright and gay all through it. It is the Giono and Pagnol world—the world they created. I keep thinking of Giono's *Un de Baumugne*, a man from Baumugne, where silence is so important because he is a man who rarely speaks, who is clothed in silence. In *The Baker's Wife*, when the wife runs away, it is finally a fisherman who sees her with her lover and comes back to tell. But he is a frightfully shy man. If he's interrupted he stops and won't go on. He's famous for that. So everybody has to be silent, because if they say *anything* he will say, "I'm cut off and from now on I'm silent." Another marvelous thing in this film is the sense of the village, the very old wars between individuals that go on from generation to generation and the excitement there is in every day's meetings. I was impressed because the *curé* who, at the beginning, is a meanie turns out to be compassionate, and, in fact, the whole village becomes compassionate toward the baker's wife when she comes back. There is something moving about this—and unexpected.

Yesterday, because we had been looking at the video, I think, we never did have our daily walk. But as Edythe Haddaway is coming to lunch she and I can walk around the house three or four times.

I was shocked to discover that I only weigh one hundred and four pounds, but I suppose that if you eliminate muscle, and God knows I have no muscle, and if you eliminate fat, and God knows I have no fat, whatever is left, bones and very little flesh, doesn't weigh very much. But because Susan has fed me so bountifully and so exquisitely I expected to have gained about ten pounds. It was a shock to find that I had not. Susan suggested that because I really didn't eat at all for a week in the hospital I must have lost three or four pounds there and that explains it. I think that is true.

The phone rang rather unmercifully on Saturday, because that's the time when people feel they can ring. Also it's still the New Year, which has to be celebrated by being in touch with one's friends. Yesterday my friend Dori, from Santa Barbara, called. She's in her late eighties. They have been waiting for rain, and the wonderful news that she gave me on the phone was that they had had two days of steady, gentle rain— just what they needed most. It seems like a miracle to think of it. You can imagine what this rain has done for the morale.

It made me think of the Pueblo Indians' dances for rain—the drum in the distance that we heard on our way to the dance, calling the people; the fervor of the dance, the Indians in their buffalo and deer masks. Wonderful days they were—those days when Haniel and Alice Long, Agnes Sims, Dorothy Stewart, and I all went to one of the pueblos, such as San Ildefonso, to be part of that vibrating world of the drum and the dance.

Pierrot is sitting on the rug by my bed with his paws tucked in, listening to what I'm saying with a good deal of interest, because his ears are turned slightly. Susan asked me how a cat shows happiness, as he doesn't wag his tail like a dog. A cat only wags his tail when he's hunting, and it isn't wagging so much as *lashing* then, but a cat shows his content by holding his tail straight up in the air. Pierrot's tail, when he comes in from outdoors, is a plume standing *straight up*. Of course, purring is the major sign of happiness for a cat.

I reminded Susan that Julian Huxley sometimes took me behind the scenes at the London Zoo, of which he was secretary in the thirties. Once we were allowed inside the cheetah cage. The cheetahs were quite tame. There were two of them standing there, and I scratched them behind their ears. Suddenly there was a *roar*—rrrrrrrrr—in their throats. I thought it was growling and jumped, but the keeper laughed and said, "They're purring, ma'am." That was a great moment.

There were of course other great moments. One was when I was brought to see bears behind the scenes—a bear and her cubs. The keeper said this was a very wicked bear who sometimes killed her cubs. I asked why they didn't breed her to a gentle bear and try to have gentler and gentler cubs. The keeper smiled and said, "But, miss, you see, the *bears* choose." I thought that was lovely.

One of the delightful things Julian did at the zoo was to set up large sculptures of animals, works of art. He also engineered the famous penguin area where the penguins could swim in a fairly deep pool. But of course the greatest success of the zoo was the panda cub. He became a national treasure, a symbol of joy and survival during the Blitz.

These days I devour catalogs of plants. It's really ridiculous. I can't garden anymore. But when the Winterthur catalog came with terribly tempting things, I couldn't resist, and I've decided to buy a single Chaste tree to replace the French lilac which died. This shrub flowers profusely in late summer with lavender blossoms and looks like a lilac. Then I decided to buy something I've wanted for a long time—a Franklin tree, which also flowers from August until frost with outstanding fall foliage. I shall plant it back of the house, where I dream of a kind of arboretum. I can't help dreaming about the garden even if someone else has to do most of the work. Diane will enjoy planting a lilac to replace the dead one. She has such a feeling for every plant and loves the garden. Lucky I am to have her.

Wednesday, January 16

A SLIVER OF SUN—a little red sliver—came through the clouds early this morning. It looks like a gray day. We wait. War has not been declared, but we wait and live in suspense.

The day before yesterday I got a charming note from Rusty Moe, a psychologist in Indianapolis, who had me come there some years ago and arranged for me to be a guest at the Carmelite monastery while I was in Indianapolis—a wonderful experience for me, which I recounted in my journal *After the Stroke.* In this note he gives me the delightful news that Alice Walker is coming to give a reading for his group, and he suggested that she might like to stay with the Carmelites. He had asked them if they would welcome her. He also gave her the passages from *After the Stroke* which are relevant, and apparently Alice Walker was delighted by all this and has accepted to go there. It takes me back into that infirmary room, which had windows on three sides, the bed facing one window and windows on both sides. In all these windows I looked out on beautiful trees. Inside the fortifications—it's all one can call them, a high wall around the monastery—there are magnificent trees, some flowering fruit trees inside, then large tulip trees. The leafy greenness was welcome. Now I have the pleasure of thinking of Alice Walker in my room. How it brings it all back! How she will enjoy the stirring conversations we had over supper every night. I think the Carmelites usually play records of classical music or someone reads aloud while they have their dinner, but when they have a guest that is not done. There is marvelous conversation, lots of laughter, and a strong interest in world affairs. I'm sure that they are praying for peace assiduously these days.

I was talking about them at breakfast just two days ago when that note came. I said they believe that prayer can change the world and that is what their whole life as nuns is about. I don't believe that prayer can change the world, but I do believe that those who pray create a radiant center. The Carmelite monastery in Indianapolis is exactly that—a radiant center. And yes, perhaps their prayers change the world, not through the intervention of God but through their influence. It makes me nostalgic for that time when I was having a struggle with pain, just as I am now and have been for so long.

Once again this morning Cybèle barked and barked. Susan was having a bath but she heard it and realized that Cybèle was saying: Pierrot wants to come in! So she got up

out of the bath—this is so like Susan—and put on a wrapper,
ran downstairs, and, lo and behold, there was the cat! It is so
endearing that there is such a bond between these two little
animals who occasionally meet each other nose to nose, but do
not know each other yet.

Yesterday I saw Dr. Petrovich. He was pleased with the
state of my heart. They will do a draining of the lining of the
lung once more. But Dr. Gilroy, whom I saw on Monday,
thinks that may be the last time, because the medicine I'm
taking now for drying it up seems to be working. That is very
good news. In fact, if I could solve the intestinal problem I'd
be well. It is strange that I don't gain weight, considering the
heavenly meals that are presented to me four times a day, for
we have tea every afternoon—often with cinnamon toast. But
I still weigh only one hundred and four—in my clothes, with
boots on. That is a very big drop from what used to be one
hundred and sixty, although of course I was always trying to
lose it and sometimes got it down to one hundred and forty-
five, but never, I think, below that in the last twenty years.

The *Smithsonian* is advertising a book about Indians, very
expensive—American Indians and their tribes. It's nearly
forty dollars and appears to be more of a showcase than the
kind of history that I would like to get hold of. Maybe Peg
Umberger, who lives in upstate New York, can direct me to
one, for she has done a lot of work with the Iroquois—especially the Iroquois craftsmen—and has helped found a museum for their arts and crafts. An interest in the American
Indians, except for the Pueblos near Santa Fe, came to me
late. Now I feel strongly the guilt that we must all bear and
the need to know more. It is a reason for rejoicing that the
northern Indians in Maine did win a very big case against the
state involving millions of dollars and that now they have the
wonderful pleasure of employing poor whites from northern
Maine in factories that they have founded, using, of course,

first of all, Indian labor. But for so long they were the hangers-on, the poverty-stricken, the rejected by society partly because of liquor, mostly because of poverty.

Once in a while I know why I go on, determined to resubscribe to the *New Statesman,* which is now called *New Statesman & Society.* I have been subscribing to this English weekly for well on forty years, more than that, probably fifty. When I was first in London it had a roster of marvelous literary critics, and that was why I subscribed. Now I subscribe in large part because of reviews of political books that I don't see anywhere else. In the last issue that I've been looking at, which is an old one, December 14, there is a review of two books. The review is called "Unto every one that hath . . ." One of the books is called *Bad Samaritans; First World Ethics and Third World Debt* [Paul Valley], published by Hodder & Stoughton, for eight pounds, ninety-nine pence, which is not too much. This paragraph is about the other book, which is called *The Poor Die Young: Housing and Health in Third World Cities* [Sandy Cairncross, Jorge E. Hardoy, and David Satterthwaite, eds., Earthscan, £9.95]:

> This volume shows hundreds of examples of self-help, in cities as diverse as Allahabad, Rio de Janeiro and Khartoum. There, people are improving their health by upgrading their neighbourhoods, in ways that are far cheaper and more enduring than any of the large-scale projects advocated by planners and engineers trained in western mould. The most vital measures for survival—clean water, sanitation, control of disease—can be undertaken by the people themselves, but only in conjunction with sympathetic local administrations.

What we do, on the contrary, is impoverish the Third World by, amongst other things, using their cheap labor, which then American entrepreneurs make the money on and deprive American laborers of their jobs. We have exploited worse than under colonialism the Third World countries and are in large part responsible for their debts and for their misery.

Thursday, January 17

WE OPENED THE WAR yesterday with a massive air attack on Iraq and apparently succeeded in bombing out their missile sites, which would have flattened Tel Aviv, they said, had they been operable. Very few casualties, a British plane and an American plane. Of course, the real war, the bloody devastating war, will take place with ground troops, and this is what one dreads. We have waited so long for this that in a way it's a relief. We've been sitting on the edge of a knife.

One of the most shocking things was a long article in the *New York Times* a couple of days ago about the cost of the war, saying that we can, I regret to say, well afford it, that even the huge amount it's costing, fifty billion this year they say, is only five percent of our total national product.

It rained all day yesterday—a miserable day, somewhat lightened by the video of *Dodsworth* which Susan was sure I would like, and she was right. It is a very good film and brings back the twenties and thirties when so many Americans were traveling to Europe and were often so uncouth. I remember one woman saying," I sent back a martini five times in Madrid because they couldn't learn how to make one." What is so depressing is the American idea that we're superior to everybody else in every way. War has not come home to us. Even the Vietnam War, after all, did not mean that children in

Duluth were bombed in their schools. When you think of what World War I did, what World War II did, yet no destruction here at home, you do not wonder that we think we can do anything and always win. That is the worst of the illusions.

The cat and the dog can now be placed nose to nose when they are in Susan's arms. It is quite hilarious.

No one comes today, except Eleanor Perkins is here cleaning, always a great help. I go and get a permanent wave at last. My hair has been standing on end like straw. I shall be much more comfortable and look a lot better, good for the morale.

Friday, January 18

I KNEW EARLY this morning that it was going to be a beautiful day. There was a sky with little thin clouds—wisps of clouds—which turned a reddish gold in otherwise a pale, green-blue sky before the sunrise.

The great event yesterday was the permanent wave. When we walked into the beauty salon in York, which is a lovely big, airy room, there was an elderly lady who is often there having her hair done, like me, and who said, "Oh, Miss Sarton, I've just taken five of your books out of the library to comfort me during the war." I thought it was very sweet. She said, "Your books are comforting." Sometimes I wonder why, because I've certainly faced some pretty tough things in them, such as, you know, death, dying of cancer, coming out as a lesbian, so I was touched by the word "comforting." It also made me think of Donna—that's my hairdresser's name. She should call her customers her patients, I sometimes think, because she has so many elderly women customers and is so good a listener, always positive and helpful in what she says. I feel cheered when I leave. It's not only because my hair looks marvelous, but because I've been given a step up.

Of course, these days are dominated by the war news. All the regular television programs are canceled. We get very long, very interesting briefings on CNN and on all the stations. It is staggering to think of the genius of the inventors of all this matériel, which at least until now has proved to be extraordinarily successful. We saw today bombs which can be guided by lasers to go around a building and in through a four-foot-wide door and then explode inside the building. It is staggering. The war is costing at present one billion a day. All one can think of, I'm afraid, is what one billion a day for five days would do for the homeless, for drug addicts, for the troubled state of the prisons and the judiciary system in general. Nothing is being done, or very very little, for any of the dire needs at home. I think continually of the bridges over the Hudson, at least one of which is in danger, we hear, of collapsing. The cost of mending even one is staggering, so the money isn't "found." Mayor Dinkins had to fire sixteen thousand city employees yesterday. Meanwhile billions go over to Saudi Arabia.

Yesterday we saw Pat Chasse for the first time in many days. Of course she's had flu twice, she's been upset by side effects of the antibiotics, but in spite of illness she looks fresh and young for her age, with her reddish hair and blue eyes. I always ask her who she's been seeing that day, because she is a visiting nurse who deals with babies, young mothers, and children. Yesterday she had been to see a young mother who was never loved by her own mother and who now is incapable of loving her three-year-old daughter who is a warm, loving little girl who runs to her mother with her arms out and then is not hugged because this mother has never been taught how to love. It's so terribly sad.

Saturday, January 19

A MARVELOUS SUNNY MORNING AGAIN—the leafless branches of the maple I see from my bedroom window gold against the blue.

Susan has taken some remarkable photographs of the winter landscape here, which she has managed to capture as poetic and even glorious. I'm so happy to have them.

Yesterday was to have been the first day this week when we had no appointments. We didn't have to go scrambling to Portsmouth, or to the store, or to one or two doctors. We were going to have a cozy day at home. And so it began, but, alas, at noon we noticed that the dishwasher had not worked. That is, no water was forthcoming. Susan generally leaves it on at night and lets it run, but it hadn't done its work. Luckily Mary-Leigh and Beverly were back from Bev's show at a museum in Florida. I asked Mary-Leigh's advice and she suggested I get Ralph Fabrizio. He is an excellent plumber and has been here often. If you can believe it—if you've ever lived in the city, for instance—I called him at noon and he was here at one from Portsmouth, took the whole machine apart and couldn't find anything wrong except for a valve, which, of course, he didn't have with him for a twenty-year-old machine. Meanwhile Mary-Leigh had decided that perhaps the thing to do was to invest in a new one. She's now looking in

The winter landscape

her *Consumer Reports* for what make they advise. I felt extreme depression, which is quite absurd, because what's a dishwasher? It can be replaced, but somehow it was frustrating on top of a hard time with illness and pain.

Susan had gotten a video called *Torch Song Trilogy*. I had not understood that it is about drag queens, and I found it terribly depressing, so we decided to stop it. It made me cry, I don't know why. After all, I greatly enjoyed *Victor/Victoria*, because it has appeal for the androgyne in all of us.

We now have downstairs the great Harrop's French-English dictionary. I only brought down the French-English because Susan and I keep thinking of French words we're not sure of. For instance, yesterday it was *dégringolade*—a wonderful word which means tumbling down—*dégringoler*: to tumble down. I suppose one might say that yesterday we *dé-gringoléd* through the broken-down dishwasher.

After we put off *Torch Song Trilogy* we watched the *National Geographic* documentary on cats, which Pat Chasse had kindly recorded for us. This is really a remarkable film filled, naturally, with marvelous photographs of cats. What superb mothers they are! I had not realized how generous they are about allowing strange kittens to suckle. But all through I was aware of how beautiful everything a cat does *is*, how wonderfully designed this animal is—from spine to whiskers. Everything serves a purpose and is beautiful. There's no animal as beautiful in all it does. Spraying to mark territory may not be, but it is very effective.

It makes me remember Tom Jones—Judy's and my cat—who later became famous as the "fur person." He was an unaltered male who had come to us for shelter and was fairly young when he came. Suddenly he began to spray. We had bookcases along a hall—this was at 139 Oxford Street in Cambridge. He began spraying the books. It happened that Elizabeth Bowen was about to come to us as a guest, and we simply *could not* expose her to the rank smell of Tom Jones signing his territory. So we had to have him altered. He was miserable. I think he got pneumonia in the cage, but he did recover, of course, and there was no more trouble. So he became, in *The Fur Person*, a Quaker cat. He refused to fight. The fact that he was a Quaker caused us considerable amusement, since Judy was a Quaker herself. Tom Jones—never was a cat so loved.

Yesterday I found a letter I've been trying to find for days—from Doris Beatty. I want to put a part of it in the journal for two reasons. One, we often think we can't do anything about the needy, the poor, and the homeless. The other is what wonderful friends I have, among them Doris Beatty. Doris had four children and lost her youngest son very tragically, when he was seventeen. His name was

David and he appears in this paragraph, so there's no doubt that she answered the appeal in the newspaper thinking of him.

... last week there was a photo and headline on the story—*Mother wants better life for son*—and showed a picture of them sitting on the floor—it just grabbed me— the boy was 9 yrs. old and very good in math appar- ently—he needed pants without holes in the knees and a bed, a folding one if possible, and she would like some dishes—there was no furniture at all—one room and a kitchenette, the article said, and she was going to be taking classes to train for job placement. It listed a social worker with the Traveler's Aid. So I got the number thru info but the social worker was off for the day. The person who answered took my name and number and the info that I did have a folding bed and some dishes. Well, in less than an hour Mary, herself, called. Clearly a person who had not had much chance for an education but a good mother, I felt, so we made arrangements to bring her these things next day and she gave me her apt no. and address—right in the Tenderloin district of S.F.— winos drinking out of paper bags, or staggering drunks— oh, my God, May, to raise a bright child, to just live here—I locked both doors on the van and Jerry, brave soul, walked back to the apt. bldg.—at least it was se- cure—a locked gate in front—the Franciscan Towers it was called yet! He carried some of the boxes of clothes (for her), and he said that the security system was good—there was someone in the lobby to check him in and out—Mary's apt was on the 4th fl.—there was an elevator, and the place was clean if not depressing. Jerry was gone for a long time, I thought, I got scared that I might have sent him into a terrible situation and that he might have been clobbered over the head. . . . not so, eventually, he came with Mary and her son, to our van and we met and talked a bit and they were able to carry the rest of the things back to the apt.

Sign of our times. Jerry said that, in spite of no furniture, they did have a color TV. I think it's lucky that they do have it because I would sure not want to have my 9 year old child outside in that neighborhood. I asked Jerry if their apt. was anything like the one that Dave had before he died—it wasn't far from there—this little boy reminded me of Dave, I guess, bright and courageous. His teacher says he is way ahead of his class in math. I tucked in as many good books as I have left here and some good games. . . . and you know Ernie and his pal from Sesame St.—they have sat on my desk for a long time—meant to go to this lad I think, don't you.

It's so moving to consider what Doris and Jerry did—she sees a notice in a newspaper about people who have nothing and takes it on herself to go and give them at least some of what they need—in the memory of her son. That, and the hundreds of other things that she does for people in need, makes Doris so lovable.

Sunday, January 20

We're in the fourth day of the war. I've been more than usually moved by the letters that come in from people who are concerned with human needs. Each of these letters gives me a lift. Each letter which says, too, that my work has been of help makes me want to get well and makes me grateful. The Sister of Mercy who wrote music for my poem on AIDS accompa-

nied the cassette with a wonderful letter about all my work—
what it meant to her. It tells me something that I found interesting and moving. Sister John Peterson says:

> For the last four years I have worked in Coming Home
> Hospice as an attendant and have been there since it
> opened. Coming Home is a hospice facility of fifteen
> beds: ten for those with AIDS, five for cancer. It is a
> wonderfully warm and homelike environment. Most of
> us who work there have worked in people's homes, so we
> insist on it remaining homelike. During the time since its
> opening four hundred people have lived and died at
> Coming Home. It has been for me a very privileged,
> graced, and moving place to be. To be with people as
> they move toward death—they seem to bring us all to
> the edge with them and draw us to live as fully and
> brilliantly as we can.

Then she tells about hearing me read the AIDS poem in San
Francisco in May of 1989 and that she had the inspiration to
put it to music, which she did. It's awfully hard to write music
for a poem. There are a lot of cassettes here stored away with
different pieces of music composed to poems of mine. None
have I found to be quite satisfactory. I presume that is because none compares with the exquisite songs Duparc and
Fauré composed for poems of Baudelaire.

Yesterday was a gloomy day—extremely gloomy—because I thought I had solved my intestinal problem. Instead I
had an attack of violent pain, so much so that I finally took
paregoric and could do nothing but lie down and hope it
would eventually work, as it did.

In the afternoon we watched on video *The Four Hundred
Blows*, the famous Truffaut film. As I was, I must admit, very
depressed because I had thought that I was on the mend at
last, this was not the film, perhaps, to see. In the first place it

was in black and white and the whole scene was gloomy—a
gloomy France of the *lycées* and little boys unloved by their
parents, unable to make a go of it in ordinary life. The little
boy is very touching but is without moral sense, partly because of the lack of love in his home. He is a terribly isolated,
lonely child, so he steals money from his parents, behaves
badly in school, steals a typewriter from his father's office,
which he finally returns because he gets scared. He ends up, it
is suggested, as a criminal. So that last night I went to bed
pretty low, glad to be able to sleep. The oxygen and a sleeping
pill do give me a sustained night's sleep. And we'll hope for
some new and better behavior of the intestinal tract today or
the next day.

Susan had put white tulips and small yellow daffodils in a
jar on the television for me to look at during the day when I
was in very great pain. I realize more and more what she has
done for me. The fact is I've become very lazy when I think of
all the things I must do when I start the day and when I end
the day. I end the day by going downstairs to turn on the
oxygen and get Pierrot in. I start the day at six or often earlier
to turn off the oxygen and let the cat out, get my breakfast,
and watch the news.

One of the people who will help me after Susan goes,
Andrea Rioux, comes today to be briefed, so that will be interesting.

Tuesday, January 22

A BRILLIANT DAY—brilliant because it has brought us, just after eight, the wonderful plumber Ralph Fabrizio, bringing the new dishwasher. Mary-Leigh managed to get it delivered today, yesterday being Martin Luther King's birthday and a holiday.

There was a good editorial in the *New York Times* pointing out that with a reputation slightly tarnished by the proof that he plagiarized part of his master's thesis, "compared to what he achieved that is a very minor thing and should be forgotten." It did occur to me that it's also true that many people have been shocked by J. Edgar Hoover's tuning in on King's women. He was a womanizer, there's no doubt. But after giving a speech like "I Have a Dream" a man must be so tense, so towering in a way, even over himself, so full of power, that it's natural that he need the release of sleeping with a woman. It's interesting that so much has been made of this in Martin Luther King's case as unacceptable, whereas the fact that John Kennedy, president of the United States, did the same—even invited women to the White House— doesn't seem to have affected his reputation. It's a strange world. But Hoover hated King, there's no doubt about that. He was out to get him, and, in fact, there are still people who believe that it was the FBI who shot him, and that is not beyond belief, unfortunately.

Meanwhile the war goes on. We can't help being terribly anxious about the ground war which is presumed to start in a few days, and it is very worrying about the oil reserve tanks. Today on CNN—which I'm glued to between seven and eight A.M.—according to one report they are all engined. All Hussein has to do is press a button and they will ignite, and it has been planned for a long time. In some cases it will take a year to put out those fires—if ever.

Lately there has been a paucity of good things to read in *The New Yorker* but the last issue contains almost too much. There are three long pieces. One is part of John Cheever's journal—the second half will be published later. It's fascinating, of course, but also *so* depressing because of the enormous waste that his alcoholism caused and the amount of guilt he had to support because he couldn't give it up. And it becomes clear—and is clear since the biography of him and since his daughter's book—that part of the alcoholism was due to his insecurity about his sexual being and his inability to come to terms with his homosexuality. It's a strange story.

The second great thing in *The New Yorker*—this is the week of January 21—is a profile of David Bamberger, who has a huge ranch in Texas devoted to the preservation of species which are about to die out. This is also fascinating.

Thirdly, there is a letter from Tokyo which is at least partly about the changes in the attitude about the emperor—what he means to the Japanese, what he can't mean, and what he should mean. I'm only part of the way through it.

Yesterday Andrea Rioux came to talk over when she could come—late one afternoon a week to cook a meal for me, and perhaps also on Saturday mornings. She says she loves to bake, and the idea of a pie is very good. Suddenly my terror of being left here alone without Susan is mitigated by all the people who are coming. They will drop in tomorrow to be briefed. Then we'll be ready to go. So things are looking up here, except for my recalcitrant tummy, which still behaves very badly.

Wednesday, January 23

IT IS TERRIBLY COLD, Nancy said—five below this morning
when she set out. I feel a little bit like a fish in a tank. The tank
is warm, as the house is warm, and I'm never out of the house,
so I'm always warm and don't realize what bitter cold there is.
It was a marvelous sunrise again today.

I watched while Susan's little dog *ran* around the lawn
below the terrace, ran wildly—a little powder puff as white as
the snow. It was thrilling to see that, not so thrilling to be
Susan and have to take Cybèle out when it's five below.

Last night Susan was tired, had circles around her eyes,
for she had had a grueling day. Fabrizio brought the new
dishwasher. Amazing that Mary-Leigh managed to get it
delivered so soon. But installing it meant, of course, all kinds
of adjustments and work that had to be done—a pipe that
needed to be replaced and so on. Meanwhile Susan was
cleaning up after the men all morning as they worked. By the
time Edythe came for lunch everything was in order again,
but Susan *must* have been exhausted.

Edythe came while Susan went to have lunch at Nancy's
and to see that charming house in the woods. At least there
was a rest there, and a delicious lunch of lobster salad. When
she came home she was on a kind of high that suggests hyster-
ical fatigue—when you're still driving yourself at one hundred and fifty miles per hour and using up the last resources of
energy. This morning she said she had not slept at all since
eleven-thirty last night. Poor Susan! She is leaving on Satur-

CREDIT: SUSAN SHERMAN

Cybèle

day, and what's ahead must be on her mind—packing and all the things that have to be done.

We didn't look at a film yesterday when she got back. I suggested we just have fun and see our mainstays: *Golden Girls,* which I never looked at and didn't like until Susan came. Somehow or other seeing it together has made us laugh and enjoy. It is followed by *People's Court,* which is also fun to watch together.

Today there has come a paper on my work from a student, a sophomore at the University of Florida at Orlando. She has written a term paper, "The Muse of Solitude." I am delighted that so many students are using my work. Two or three times a month I get a term paper on one aspect or another of it and usually from a student who has only recently discovered Sarton. Often a friend has given her a book of mine. The word gets around.

Today two of the people who are going to come and work here for a few hours are coming to talk things over at one-thirty.

I listened to the war news on CNN while Susan was getting my breakfast. The bad news is that a missile did real damage in Tel Aviv. The most dangerous thing going on now appears to be the burning of oil in Kuwait which Saddam Hussein is doing, well by well. If it can be sustained over the long run it will do permanent damage. There have been terrorist attacks by people connected with the Gulf war—terrorist attacks put the whole world on the alert.

Thursday, January 24

ELEANOR PERKINS is here cleaning. Everything is going to be spotless. This is always the way.

I feel more or less squared away as far as people helping me, but I was very tired at the end of an hour of explaining. I feel for these two women, one so young, with two little girls two and six years old. Her name is Jerri. She is a nurse's aid and she tells me that her husband is wonderful about helping with the little girls when she is at the hospital. The other one, Joan, is a secretary at the hospital, was a schoolteacher in the early grades, has seven children, most of them grown-up, and loves to cook. So she's a cook in reserve. She also likes to get up early; Jerri doesn't. Joan will come on Monday morning at seven-thirty and get my breakfast. On this Monday Susan will be down in Florida already, with her parents.

Nancy will take me to the hospital, as they are going to drain the lining of the left lung where liquid accumulates. The medicine, Nolvadex, which they have recently prescribed does help take care of the liquid. Dr. Gilroy said, when I saw him last week, that he thought this would probably be the last time the liquid would have to be drained. So that's good news indeed. While Nancy takes me to the hospital, Jerri will be making my bed and tidying things up here.

We did see parts of a moving video, *I Heard the Owl Call My Name*, which I remember reading as a novel. The Indians of the Northwest believe that when the owl cries it means that you're going to die if you hear the owl. It's a warning. This is a film, almost a documentary, about Indians who have fished for many generations and for whom fishing is life. Children get no education beyond the seventh grade. There's a teacher who teaches all seven grades in a one-room schoolhouse.

Once again we are confronted with the complex problem: Is it better for these Indians to keep their own ethnic ways, to bury their dead with their own ceremonies, or to send their children, after the seventh grade, to a town where they would get further education? The Indians feel this would ruin the children. They don't want any part of the white man's world. They want to stay in the world which their ancestors created. There's much to be said for both sides of this argument. I don't know which side I'm on.

It doesn't seem possible, as it did for the Pueblos, to combine the two, for the Pueblo Indians have kept their dances and kept their crafts and their architecture, and at the same time have, for example, volunteered into the armed forces. They were pilots in World War II, for instance, but actually came back after the war and opted for their Pueblo life.

Saturday, January 26

THE FATAL 26th of January when Susan leaves! It has been a marvelous time. She's taught me a great deal about love, and perhaps I've taught her a little. We've exchanged so much of the precious inner person who is exchanged very rarely with anyone. It's been far more than only a time in which I was helped to get well, though there is no doubt that I'm better than I was when Susan came. Everyone notices that my voice is louder and that it has resonance. That scratchy sound of my voice was one of the hardest things to handle, the sign of greatest weakness, during the months before she came. I feel ready to become the captain of my ship, and in some ways, of course, I'll enjoy resuming my solitude after these months of precious companionship and care.

Tuesday, January 29

AGAIN A BRILLIANT DAY, but I have been in one of my periods of torment since last Friday when I had a really terrible attack of diverticulitis, had to stay in bed and didn't eat anything. Finally, after taking a great deal of the regular painkiller, Tylenol with codeine, I resorted to paregoric, which did at least stop the pain for the rest of that day, and I slept well.

Susan left Saturday. I was still in pain and unable to get up to say a proper goodbye. Nancy described her car—Susan's car—as packed to the gills and more. It was very hard to see her go. I miss her and all the things we did together—like looking at CNN and—to go from the horrible to the ridiculous—*Golden Girls.* All the things she did to help me are here, like fruit juice, everything at hand, a whole stuffed chicken, which, unfortunately, I've not felt well enough to eat. But today I'm hoping to have a real meal.

It's the fourth time I've had the lung drained, and this time, unlike the others, it was *hideously* painful. I had to cough but was asked not to, which was difficult. Even to try to warn ahead for a cough was impossible. I held it and held it—in awful pain—and finally had to cough. So it seemed interminable, but the surgeon did it, I think, in about a half hour. He drew out six hundred cc's of liquid.

There are monstrous happenings that one can't control: in this case an extremely efficient and nice nurse who happened to have halitosis. As she was bent over my head, holding my arms during the whole operation, her breath was nauseating. That was the final straw and the final hell. At last, home— Nancy drove me back. I crept into my bed, and oh, I was relieved, still in pain, and I still am. However, I slept very well, thanks to oxygen, another thing that Susan did for me.

I notice that talking even this much into the recorder is making my chest hurt.

Yesterday, the supreme irony, just as I was starting to relax a little and had a hot-water bottle to help, the phone rang twice in quick order with things which demanded of me attention and savvy which I was in no condition to provide. The first was the National Shawmut. I've been considering leaving them, taking the trust and putting it under the management of Mark Meizler, the man who does my income tax, because the Shawmut charges such an outrageous amount for handling the small trust I have built up myself. They talked to me, and by late afternoon I decided to stay with them, but the call was agitating.

Immediately after that ring, another came and it was Eric Swenson, my editor, and vice president of W. W. Norton & Company, saying that they needed a two-paragraph biography of me for the jacket of *Sarton Selected,* a book Brad Daziel has edited and which is coming out for my birthday this year—my seventy-ninth birthday. Here I was, in tremendous pain, having been told to rest for the remainder of the day, being suddenly confronted with providing a very difficult thing in a few minutes—a brief autobiography. I did it—I had said I couldn't—but then I woke up and jotted down notes for it and am about to organize them and give them to Nancy to type. I'm amazed that I managed to do it. I'm better than I thought!

Wednesday, January 30

THIS IS THE 30th of January; we are hurtling into February. A gray, rainy day.

Yesterday was a hard day, partly because I managed to do that biography Eric had asked me for. But it's always invigorating to manage to achieve something that seems to be impossible. I make a good point in it, I think. Having an English mother and a Belgian father, I have been for forty years a builder of bridges—a builder of bridges between one kind of life and another, between Europe and America, for example;

another between the homosexual and the heterosexual life; between solitude and communion with others. I lead, on the whole, a solitary life. At the same time I have an enormous number of friends and an enormous number of people who think of me as family and whom I think of as my family. One of them is coming this weekend, Karen Saum, who made a sensitive videotape of me called *She Knew a Phoenix.*

For the first time in a long time I've ordered flowers for the house from Foster's. Dear Susan filled the house with flowers. Now there are none. I need one bunch in my bedroom and one downstairs, so I have ordered a few tulips.

The main news yesterday was finishing that brief biography. Today I feel empty and alas not well because of the bowel syndrome, but I think that it may be the new medicine, Equalactin, is going to help in the long run, since I'm taking no laxative at present, only the medicine itself. If it could get me onto a regular rhythm, wouldn't it be marvelous? So, let us pray.

Friday, February 1

IT SEEMS AS IF the year were already on its way out. I haven't been talking to this little machine, because I have been so ill. I think that having the operation on my lung on Monday did something to the whole chemistry of my body, because I had had such violent diarrhea at two A.M. and then had to hold everything in while the surgeon dug into my back and got out a surprisingly large amount of fluid. Since then I haven't been able to function at all. I live on warm prune juice. I'm taking less painkiller, Tylenol with codeine, because they say it's constipating. So it's the old story of "you can't win." I live in a cocoon of pain most of the day and look forward immensely to the night. Luckily, thanks to oxygen, I sleep very well.

Jerry was here today—for the last time this week. She is the most wonderful worker. Today she cleaned the copper, and it now *shines* out. She watered the plants and also gave them some nourishment, which it's high time they had. So things are being looked after in a splendid way.

Tomorrow Karen Saum, who lived here for half of the week for a year when she was working in Augusta, is coming for the weekend. We'll catch up on everything. Since then she's written a whodunit which is apparently selling very well and she continues to work at H.O.M.E. as she has for many years now.

I have a couple of things to read for blurbs. One is *A Noel Perrin Sampler.* I have always been an admirer of Noel Perrin. It's a completely original voice. How rare it is when such a thing as an original mind finds a means of expressing itself as Perrin has—entirely, really, through essays. He publishes in all kinds of unlikely places, such as the *New York Times* Sunday magazine section. I was particularly moved to see that this book is dedicated to Rachel MacKenzie, who must have been his editor at *The New Yorker.*

This gave me a glow of pleasure, because she was such a wonderful editor and such an extraordinary woman, fighting very severe illness all her life. It was her heart. She wrote a book, actually, about the almost fatal heart attack and the long time she spent in intensive care. This is an extraordinary work of art and also of memory. I think we tend to forget things that happen in the hospital, especially if they are painful. Rachel managed to remember.

One of the things I'm proud of in my life is that when Katharine White, E. B. White's wife, who was the chief fiction

editor of *The New Yorker* for many, many years and edited
the pieces they bought of mine, incidentally, was retiring she
must have written to a great many people to ask them
whether they could think of someone who would be able to
take her place, and I was included. I wrote a letter such as
I've never written in my life saying I *had* the person—she
would be absolutely perfect. This was Rachel MacKenzie,
who had spent the two or three years before this in bed on the
Hill in Boston being taken care of by a doctor who actually
came to see her and who paid for the medicine because he
wanted to help her. She had a strange virus she had caught in
China. In my letter to Katharine White I said that the first
impression might not be wonderful. Rachel had an owl-like
face and wore glasses, was very sure of herself, but quite shy.
Katharine White did hire her, and she was a tremendous success at *The New Yorker*. Once in a great while life brings one
an opportunity like that, and how splendid when one can
meet it! I'm so grateful.

Sunday, February 3

OH, IT'S LOVELY to have Karen Saum here! About ten years
ago she lived here on the weekends—the year when she was
working at CETA and would go to Augusta every Monday
morning and come home on Thursday sometimes, more often
on Friday. She did all the cooking on the weekend. She loves
to cook and is a very good cook. And she could work. The only
trouble is that the guest room is the warmest room in the
house. It seems to be impossible to get it fixed so that it isn't

something of a sauna. Karen had to work *naked* at the desk because it was so hot, but in the very cold winter this was not altogether a bad thing. She is now a grandmother, a little over her mid-fifties.

It hurts that so many people who seemed terribly well and, I'm ashamed to say, on whom one could lean are themselves facing the gradual dilapidation of the old body. Karen has had a go with sciatica this year, which frightened her very much, as she had no idea of what was wrong and, of course, the pain is acute. However, she felt a lot better once it was diagnosed, and she's now gone off for a walk just after the sunrise.

Professor Earl Ingersoll at New York University at Brockport has edited a book of the interviews with me over the years. He tells me it will be published by the University of Mississippi Press. What strikes me as I go over the list and answer a few of his questions is really what an immense difference the interviewer makes. The ones that are good— notably Karen Saum's in the *Paris Review*—simply show that the interviewer has a good idea of what the vision back of my work is and has been, and is therefore not trying to ferret out something that is not already there to be seen, if one can read.

Yesterday we had lobsters to celebrate Karen's being here, and they did taste awfully good even though I was, as usual, not feeling very well. What was best was showing her the videotape of me at Gainesville last July. When I first saw it I thought that I looked so old it depressed me, but now I see that something comes through that is valid, although I sometimes look to myself like an old turtle with very small eyes, and my voice is that of an old woman. I did not imagine it would ever lose its resonance.

I don't feel like talking today. The war lies like a pall over everything, a black fog through which one cannot see ordinary things anymore. Today on CNN there were terrible pictures of a village south of Baghdad that we have bombed to pieces. I'm glad that such things are being shown, that we are being told a little bit at least of what has been happening.

Wednesday, February 6

DEAR JERRI has just come at seven-thirty and made my breakfast and brought it, has done a small laundry and folded it. Although it's rather difficult to find *enough* for people to do, part of what I need is simply somebody coming to see I'm all right. Last night Andrea came with a wonderful lamb stew I had commissioned and which Susan and I will have Friday night.

I felt ill and depressed because of my staggering loss of weight. I'm ninety-four pounds now. I'm afraid that means that the lining of the lung, which they drained on Monday, is cancerous. I'm seeing Dr. Gilroy on Friday—Nancy will drive me—and we'll see what he has to say about this. I suppose if it is cancer, there are things that can be done, but I'm not going to go in for chemotherapy.

I've been wanting to put on the record a charming old English blessing that came to me in a note the other day from a fan. This is it:

> God bless thy year!
> Thy coming in, thy going out,
> Thy rest, thy traveling about,
> The rough, the smooth,
> The bright, the drear.
> God bless thy year!

As I read it, it made me think what an enormous number of blessing I *have* even though I feel so ill most of the time, and so at a loss as far as energy goes. But here I am in this beautiful house, and here is Nancy, this absolute angel. Two days ago I got into a bind over the income tax, because I'm not good at using even a small machine to do numbers, so I've been adding everything up, and I finally felt, as I said to myself at the time, like a drowning sea turtle at the end of an hour and a half of figuring. Suddenly I realized, I can ask Nancy to do this. She has a little adding machine, and yesterday she did in one morning what would have taken me a week. She also wrote an important letter I would have found hard to do. So there she is oiling the wheels and making wheels go round even though the machine—I'm the machine—is creaky and pretty much out of the running.

Friday, February 8

AFTER A RAINY DAY YESTERDAY, brilliant sun this morning.

I was to have seen Dr. Gilroy at ten-thirty. I'm anxious to see him, because I have so much pain in the left side where the lining of the lung—the liquid there—may well mean cancer. So I was all geared for getting some help and perhaps being advised to go to an oncologist, when the phone rang and I was told Dr. Gilroy had been called away on an emergency and couldn't see me. Nancy doesn't work in the afternoon and I didn't want to ask her to, so we put off the appointment until ten forty-five on Monday.

Meanwhile I needed some drugs—those with no more refills. Very soon I'll take the painkiller again, but I feel profoundly depressed, and when it turned out that I wasn't going to see Dr. Gilroy after waiting nearly twelve days in constant pain in the left side, I began to cry and couldn't stop. I don't think it's unnatural that I feel so neglected. Since both doctors said there was no liquid—almost none—and then the surgeon finds a whole lot and they don't even bother to call me, I feel abandoned. But that sweet girl Jerri came and brought me my breakfast and changed the sheets. So we're starting out fresh. Susan will be coming tonight for some of that fabulous stew. Things are going to look up over the weekend if I can feel just a little better.

I did manage to write the blurb for Noel Perrin's new book—a sampler of his work. What a marvelous essayist he is. In the blurb I compare him to Montaigne, who also wrote autobiographical essays. There aren't so many people who do it and, since E. B. White, perhaps none with the humor and grace that Noel Perrin does. Who would talk about a kindling of kittens except Noel?

Two days ago when I was waking up at about half-past three from my nap and feeling very low in my mind, I heard Anne Woodson calling from downstairs. She and Barbara stopped by on their way home from the Cape. I began to cry as soon as I saw them. I had reached a patch of deep-down hopelessness. It has been hard to handle it, but warm hugs and a good talk worked wonders. I so wish Anne and Barbara lived nearer me. They are lifesavers and always have been.

In the afternoon when I go to have my nap I often have extraordinary dreams. They are far more interesting and mysterious than anything I read these days. I wish I could remember them better.

We now wait for the ground war. This morning on CNN a high-ranking Arab officer briefed us. The one good thing that may come out of all this is a greater understanding between Arabs and the West. I should say it the other way, that we in

CREDIT: JANICE OBERACKER

May Sarton with Barbara Barton and Anne Woodson, May 1984

the West may begin to think of the Arabs as more human and get beyond our usual emphasis on their treatment of women. This man was so civilized, honest, and persuasive that I was glad to know him.

Saturday, February 9

IT'S A GLORIOUS SUNNY DAY and it's the day of roses as Susan arrived for supper last night with one hundred and eight roses of every color imaginable! Now the whole house is *embaumé*, as the French would say, filled with the scent and the marvel-

CREDIT: SUSAN SHERMAN

The day of roses

ous form of all these roses: white, two or three different shades of pink, dark red. I had run out of flowers except for the plant window, which I had remade and which now was glorious with cineraria—four different blue and purple. But cut flowers there were none.

It's wonderful to see Susan coming back from her first week at school looking *so* well and radiant. She got a tremendous welcome, her students were so glad to have her back.

I don't feel well, alas, but at least I know I shall see Dr. Gilroy on Monday and perhaps find out something about what's going on. I do believe that the medicine is helping the digestive problem, and that's a big step. So we have to rejoice in that.

Tonight or this afternoon Susan and I shall see a movie which she brought.

Pierrot was, I think, glad to see Susan and the little dog—from a distance. Often he sits quite close to the door of the guest room where Susan works and Cybèle has her nest on the bed.

On this day of roses I am filled with serene joy. There is so much beauty—how can one really take it in? But I must go upstairs and send some valentines. I got pretty cross at Wellby's because the valentines were all addressed to "my niece," to "my aunt," to "my wife," nothing about friendship apparently.

One of the advantages of tidying up my desk, which I've been trying to do lately, is that I find things that should have been answered. Two days ago I found a dear note from Kyoko, my Japanese guide. She was eighteen or twenty when she was my guide. Now Kyoko is married and her son has gotten married! I can't believe it. She teaches in a university in Tokyo—English and American literature—and has taught books of mine. So she wrote partly to say that one of her students was writing a paper on me and would like to communicate with me. Wonderful to think of somebody in Tokyo, a young woman, discovering May Sarton!

Of course, all this led me back to Kyoko and the wonderful time we had when she was my guide in Kyoto. I was forty-nine then. I celebrated the year of my fiftieth birthday by going around the world from east to west so that when I climbed the Acropolis on May 3, my fiftieth birthday, I felt I was standing at the birth of our civilization. I had come from India and Japan, so ancient Greece felt young as though yesterday.

May in Kyoto, Japan, 1962

Luckily Kyoko and I saw things in very much the same way. We stayed at a Japanese inn, and this is an adventure in itself: everything taking place on the floor, your clothes folded away behind screens, your table a foot from the floor—you sit on cushions. You are given by the inn a kimono, and there is a little charcoal container beside the table where food is kept hot. The servant brings your extraordinary meals, each one, each serving, in a different piece of porcelain; and kneels to serve you. I remember that our dessert one day was one strawberry in a little basket. The Japanese strawberries are very good. They are long and they hang, I guess, on trellises. Kyoko taught me a great deal. She didn't know all about what we were seeing, especially in Kyoto, and that was good for me because I hate being "told." I was to suffer in Greece from a guide who knew, of course, much more than I did. I got tired of always having to listen and be told: "Look at that, that's the great thing you must look at!" I like to find things myself.

Kyoko was perfect in that she understood what I like about life in general. Those Japanese meals were elegant but they were not filling. It was March, and by evening we had been out in the cold for hours of sightseeing, walking, and taking buses. By the time we got home and had an *extremely* hot bath and then had our supper we were ravenous. We had steak and mashed potatoes for lunch at a *not* elegant restaurant so we could summon the grace needed for a sumptuous supper of very small bits and pieces in lovely surroundings. Kyoko taught me many things. She was shy, very shy, and it took her quite a while to *dare* to tell me that in Japan it is not polite to talk while you eat. It had been a terrific effort for me, at the end of the day, to feel that I had to be entertaining at supper, so to be silent and enjoy was a relief.

What an amazing trip that was, that I designed for myself with the help of Thomas Cook in Boston. I went alone. It was quite daring, but there were stopovers. In Japan I had help from Kyoko, and in India I stayed for ten days with my friend Cora DuBois, the anthropologist, who was studying with graduate students on a Ford Foundation grant in Bhubaneswar, that very old religious city south of Calcutta, in Orissa. I had a chance to explore the early-morning life of the village in a very untouristy environment. We set out in a rickshaw at five every morning to beat the heat—it was a great time. I felt newborn at fifty. That is a long way back from seventy-eight.

Wednesday, February 13

A VERY BAD DAY for two reasons. One is the news of the bombing of a shelter in Baghdad in which hundreds of people were burned alive. We may be told that civilians are not targets, but the fact that so many die brings what war means closer everyday. And that toll is continually underemphasized.

The other reason for grief is different. A dear friend of mine and his friend have been diagnosed as HIV positive and can expect perhaps three years of life. In the letter in which he tells me this he says,

> In some ways it is a privilege to know that death is close. I've always quoted to my students de la Mare's "Look thy last on all things lovely every hour," which you use twice in *A Reckoning* and I think once in *As We Are Now*. M. and I feel its truth keenly every day. Every moment of life has become doubly precious to us and we have felt much of the time neither defeated nor dispirited. After hearing the news we were dumbstruck, of course, but we were still able, over a four-month period, to finish the construction inside of our new sunroom.

It's marvelous to see the brave, life-giving reaction of this man, but also I have the aching sense that the earth is becoming depeopled.

In the mail today came an anthology on old age—a good one—published by Penguin, with excerpts from a great many famous writers. I'm glad to see that I'm quoted in it. In the quotation, which is from *At Seventy* and has to do with my seventieth birthday, I remember many old people who were dear friends of mine, such as Lugné-Poe, *mon éléphant*, as I called him because he had a very big nose and he signed his letters with an elephant's head; Koteliansky, of course, who seemed older than he was with his grizzled hair standing straight up as though he were perpetually electrified, as he was, by life; Jean Dominique, who died at nearly eighty, really the dearest person on earth to me. So many have gone, and now a dear friend has AIDS.

The day before yesterday I saw Dr. Gilroy and yesterday Dr. Petrovich, who, as always, was consoling. He feels that it's useless to see an oncologist, that it may be that the liquid in the lining of the lung contains cancer but if so there's almost nothing they can do. The area is too large for radiation; chemotherapy at my age and frail as I am is really out of the question. I must say I heard this with great relief, dreading having to go to Maine Medical Center and have a lot of tests. I have known, after all, for some time, I think, that my time is limited. I'm not going to be here forever, let's face it. But also Dr. Petrovich reminded me that the last time the lung was drained I also felt terribly weak and sure I was dying and had a good deal of pain. The pain since the operation has been bad. He feels that it's possible that the surgeon brushed a nerve or something. In other words, I'll get better rather than worse as the days go by. I came home very much encouraged.

Then Janice, whom I haven't seen for ages, came for tea. She is in a very difficult job, exhausted with the responsibility and all that is asked of her. I wish she could get a real holiday.

Today there was a small flotilla of valentines. The white roses that Pat Chasse sent are absolutely pure and beautiful. Apparently she ordered them a long time ago, and perhaps this is what made them really fresh as many roses from Foster's have not been lately. I'm enjoying them greatly, so crisp and elegant.

Meanwhile Susan's roses are beginning to die, but are very beautiful in their deaths, their petals still so alive and crisp, not drooping.

Thursday, February 14

A WILD RAINSTORM—although inland they must be having heavy wet snow, as Nancy said. Very comforting that both Eleanor, to clean, and Nancy got here through the storm. There's a sort of desolation about a day like this, although we've been spoiled by many, many beautiful days and beautiful light.

There are marvelous flowers in the house. Susan sent huge purple anemones, and white tulips and some lavender ones. The combination is staggeringly beautiful. One could sit and look at it forever, at those dark hearts of the anemones.

The mail today brought a great many valentines. It is lovely to be remembered by so many people.

Yesterday Maggie came for lunch, bringing oysters and a wonderful clear chicken broth with carrots in it and wine jelly with dear little cakes that she'd made. The trouble is one gets spoiled by homemade soup. Last night I had for supper veal stew that she'd brought made with sour cream, onions, and mushrooms. It was awfully good.

These have not been very good days as far as health goes. It would be nice to have a couple of good days in which I might achieve a great deal. I'm getting along with the income tax, and of course it's taking me back to wonderful things that happened last year, particularly the trips to Seattle and Portland, Oregon, on which I took Nancy along to take care of me. She was marvelous, wheeling the wheelchair, I remember, one day when we went to a movie in Portland. She had to push it uphill some of the way, and it really was tough going. But it brought back the hotels also: the Heathman in Portland, a modern hotel with really very nice rooms, and an old-fashioned hotel in Seattle called the Sorrento. It was furnished with Victorian furnishings. It was spring there. Here we were still in the depth of winter and mud season, so that I remember seeing the small flowering fruit trees in the streets of Seattle with stupendous excitement.

I want to go back to Kyoko, whom I was thinking about in a recent journal entry—my Japanese guide. One of the best things about having her was that since she could speak Japanese she could find out what bus would take us to where we wanted to go. So we didn't have to take taxis all the time. Then the population of buses is a good way of getting to know the people a little. One day we got on a bus on our way to a temple. It was full of Japanese; I the only Aryan there. We sat next to a little boy, perhaps three years old, who was fascinated by my face with its huge sharp nose, utterly strange to a Japanese child. He looked and looked and finally he couldn't bear it any longer and reached over and stroked my nose. Of course the whole bus burst into laughter, a wonderful moment.

Friday, February 15

STILL SOME LATE valentines pour in. Valentine's Day is my favorite of all the festivals, because there's no obligation to send a valentine, only when you want to, to someone you love.

I am enjoying tremendously the flowers in the house—two cineraria, one brilliant blue and one magenta with white centers, and a very bright pink cyclamen. The plant window is glorious right now.

I've been thinking about something Pat Chasse asked me last Sunday when she came for tea. It was that she is aware that I emphasize solitude and talk a great deal in the journals and also other books, and in person, about how precious it is to me, and yet I have so many friends and, she said, see so many people. She evidently couldn't put this together. I'm not a recluse, that's one thing, but I think the main point is that Pat herself is a visiting nurse, she sees people all day long, so when she gets home at night she naturally treasures being alone, not to have to respond to people, whereas I, in my normal life, am alone all the time. I work alone. Therefore, when someone comes for tea and it's the only person I see all day, that is precious too, because solitude without society would be meager and would, in the end, make for a dwindling of personality, perhaps. You can't eat yourself all day and all night. There has to be something coming in that brings life-food from the outside.

Of course, Pierrot does this. Right now he's having the most wonderful time with a catnip toy—the first time he's ever responded to catnip. He leaps in the air after it, he throws it up the stairs, he lies down and chews it, and is recklessly happy with it—so much so that he didn't even have his breakfast. He played and played, and then wanted to go out again.

My life is very complex. Whenever I went out lecturing, which was every year—in March and in November—I made new friends. Now I'm seventy-eight, nearly seventy-nine, there's a great collection of people who feel warmly toward me and to whom I feel warmly and with whom I feel it a riches to keep in touch. It dawns on me that many of the people whom I think of as intimates came to me first through my work, and they are men as well as women. I have no immediate family, so I keep borrowing families and adopting families. That also makes for *not* a solitary life in some ways. Distant cousins become precious. Yesterday I wrote to my cousin May Pipe, who had made a second pair of bed socks for me because I am so pleased with a pink pair she made for Christmas.

Monday, February 18

Presidents' Day. It's a holiday—a perfectly beautiful day. It makes one's heart sing.

I enjoyed being alone this weekend, although I was happy to see Joan arrive to make my breakfast this morning at seven-thirty. Yesterday I had done the whole job myself, including making the bed and doing a laundry, but I was very tired at the end. I didn't even say anything to this recorder, although I thought about it.

One of the things I think about a lot now is how to make my feelings clear to someone who has the illusion that she could help me by coming here and suggested staying the whole day. "Oh, I wouldn't bother you at all. I would just be silent and do anything that needed doing." How to make it clear that I can't handle this idea at all? What she doesn't realize is that a stranger coming to the house is inevitably something of an invasion of privacy, however kind she may be. The second thing is that there is a misunderstanding, which is my fault. In my books I appear to be very open, very available, if you will. I give away a lot of my inner person and a lot of my life here. People who read me feel that they know me and that I'm their friend. In order to maintain the kind of life I lead I have to be fairly ruthless about not inviting Tom, Dick, and Harry over—even though Tom, Dick, and Harry would give anything to come! I have *never* learned exactly how to handle this.

In a few minutes Karen K. is coming to take me to the bookstore, because I still have a check that Janice gave me for Christmas, to buy books with. This will be an adventure. Then I'm going to order a leg of lamb for Friday when Susan comes, and do a couple of other errands. I wish I didn't feel quite so shaky. It's really too bad. I always hope, "Today I'm not going to be so shaky."

However, I did go out and throw down a lot of peanuts for the squirrels. These peanuts turned up when Joan was tidying up a basket of scarves and gloves that sits by the door. In it, hidden away, was a bag of peanuts. I have to give them to the squirrels, my enemies who empty the bird feeder. What else can I do?

Thursday, February 21

I CAN'T BELIEVE the month is slipping away—time slips away. But it isn't a good time right now, and strange things happen which make it worse.

I was in the middle of my nap yesterday when I heard a faint tapping at the door and thought it might be UPS, who often come about two-thirty. It was a woman, and when I opened the door she said, "I'm Helena." Well, she has been offering to come and help me out, has been rather insistent about being anxious about my health. She is a fan, and I recognized who she was.

I said at once, "How did you find me?" because only once before has somebody been able to find me. The post office is very good about not giving out where I am, and so also are people like the cleaners or the IGA. They all know. I think she said she asked an older couple who thought that I lived on Western Point, and of course I do not, so she went there and couldn't find me. Then she let it fall that she'd expected me to be part of a friendly neighborhood instead of living far from other houses alone on a little hill, Wild Knoll as it's called, looking down a long field to the ocean. She found herself out of her depth, let's say.

What she said was, "This is not a visit. I just brought you a few things." So, with tears streaming down my cheeks—I really was very upset—I explained that I had to rest and she could go in and leave anything she'd brought, but I couldn't talk to her. Well, she was there half an hour, and in that time

Wild Knoll

she disposed of a *ton* of food. She *invaded* the refrigerator and *planted* I don't know what—several meals there and innumerable other things, among them cheesecake, which I don't like, and she left twenty pounds of birdseed in the hall. I only give the birds hearts of sunflower seed, because the shells of regular wild bird seed make such a mess under the bird feeder. So there's twenty pounds of seed that has to be disposed of and I can't lift things. Thank goodness Nancy has promised to take it.

But an invasion like this is *not* kindness. Giving too much is not kindness. Within the last year I've said to one dear friend, "The only way we will ever lose each other is if you try to give me too much." It's not good. Yesterday what happened was a storm of tears and a wish to commit suicide—to run down the field and drown myself because I felt that there was no privacy anymore, that I simply was a *prey* to anybody who builds up this kind of obsession, for that's what it is. She didn't know how ill I was, what was the matter with me.

Later I called her and tried to explain gently what was wrong with what she'd done and that she would be invited later to come here but not now. She said, "I didn't know you'd been ill for so long." Well, why did she brings tons of food if she didn't know anything about my condition? I was terribly, even ridiculously, upset and couldn't pull myself together. My whole intestinal tract was tied into a knot. I've been in pain ever since, but this morning came a saving grace, a letter from Gracie Warner to thank me for a valentine. She says in it, "All of my animals are fine. I must start cutting fence posts up on the hill across the pond so I won't have to do that when the weather gets nice and there are so many things to do on the farm. I usually cut them and get them all ready so they will be ready to mend my fences." I love this idea of being ready to mend one's fences. I never am, but I'm certainly a little more ready because of Gracie Warner and thinking of all those animals she takes care of, the wonderful concern and care she has for all living things and all that farm means of real life.

Now I am off to the hospital to have an X-ray of the lining of the lung made, to see whether it's already filling up again. Let us pray that it isn't and that I'm out of the woods on that score anyway for a while.

Saturday, February 23

ANOTHER GLORIOUS DAY with sunlight streaming in the window through the paperweights—the crystals that hang in the window and have now covered the ceiling with their lights and even float across the roses. "Light birds," my mother called them.

What a wonderful moment it was when Susan arrived about five and filled the house with roses, and with her dear little dog, Cybèle, who has been very ill, but ran around the lawn and was happy to be here. Suddenly the house, which has seemed rather sad these days, is all lit up and happy. I had a roast lamb in the oven and it proved to be a great success.

Susan is delighted with the curious rocking chair without arms that I ordered by mail because I was looking for something which would make a third chair possible on the porch, where I sit in my chaise longue and where also the dining table—a round teak table—is. I did not want that corner where the table is to be snuffed out by a big chair. This is absolutely perfect, because it's low on the ground, has no arms, and leans against the heavy oxygen tank. It's covered with imitation black leather and is quite stunning. Susan was delighted. Of course, she notices everything right away and rejoices in it with me if there's cause for rejoicing.

I've been thinking about happiness—how wrong it is ever to expect it to last or there to be a time of happiness. It's not that, it's a *moment* of happiness. Almost every day containing at least one moment of happiness. That moment yesterday

Light birds

was when Susan sank down into the new chair with cries of
joy, and another moment was when I walked into my bedroom to rest for a quarter of an hour before supper and there
was a great bunch of roses—red, pale pink, deep pink,
white—so beautiful, right at the end of the bed. Pierrot was
very glad to see Susan. He came right to her, which is really
amazing for him.

Susan brought breakfast up on a tray and we sat and
looked at the war news on CNN, so terrifying. For the first
time yesterday I envisioned what it would be if all those
men—our men—were on their way home. Instead we face in
about three hours the start of the ground war, and I don't see
how it can be stopped, because to give Hussein twenty-one
days to get out of Kuwait is impossible. He'll simply blow up
all the oil fields and God knows what, destroy, and then be a
hero in the whole Moslem world, his power undiminished.
That is what is frightening, so I think Bush is right. But what a
responsibility.

One of the compensations for my having become such a
wraith, losing so much weight, is that I can give wonderful
clothes away. I gave Karen Saum my bright red Ultrasuede
jacket. She'll look wonderful in it, I know. Today I've been
finding some of the Bleyle suits to give to Janice, who will be
coming again in the morning, because she, unlike me, has
gained weight. She's outgrown some of her clothes. Mine, I
hope, will fit. That will be a moment of happiness.

One thing that Susan noticed this morning at once is a bird
which gives a loud single peep early in the morning. I don't
know what it is, but it's interesting that she noticed it right
away as a new bird.

The other side of happiness. There are tears, and I've
been distressed lately because I'm so close to tears all the
time. When I went for the X-ray the other day and it had to be
retaken because there was a little flaw, I could feel the tears

pricking my eyes—so ridiculous. Because I' so vulnerable, anything, any rough word or touch, makes me cry. *Then* I've suddenly remembered, as I was thinking about this, our visits—our painful visits—to my father's Tante Hélène, who lived in a convent in her old age in Brussels—a pathetic dried-up old lady—and who was my first experience of old age at its most painful. She was not ill but she was terribly depressed all the time, convinced that the nuns were stealing her money, which she kept in a trunk in her room. The nuns couldn't have been kinder, but she was difficult partly because of discomfort, I'm sure. What struck me—I must have been about seven when I was taken there when we went back after the war to rescue what we could from the house in Wondelgem— was that I saw that she was trying to cry but that she was so dried up that there was no liquid in her eyes—she couldn't cry. Suddenly I realized that tears are very beneficent and we should be grateful when we're still able to cry. There is that moment of being full to the brim.

One can weep also from joy. My first experience of that was at the Shady Hill School. I was probably in the fourth or fifth grade when Lorraine Warner heard that her father was coming home from China earlier than expected. She burst into tears—tears of joy—because he'd been away for over a year. It was a striking moment for me of what pure joy can be. I've never cried for joy exactly, but I did cry that same year when we went back to Belgium in 1918. The ship we were on went up the Scheldt River and there were the low Belgian lands— Flanders—all around us. I felt tears in my eyes—the tears of the Flemish little girl I was. Never do I go back to Belgium without that same experience happening at least once—the tears of recognition and of joy.

Monday, February 25

I'VE BEEN READING the text of this journal—proofreading it, I suppose one might say. I think it's not very bad but also I'm rather disappointed that it isn't better. Perhaps I've always felt like that. In any case, here it is. I've read one hundred and some pages now, and it will be three hundred by my birthday, when it will presumably go to Norton to see what they think about publishing it for my eightieth birthday. There is now also the question of a title, but we'll see.

I think what does *not* come through—and that was because I was afraid of overemphasizing my physical distress—is that it really does not give an idea of how very ill I've been—unable to function as a normal human being. That means physically extremely fragile and shaky. If somebody even touches me I react as I do to a bump in the road if in a car. It hurts. Everything hurts. If somebody puts an arm around my shoulders it hurts unless it's done very gently. It's difficult for me to get in and out of a coat. And, of course, the everlasting problem which is never solved, no matter what I do, is the digestive problem. About this I really don't know what to do. Continual intestinal pain is such a drainer of energy it's unbelievable. I live from hot-water bottle to hot-water bottle.

Susan was here for the weekend. What a weekend it was, although I was really knocked out the whole time. I did cook a roast lamb for her when she arrived on Friday, and we had a good talk then. Yesterday most of the time I could only lie on my bed until she left right after lunch.

I have to remember—and I think there's every reason to be honest, since she's such a major part of my life—that without Nancy my life here would really be impossible. My whole instinct would be, if she disappeared out of it, to get rid of all the files, stop being the writer I am, altogether. In some ways it would be a relief, I must admit. In other ways, of course, it's very exhilarating that so much is still asked of me, that so many books are in the works, such as one putting together all the interviews with me. All this is quite amazing. If for just a week I could feel well, lead a normal digestive life—it makes me laugh to say that—I think I would be full of energy and even perhaps start to write poems again. As it is, I've been lying on my bed—it's now eleven—since Nancy came at nine and I've been reading the journal.

I first read the mail. There was nothing staggering there, by letter anyway, but there was, however, a collection of photographs by Susan. Susan is a genius at photography and has recreated the whole life of this house, every object in it and Pierrot, of course, in all his glory—and me looking sometimes quite possible, at other times very old, wrinkled, and ill, which is what I am.

I'm deep into the life of Edward VIII. It's extraordinary that I should have wanted to read this, but it is an excellent biography. What it has done is to make one see very well what hell it must have been to be the Prince of Wales at the time he was, with a father who didn't understand what it meant to go on the tours he was forced to make of the empire, where he was on show for twenty-four hours a day, where he never had a rest, and where the excited crowds—although it was in some ways exhilarating—almost killed him. They actually tore off the back of his open car; everybody wanted to touch him. At the end of the day he was bruised and had to be massaged and his hands bound up. Also what's touching is that he was such a faithful lover. There was only one woman for him at a time. Mrs. Dudley Ward for ten or eleven years, maybe more. So that his reputation of being a philanderer really wasn't true. He comes through as caring far more about the people than any ruler since or before. He would have made a good king had it not been for Wallis Simpson—her ambitions and her lack of understanding of what his responsibilities were.

Tuesday, February 26

WHAT RUNS THROUGH my head is that French phrase *Tout passe, tout lasse, tout casse.* It's interesting that sometimes the hardest blows are in a strange way exhilarating, and as a door slams shut, another opens—a door into a further demand on courage and the ability to withstand trouble and go on. Nancy has decided to retire at sixty-two. Her birthday is November 4, so she will be with me here until November 1. That does give me some time to find a substitute. I'll find somebody who can do the routine things. Nancy is quite right when she says that the files are very much in order. She's worked on them for years, and she will leave a plan by which somebody looking for something can find it. What she does for me, what she has done, really cannot be measured. It's been exceedingly helpful: the fact that she was here for a half day and we worked so well side by side, in spite of our extreme temperamental differences. Everyone who knows me has realized this and many people mention it when they write to me or talk to me. But, as the French say, *Tout passe, tout lasse, tout casse.* Everything passes, everything tires, everything breaks—even a relationship that had seemed stable enough to accompany me to the end.

Thursday, February 28

YESTERDAY THAT WAS MUCH in my mind. For hours tears streamed down my cheeks, but I did try to understand that bad news—or the shock of bad news—is sometimes better, more invigorating, than good news. It's good news that is hard to handle, partly because good news is much harder to share. If you say, "I've just won a huge prize," your friends are glad, but it doesn't *send* them, so to speak. Whereas if you say, "I'm terribly upset," your friends will rally at once, as Eleanor Perkins, who came to clean this morning, did when I told her that Nancy was leaving. She hugged me. The bad thing is that I'm so old and ill. I used to feel the invigorating quality of bad news. Now I don't have the same strength, the same resilience, so I feel as if I was being gnawed to the marrow of my bones. Well, I laughed last night when I thought this house ought to be called the Ice House instead of Wild Knoll.

It is terrifying to foresee being without Nancy, but she is right when she points out that she has been working here for more than ten years sorting things out. The library is organized, the files—which were very complex—have been organized so that a person coming in will find little to do except the day-to-day things. I have not asked Nancy to write many let-

ters. This could change if I find someone who writes good
letters when Nancy leaves in November. As her father died
very old she might count on thirty years of only volunteer
work, if any at all, and of a chance to travel. So I'm happy for
her. I'm happy for anyone who feels well and can meet the
challenges joyfully.

I am having what feels like the worst time I've ever had. I
am trying paregoric as Dr. Petrovich suggested and I called
Dr. Gilroy to try and get a prescription for that. A strange
time. If you believe—someone just wrote me this in a letter—
that growth is change, if you believe that, I'm facing having to
grow willy-nilly. Of course, I've been very dependent on
Nancy—on her steady grasp of things and her being there
every morning, bringing the mail. I shall have to go back to
getting the mail myself or finding someone who can do it. But
it is good also that I found Joan, Jerri, and Andrea to help me
with the household.

Now I'm going in a little while to mail that magnificent
book of photographs of Katharine Hepburn which I got for
Lee Blair's birthday, because she knew Katharine and I think
she will be fascinated by the book. It's quite amazing that
Katharine Hepburn, with her sense of privacy, has allowed a
book which gives us such an intimate picture of her life as she
lives it to be published at all. There are wonderful photographs. The book is like a novel. I'm so glad I saw the review
and got hold of it.

I keep on with Edward VIII with more and more interest,
much to my own surprise. It may become less interesting after
Wallis Simpson arrives in the picture. What a tragedy that he
didn't fall desperately in love with a woman a little more
worthy.

Friday, March 1

AN EXTRAORDINARY SPRING DAY! March has certainly come in like a lamb and not like a lion. March has come in with so much good news that it is like a cornucopia laid in my hands. In the first place, the extraordinarily complex and terrible war is over—that it can be over, as far as intense fighting goes, in a hundred hours seems almost incredible. It does show what very good planning and technical expertise can now do. But we still have to wait and see what happens to Hussein himself—whether there's any possibility that Iraq can go on with him as leader. One very much doubts it. However—the relief—I feel it suddenly. It comes over me: the war is over. I imagine so well what it's like for the families of the service men and women not to go to bed every night with dread.

Other news of a very different kind—other good news—is that I had a letter from Eric Swenson and they are seriously interested in doing the book Susan has been working on now for years, which uses selections from my letters in my archive at the Berg Collection to communicate my vision of life. Eric suggests that we try to get photographs of everything. Lately Susan has been taking marvelous photographs of the house—of all the details of the house. These photographs are in color. Now she must try, when she comes for a week in March, to get some in black and white which could be used. Of course, there will be all summer also.

It appears that *MS* has taken four poems from the *Sarton Selected* for an issue in celebration of May Sarton in May/

June: Vol. I, no. 6. This is news for me. I had no idea.

.   In the mail a letter which has been sustaining in this hard
time from a woman called Eleanor Davis. She says, "Somehow as I read your journals and novels I am filled with a peace
and contentment that is overpowering." It's very curious, because, after all, I deal with difficult subjects—in the case of
the last novel, the life of a homosexual woman. Eleanor Davis
goes on to say, "I had no idea what *The Education of Harriet
Hatfield* was about, but, as I read the book and settled in with
this woman, I wished I could go into her bookstore, sit down,
have a cup of tea with her, and just talk. I am sixty. In the past
few years I've had to come to terms with my life—face challenges and change. Thank you for a splendid book." The thing
that amazes me is that people find peace through my books.
Strange, since I often write about painful things.

Today I'm certainly, comparatively speaking, on top of
the world. I thought last night when things did go well with
my recalcitrant bowel that I might be in for a change for the
better. That may be true. Let us hope.

I suddenly remembered that it is Edythe's birthday on the
3rd of March. We're having lunch today and I had forgotten
all about it. This is typical of me now. Things slip out of my
mind. But fortunately it is only March first. I went down to
Foster's and got a lovely arrangement of yellow daisies,
freesias, and two white orchids. It's adorable, and although
Edythe isn't moving for a month, her house is being disman-
tled for the move. Having some flowers to enjoy for the next
week or so should be a pleasure. I hope so. What I hope to
give her later is some kind of tub, or tubs, which she can use to
plant things on her little porch. This balcony will be in lieu of a
garden, for Edythe has become quite fascinated by gardening
in the last few years.

Two days ago I thought quite often of Stevie Smith's famous "I'm not waving, I'm drowning." Today, now, I feel just

the opposite. I'm not drowning, Im waving! Now that every-thing has come to a peaceful and loving solution with Nancy, that Norton is going to do Susan's book, using my letters. It's very thrilling. I'm not drowning, I'm waving. I'll be waving even harder if what looks like a little improvement in my digestive problem proves at long last to be true.

Monday, March 4

WE'RE HAVING THE MOST staggering rain and wind storms—yesterday and today. Deborah Straw came to be with me overnight and bring supper—a mild chicken curry she's in-vented that she thought I could eat—quite rightly—and a glo-rious apple pie. I felt well taken care of. She brought the videotape of an English actress playing Virginia Woolf, who reads the whole of *A Room of One's Own* as a one-woman monologue as if addressing a group at Girton College, as Woolf herself did with that essay. I did not like the actress as much as most people do because she simply does not sound or look like V.W. There is no sparkle. The voice is not quite right. I mind because I have such vivid memories of Virginia Woolf.

We have had wild rain, and twice the power has failed. Yesterday when I was expecting Deborah, at about two o'-clock, the lights went out. I was nervous, because if the power stayed out, as it might well have, we would have had to go out to dinner, which I was not anxious to do. The lights came on in an hour. Then it was good to have Deborah to talk with, spe-cifically about Virginia Woolf. She is going to be part of a seminar in New York in June, in which Woolf's relationship to

younger women writers is being discussed. Deborah is dis-
cussing Virginia Woolf and May Sarton. I did not think, and
told her so when she first talked about it, that there was
enough material, because, although I saw V.W. for tea once a
year in those years before 1940, from 1936 to 1940, I was not
an intimate friend and there is almost no correspondence.
There are a few postcards at the Berg saying come for tea on
such-and-such a day.

Deborah has used the word "mentor" in suggesting my
feeling toward Virginia Woolf. This is not accurate. It's a little
bit like saying that Greta Garbo was a mentor. Greta Garbo
simply seemed to me a dazzlingly beautiful woman and a very
great and moving actress. Virginia Woolf was *the* literary star,
the only one I wanted to meet, so it was amazing that I did
meet her. She was the only writer or critic whose opinion of
my work mattered to me. But she died when only two of my
books—my first book of poems and my first novel—had come
out. I have described elsewhere the extremely stiff tea we had
that last time I saw her because she knew I was waiting for
some comment on *The Single Hound* and I was too shy to ask.
At the door as I was leaving she said that she thought the
second part, the young man's love affair, was the best. And I
sensed that she did not like the portrait of the three old ladies
in the first and third parts. In the second part there is one page
describing the character based on Elizabeth Bowen walking
down a staircase which is pure imitation Virginia Woolf. I
wasn't aware when I wrote it that I was imitating by osmosis.
I never did it again, but when the book came out I certainly
saw it. It was noticed, not unkindly, in the review in the *New
Statesman.*

What did Virginia Woolf want of me? After all, why did
she see me for two hours each spring? I think it was the novelist in her who was curious about my life. She was full of questions. Where did I buy my clothes? With whom was I in love?

Whom was I seeing? What was I writing? All cozy, amused, and not malicious, so in some way we didn't connect, but in other ways we did. In one of those years her novel *The Years* came out. One reason why I adored Virginia Woolf and missed her so much after she died is that every book was a new adventure in technique. You never knew what the next Woolf would be. The proof of this is *The Years*, which had followed on her most experimental novel, *The Waves*. She told me at that tea—the last time I saw her—that she had written *The Waves* because a friend had called her up on the telephone and said, "Virginia, you're getting too far away from us. Come back." This plea haunted her, and *The Years* was an attempt at a conventional novel. It is intensely autobiographical, of course. I found, on rereading it, that the descriptions of the dying mother, obviously her own mother, were unbearable. I wasn't able to go on with it. Most fascinating was that Virginia said she'd written the novel *not* in sequence. It does seem like patchwork, in a way. She worked on one year, or one period, then put that away and worked on another one, not necessarily in sequence. That may explain why the novel lacks momentum.

Deborah did bring up the emotional tone of the poem I wrote when I heard that Virginia Woolf had committed suicide. I was in Chicago. The news came as a tremendous shock and sense of loss—in a selfish way—because I thought: Now there is *no one* whose opinion about my work matters a hoot to me. A star in my heaven had gone out forever.

Tuesday, March 5

WE'VE HAD FORTY-EIGHT HOURS of rain and it's still gloomy
outside, but we're promised a surcease this afternoon.

Yesterday I opened the *Times Literary Supplement,*
which has not delighted me lately as it used to do, to a charming review of a book about David Cecil. The review is titled
"The Delightful Lord David." I met David Cecil at Elizabeth
Bowen's, at a dinner party. Of course, he was an unforgettable man. In the first place he was so voluble, speaking so
rapidly that it was hard for me to understand him. But I still
hear him talking, with a ripple of Bowen's laughter under it
the whole time. The opening of the review, by Jonathan Ke-
ates, is:

> None of us attending Lord David Cecil's Oxford lectures
> during the late 1960s went purely with the aim of taking
> notes. The lecturer himself was as absorbing as his dis-
> course, a tall figure with a high cranium, dished nose and
> oddly sensual mouth, the sleeves of his gown working
> like the flippers of some elderly seal. The strongest and
> most compelling feature of all was his voice, embracing
> an extraordinary tonal range within its staccato barks,
> but coming to rest comfortably somewhere between a
> growl and a yelp.

This made me laugh because it brought back that evening in
London so vividly. It's a marvelous description of how he
talked. It was somewhat how Isaiah Berlin talked, who was

also there at that memorable dinner party where I, the naive American, could barely understand anything that anyone said because of the eccentric Oxford accent. But to go on with the review:

> Even if what he had to say appeared to some of his less sympathetic and patient listeners merely a limpid statement of the obvious, his manner of delivery and the conviction and charm which animated every phrase made the experience of hearing him on Shakespeare, Scott, or his favorite Jane Austen always a memorable one.

He was the younger son of the duke of Salisbury and in the very center of the literary world, but his fame—according to this book—the praises that are lavished upon him—rested chiefly on the fact that he was such an inspiring teacher and cared so much about students. We think about Hatfield House when we think of the Cecils, one of the great English names. The writer of this review remarks:

> What the Leavises and their sneering, illiberal acolytes, who portrayed him as a twaddling aesthete, probably resented most of all about David Cecil was his title. The *gratin* assembled here, Anthony Powell, Desmond Shawe-Taylor and Frances Partridge seasoned with Cavendishes, Pakenhams and Tennants, would have made them distinctly uneasy.

He was absolutely not a snob, he was such a genuine person. His enthusiasm was endearing and lovable, but even more extraordinary he was one of the few people of eminence I've ever known whom one could call happy. David Cecil seemed to be a truly happy man. He loved his work; he wrote memorable, although not great, biographies of writers he loved, such as Jane Austen and William Cowper, and also a book on the Cecils in which he speaks very amusingly about his family.

What a background to be brought up in—and to maintain oneself in as an individual! What genius that took! The review says, for instance:

> While the child David's quirks and fancies—a paradise for golliwogs situated above Heaven so that they were forced to pray with their hands pointing downwards, a set of special tunics to gratify his profound dislike of being a boy—flourished unchecked, his intellect sharpened itself on the rich flow of Hatfield conversation. "I remember he talked a great deal whilst sitting on his pot," notes one cousin; while another recalls his uncle Hugh scouting David's declared aim of making as many people as happy as possible with a crushing "Any competent licensed victualler could do as well." "It was a tough school," she adds, "being brought up in that family."

Of course, he went to Eton and then Christ Church Oxford. He was everything that one imagines an English aristocrat ought to be, and that so rarely they are, or were. He loved Elizabeth Bowen; she dedicated *To the North* to him. He knew her when she and Alan, her husband, were living in Oxford. It was joy to watch Bowen responding to him that evening at Clarence Terrace in London.

Wednesday, March 6

A BEAUTIFUL DAY. The little crystals that I have hanging in the windows are making light patterns all over the ceiling. It's so beautiful. When Pierrot was a kitten he chased them, and it was really one of the most charming sights I've ever seen. He would leap in the air because, of course, a lot of them were on the ceiling. But he never caught one.

Heartwarming news about Kuwait or Iraq is rare, but last night on television there was a report of two Kuwaitis, one we saw in a big white turban, and his brother, who decided that something had to be done about the zoo animals. It's horrifying to think of them, who would have died in their cages, unable to escape, with no water, with nothing. These two men—it must have been horrendous work—cleaned out the cages and fed the animals. An Iraqi shot the elephant. It didn't die. The bullet is still in its side. One Iraqi used a monkey as target practice. It's bestial and terrible to think of. But then there are these two men. How did they get meat for the lions? It was heartening to hear this marvelous tale last night.

Yesterday during my rest something happened which might be serendipitous. Penny Morrow called. She is an Englishwoman whom I've only met briefly—partly because I kept forgetting her name. That's typical of me these days. She does holistic massaging. I guess that is what you call it. She calls it *reiki* and has offered to give me one. I'm conservative, even inflexible, let's say. If people suggest a diet, I withdraw and don't even want to hear about it and so am hard to help. But when Penny called I thought: The time has come when you've got to change. I had said no at the time, so I called her back. What I called her back about was not only accepting her generous gift of a massage but also saying I was ready to try the holistic doctor we have in York. She is a woman, a chiropractor, but now concentrates on holistic medicine. She might be able to help me with my never-ending bowel problem. I was depressed yesterday because I had an excellent beginning to the day and a breaking of the stopped rhythm of my digestion. But I had such terrible pain all day that it might as well not have happened.

One wonders, of course, every day what's going to happen to Hussein. There doesn't seem to be very violent feeling against him. Probably people are so tired, and then, what are the alternatives? No leader has appeared who might take his place. So it's going to be a difficult time, and Bush's task is by no means done.

Thursday, March 7

I WOKE TO WILD RAIN at five—no, I guess it was four—when the cat meowed. I went down with him and was sure he wouldn't go out. It was pouring! But out he ran. He doesn't seem to mind rain at all. However, he was waiting at six when I went down. Luckily, the front door is sheltered so he can wait there. Then he meowed very loudly to express his dismay at the weather.

I enjoy doing my shopping, which Susan was so kind as to

do during those three months when I was most ill. But the fun
is seeing the people in Dave's store, where I get groceries and
everything to do with the household needs. Many of the people are my age and some of them older. There's a warm and
welcoming atmosphere in that store. The other day I had on a
wool jacket with a silver dragonfly pin that I'm fond of on the
lapel. I noticed a quite old man who was next in line looking at
it with a twinkle in his eye. Finally he said, "I don't dare tell
you what that's called." I said, "Why not?" "It's a darning
needle." That is apparently what dragonflies used to be
called. The person at the counter laughed and said, "Yes, if
you talk too much the darning needle will darn your mouth
up!" I'd never heard that before. It was a real pleasure.

I've now given up on Edward VIII because of the mean-
ness of Wallis Simpson. Apparently Edward was so furious
that his father had left him no money—when each of his
brothers and sisters got seven hundred and fifty thousand
pounds—that he took his revenge by cutting expenses. He cut
the salaries of all his employees, the food budget was cut way
down, holidays were cut down. Apparently Wallis Simpson
was very much involved in all this cutting, and she was not
good with servants. That's my final test of a good person and,
of course, especially of an aristocrat. The fact that she was a
bad employer is shocking. Also shocking—it comes out in the
biography—that their relationship was a sadomasochistic one.
She treated him like dirt in front of other people, at dinner
parties, treated him with contempt. I never realized that. I
thought she was so proud of having forced Edward to resign
as king of England rather than lose her that she must behave
as his willing servant. Not at all! All this goes back, according
to the biography I'm reading, to the fact that she was an im-
poverished aristocrat in the South, in Maryland, and had suffered so terribly from not having money. But it could work the
other way. For instance, I am certainly not an aristocrat, but

we were not well off at all when we first came to America. My father got off at Ellis Island in 1915, I think, with just one hundred dollars in his pocket. Money problems were always there. They were there for me with my theater company. But the result is, I'm afraid, that I've become wildly extravagant. I like to think of money as always in flow, never to be held back, but to flow out into life. I enjoy giving and I have been able to help a lot of friends and also a lot of organizations.

One of the ones I'm most interested in is Christ House in Washington, D.C., which takes in people with AIDS and street people. I'm also glad to help the New Forests Project. A tree has been discovered which grows extremely fast and can make over a desert in, say, a generation. This could solve the problems of a lot of Africa and also, of course, of the Near East. It's so worth doing. I would like to be able to give them more than I can. Of the same ilk is Carter's Habitat. There are a great many really good things going on. There is comfort in remembering.

As for this journal: I'm in two minds about it. I had thought when I started it that I must be frank about illness. After all, this is the problem of this journal—far more than of *After the Stroke*, when I was getting better all the time. The psychological problem here is that I don't get better, that I stay on a plateau of constant discomfort. But there may be too much about illness. I'm somewhat disappointed in the text, even apart from that. Dictation is hard for me. Sentences are often not sentences. I can revise the text, but it looks clumsy. I must go on nevertheless, and believe all I can.

something that has read the first time. One has been
persuaded into it.

Friday, March 8

TODAY AN UNEXPECTED PLEASURE, a visit from Connie Hunting, who came around noon. Luckily I had some soup left
over—the wonderful Cape Neddick Inn soup—in this case
chicken curry and awfully good. So we sipped a little sherry
and then she ate some soup. She looks absolutely beautiful!
There are people who get more beautiful as they grow older.
Connie, I suppose, is fifty and looks radiant: those blue eyes
and the wonderful bright, pale yellow, almost white hair. It
was a present from life to see her, we had such a good talk. I
felt life is worth living, having her here in the house. I showed
her the video of me, *Writing in the Upward Years*. She was the
ideal person to look at it, because she really has been such a sup-
porter of my work, has written so beautifully about the poems.
Seeing the way she watched it was a great joy for me. The only
sad thing was that Pierrot never put in an appearance, and
she was longing to see him. Connie is one of those people
who—as she often says of herself—are late bloomers. She is
the director and manager of the Puckerbrush Press, which
she founded. She publishes many things, including *Writings
on Writing* and my mother's letters to me, both of which
have done remarkably well, especially *Writings on Writing*.
It's now in its eighth edition. She has published poetry, and
now a big new book of her poems is coming out from Asphodel
Press. I hope that somehow or other it will take her over
the top. She's such a good poet: brilliant—a little strange—a

brilliance that has a strange and very moving quality about it.
You go back and reread her poems and always understand
something better than you did the first time. This has been a
red-letter day.

Monday, March 11

MUCH TO MY AMAZEMENT there's a little—about an inch,
maybe—snow today. It's a white world here as we're on our
way to spring. This so often happens in Maine. We get our big
snows in March. There is one expected—a real big snow—on
Wednesday night and Thursday. I must admit I dread it.
That's because I'm really so weak in every way. It's the tail
end of strength in me. I don't see where it's going or how I'm
ever to get better or be able to cope.

It's ironic that every machine has given out in the last few
weeks—the last thing was the washer-dryer but somebody
did come and mend it. On Saturday there was a tremendous
to-do because Beverly Hallam and Diane, who gardens for me
and for her and Mary-Leigh, were cleaning out their side of
the garage, which had been a great assemblage of boards and
things. They did a magnificent job and that side is now neat.
I'm asking Diane to do my side. I had thought I could do it
myself, but of course I never will. Diane has promised to sow
the annuals for me again this summer, so there will be some
flowers to pick. I look forward especially to the smell of nasturtiums and also to scabiosa, which I've ordered again.

But the weekend was difficult, because I was overtired.
There have been workmen here also indoors in both the bed-
rooms, fixing windows that have rotted in all the rain. It

meant that I was not free to lie down in my bedroom or use my bathroom. As this was a day when I was feeling extremely ill and needed the bathroom, it was hard. I didn't get to rest, to go to my own nest, until one o'clock, and Maggie was arriving at half-past four.

She did, and we had tea. She had brought mussels—wonderful mussels. We had mussels and delicious, chopped-up fresh spinach, and a very elegant cake for our supper. But it turned out to be about three and a half hours of talk—every moment of which I enjoyed—but I was overtired by the time I got to bed at my usual time.

Then yesterday—Sunday—I had thought that Maggie would bring soup and we would have a simple lunch before she left for home. But, bless her heart, she had brought chicken legs to cook. This took time, because we had gone out to get the paper, so it was one before we sat down. I have to eat more often than four or five hours between meals. In the middle of the lunch I couldn't go on. I couldn't eat and started to cry. It's so absurd and so shameful. But Maggie does understand. She's had problems herself with diverticulitis. Who doesn't, over seventy? She could not have been more understanding. I suffered a mixture of feelings: wanting her to leave so that I would not have to keep up a front; and hating her to leave because I feel so abandoned, immediately after a guest goes, and so frightened. I was a wreck yesterday.

Today I'm no better, but Joan was here to do a laundry and make my bed. She's such a comforting presence. Nancy got through the snow and put in a new cassette for me so I could start again on the journal. The hardest thing—and I guess the deep reason for depression now—is that I don't think this journal is very good. That is a real blow, because I had counted on it. I may be wrong, and I am correcting all the time. We'll just have to see and hope.

Tuesday, March 12

Again a brilliant morning. It's curious how some words haunt.
The word that's been haunting me is the word "grace." Someone has said—and I can't remember where I've read it—that
if you are to grow old well you must enjoy small comforts. In
other words, you mustn't be a Puritan. I laughed at Maggie
because she went to an early meeting at eight in the morning
at the Maine hospital in Portland and when she came home
was disgusted with herself because she fell asleep—I suppose
it was the middle of the morning. "Well," I said, "you've had
a major operation, you've made a marvelous recovery, and
you're tired." She said, "The Puritan ethic makes it very difficult to sleep in the daytime." Luckily I'm not a Puritan, and
the small comforts are important to me, and the graces.

In thinking about grace I remembered a poem—a Victorian poem—by Lord Chesterfield which I found ages ago. It's
called "The Graces."

> Daughters of Zeus, you know what man's life is,
>   How brief and yet how long the while—
> Its epics, falls of sparrows; its tragedies
>   Half farces and half vile;
> How every hero's sword at last grows brittle,
> How his dream fades and night comes in a little—
>   And you smile.
>
> All else turns vanity: but yours the day
>   Of little things, that grow not less.

Maggie Vaughan with Hyacinth and Cricket at the farm

Our moments fly—enough if on their way
  You lent them loveliness.
Alone of gods you lie not; yours no Heaven
That totters in the clouds—what you have given
  We possess.

It's a charming poem—one of the good examples of what one would call charming verse. It's not quite poetry. What makes it not quite poetry is the phrase "and night comes in a little," and yet that's what makes it charming, "night comes in a little."

I'm thinking about all the graces. Susan is coming on Friday. She is very aware of the graces and makes them come and inhabit wherever she is. Of course, the chief grace for me

is flowers. But I like to think of other graces: the grace of
people. It's a grace when Joan, one of the women who comes
to help me in the mornings, knows I'm feeling particularly bad
and hugs me before she goes. This is a grace and I accept it as
a grace and love it. When Pierrot rolls over on his back and
wants me to scratch his tummy, that is a grace. And the way
he walks, as if he ruled the world, with his plume of a tail in
the air. That is a grace.

Living here is a constant procession of such charms. When
Maggie was here she helped me put up the crystals again: the
little crystals, the many crystals that hang in the window.
There are five of them. They make light birds on the ceiling
and remind me of Pierrot as a kitten, trying to catch the light
birds with his huge paws.

Grace as behavior is quite rare, and it's getting rarer, just
as good manners are getting rare. Grace is not in the thing
done, but in the way it's done. My mother, for instance, was a
person of infinite grace. Everybody who knew her would have
known that and would have wanted to give her signs of grace
when she was dying. She died of cancer of the lung, over a
period of months. Friends did such imaginative things, I still
rejoice in them. Molly Howe sent half bottles of champagne
because, near the end, Mother could not eat at all. The only
thing she could swallow—she who never drank—was a sip of
champagne and an oyster—most extraordinary—but these
did sustain her in the last weeks. And of course flowers. That
was why it was so terribly hard when she said a few days
before she died, "Take the flowers away." But it was a long
time before she said that. Once a well-off friend of ours in
Cambridge sent her butler with a single, gigantic chrysanthemum. There was something about this man at the door with a
huge chrysanthemum—it must have been about five feet
tall—which was a grace. As again, another time, the same

friend sent blue morning glories in a lovely bowl. A single
gesture often brings us a moment of grace.

> . . . the day
> Of little things, that grow not less.
> Our moments fly—enough if on their way
> You lent them loveliness.

Wednesday, March 13

ANOTHER GLORIOUS DAY—with the light birds all lighting up
the ceiling. Brilliant sunshine and Jerri here to give me my
breakfast and change the bed—says that it's warm out. So
that's good.

All kinds of good news have happened. *Mrs. Stevens* is to
be translated into Japanese! Now I've been translated—or
shall be soon—into Japanese, French, Dutch, and German.
The one I really wanted was French, so I'm so happy they're
doing *As We Are Now*. But isn't it curious that the Japanese
would want *Mrs. Stevens Hears the Mermaids Singing?* It
may be because it's been so much used in women's studies. I
must certainly tell Kyoko—she will be thrilled.

I said the other day that the charming Lord Chesterfield
poem was verse, not poetry. I found, looking through collec-
tions of old poems I've liked, a marvelous *true* poem—
adapted from the ancient Egyptian by A. Alvarez. I want to
die, there's no doubt about that. When you have as much pain
as I have and there's no way out you *do* want to die, if you're

as old as I am. You do want to die. There is that hope that someday, while you're asleep, the old heart will stop beating. But I don't have any idea of what will happen afterwards. I've always felt we shouldn't probe into this. We shouldn't try to reach those who are already dead. This is the final mystery. We must let it be a mystery until we cross over and find out what it is. Here is a wonderful true poem called "Dying":

> Death is before me today
>   like recovering from an illness
>   and going into the garden
> Death   the odour of myrrh
>   a sail's curving shadow on a windy day
> Death   like the scent of the lotus
>   like lingering on the shore of drunkenness
> Death   a quick, cool stream
>   a soldier coming home
> Death   like a break in the clouds
>   a bird's flight into the unknown
> Death   like homesickness
>   like homecoming after captivity.

It does speak to me. I recognize it.

Friday, March 15

TODAY HULDAH is having a radical operation on her neck to try to cure the arthritic pain. It involves the moving of bone from the thigh, as I understand it, and somehow fitting it into the neck. It sounds grueling, but she was determined, the pain has been so bad. I can well understand that. If I was told I could have an operation I'd have one immediately.

These have been very hard days but everything has changed because, conservative though I am, I have reached the end of my tether as far as ordinary doctors go. I am engaging in two things. Penny Morrow has been suggesting for a long time that I go to a holistic doctor who is here in York. Penny does a Japanese massage in which you don't have to undress. I'm ashamed to say that this was very persuasive to me—that I could have it without undressing—as I am nearly a skeleton now and have a pretty devastated old body. So Penny came the other day and I must say that it was a very good experience—a whole hour in which you lie first on your stomach and then on your back. Her two hands find certain points in your anatomy and press. The effect on the patient is a great warmth—really a tremendous vibrant warmth, especially on the soles of my feet. That was the end and it was the best of all. I was perfectly relaxed. That's what she said: I'd feel rested after it. So I've decided to have one every two weeks. It's expensive but it's certainly worth it.

But that isn't all. In the euphoria of getting in touch with Penny again I've decided to go to the holistic doctor whom she recommends. This is to take place on March 26.

Life is full of miracles. A few days after I'd made this decision and made the appointment for March 26 to see the doctor, the phone rang. It was Vicki Simon, whom I haven't seen for about a year. She's a married woman with two children and is a busy psychiatrist in Portsmouth. So Vicki called, and, of course, remembering that she had talked about holistic medicine, I told her I'd made this decision—tremendous for me, the old conservative—and that I had an appointment. Vicki was delighted and proceeded to tell me her story. This has given me hope. I feel hope for the first time in a very long time. Some years ago Vicki wasn't able to eat—for nine months—and had terrible digestive problems, obviously. By going to not my doctor but the master of my doctor, who lives in Eliot, Maine, Vicki was completely cured. She can eat anything. She's very well. Well, you can see why my heart leapt up.

Saturday, March 16

SUSAN IS HERE. So it's Susan time and rose time. When I went down to let Pierrot in at six the sun was rising and touching a bunch of yellow roses in the room where the flower window is, on a little table there. It was glorious. Now here in my bedroom I have a bunch of red, that extraordinary pink, and white. There haven't been many cut flowers around lately, so this is a real feast.

It was a different kind of feast but a very precious one that Susan was back sitting in the rocking chair by my bed having her coffee, having brought me my breakfast. We had a little talk, partly about movies she had had sent that we can see while she's here. For she's now here for twelve days. A great event. A wonderful pause. We can call it a kind of pause in pain. The pain is still there, but Susan is here. So it's much easier to bear.

For some reason I've been thinking about Thomas Hardy and particularly one poem which I thought of years ago as a signature, almost, of my own. Hardy is one of the few good poets who is also a great novelist, sometimes I think a greater poet even than a novelist. It's so rough and rugged and so terribly honest, the poetry. Here in America I suppose Penn

Warren is the only equivalent of someone who is a genius in both fields. They take such different parts of the person. As I am a poet and novelist I know this well. Here is Hardy:

When the Present has latched its postern behind my
    tremulous stay,
And the May month flaps its glad green leaves like wings,
Delicate-filmed as new-spun silk, will the neighbours say,
'He was a man who used to notice such things'?

If I pass during some nocturnal blackness, mothy and warm,
When the hedgehog travels furtively over the lawn,
One may say, He strove that such innocent creatures should
    come to no harm,
But he could do little for them; and now he is gone.

If, when hearing that I have been stilled at last, they stand at
    the door,
Watching the full-starred heavens that winter sees,
Will this thought rise on those who will meet my face no
    more,
'He was one who had an eye for such mysteries'?

[Part of "Afterwards," No. 511 in *The Complete Poems*]

One of the delights of Susan's arrival was Pierrot, who gave her the big hello. He meowed—it was like a conversation—maybe ten times, rubbing against her and showing in every possible way that he was very happy indeed to see her. That was lovely. Then it was lovely to see Susan coming in with Cybèle in her arms, those dark eyes—dark, tender eyes—looking out under the white crown of her hair.

I heard yesterday in the middle of the day that a former student of mine at Wellesley, Nancy Ellis, had committed suicide, a woman of fifty with two teenage, or perhaps even grown-up, children, divorced, a medical doctor. The friend of hers who called me—and it was kind of her to do that, as I might have seen an obituary somewhere—said that she had left a letter three pages long to explain why she couldn't go on.

In a strange way it has made me more determined than ever to cast aside my fantasies of suicide as a way out of the constant chronic pain. In the first place I don't know how to do it, but somehow or other I feel one must have one's death, one must not make one's own death. One must let death come when the time has come. It's easy to say that if one is not in too great agony.

Saint Patrick's Day, Sunday, March 17

YESTERDAY WHEN I CALLED the friend who is house-sitting for Huldah I heard that Huldah has survived the operation and is doing well. I had been suspended in my mind on this event—hoping so much. So that was a relief.

Otherwise yesterday was a perfect Susan-May day. It began with our going out after I got dressed to see—as Susan had found—that snow crocus was out all along the outer perennial bed below the terrace. Such a welcome sight of mostly yellow and white—those small crocuses that are the harbingers of spring. Now today with the sun out again it may be that the snowdrops will finally open and show their lovely white cups, which are still firmly closed.

Well, the day went on with our having a little time, each of us, to work; Susan going out to get the mail; Andrea bringing what looks like a wonderful soup we'll have today, from the Cape Neddick Inn. I had a good rest, but I must admit it has been a time of pain. There's no way out of this until, I hope, I see the holistic doctor and it begins to get better. But I rested and at half-past three got up and we had our ritual tea with cinnamon toast while Susan put on the film *Elvira Madigan*. This is that romantic Danish film which made of Mozart's 21st Piano Concerto a best-seller, number one on the popular music charts! I had never seen it, and I must admit it is extraordinarily visually beautiful. It's like a long lyric poem in which every frame is a masterpiece. A walk down a road with trees on one side of it; chasing butterflies in a field of long grasses and then rolling over, the young Swedish count deserter from the army and Elvira Madigan, who has run away from a circus where she had been performing. There is always the shadow of tragedy, as how will they live? They have no money, and finally they are starving to death and the only way out *is* death, so it ends with his shooting her and then himself. But somehow it doesn't matter, because they have had such an extraordinary time of joy and of sharing all that each had to give. It's like a series of French Impressionist paintings. First you see a Monet *Dejeuner sur L'Herbe*, then you see a Manet of Elvira walking on a lonely street, always beautiful, always immaculate. He's always in a pure white, newly ironed shirt. It's a fantasy but one accepts it as a fantasy and can't help but be moved almost to tears by the sheer beauty of it. So that was a wonderful way to end a Susan-May day.

Meanwhile this morning I went up to my study and took out of the file Nancy Ellis's letters. During the late seventies and early eighties she wrote me fairly often. She was a former student of mine from Wellesley; at the time she wrote, a doctor, dealing chiefly with terminally ill children and finally realizing that she couldn't go on, that she was burned out, and thinking that she might go another route through Hospice. Nancy Ellis was an extraordinary woman, of extraordinary intuitions and intelligence and sympathy and love, who ended two or three days ago by taking an overdose of barbituates and committing suicide. It is terribly tragic. She was only fifty

but I feel that she *had* a marvelous life and, more unusual,
that she gave an extraordinary amount to life. It's not a *failed*
life but it's a life which came to the point where it could no
longer carry whatever she, Nancy, had imposed upon herself
as what she *had* to carry. In one of the letters she says, of
working with Hospice, "I am hoping that, by doing this, I can
'get rid of' some of the enormous anger which I still carry
around toward the 'officials' of the medical profession who
consider supportive care to be no care at all, or 'merely' the
province of nurses and priests." Of course, this is what I've
come up against with my doctor, a general practitioner, who
simply is not interested in chronic pain. Nancy was fighting
this all the time and finally began to write poems. I think that
is how she began to write to me more than before. The poems
are sometimes very painful, but to show how talented she was
and how much she already was able to give, I want to read
one which refers to Nebraska where she was born and shows
that she had enormous talent.

Home

In Lincoln, Nebraska, there are rows of
Streets lined with tall old elm trees which
In high summer interlace their topmost
Branches across the concrete or macadam

To form lovely arbors of cool green shade
In the midst of sweltering humid heat. I
Wandered for years within this cave of
Mercy, saved from broiling in a southern sun.

In that God's country, thunderstorms pile up
Toward the west, in the steamy afternoons.
Pillars of cloud mix with airbourne dust,
Yellow verging on green, gold, and orange.

The light turns a sickly ocher, and goes out.
In sudden dark, howling wind whips branches

Audibly against each other, and finally,
Finally, finally, at last we hear the

Drum of rain upon the upper limbs, heralding
Drenching downpour which miraculously relieves
The built-up tension and restores creation's
Equanimity. Earth relaxes in the embrace of rain.

What a marvelous evocative poem this is and how much I long
to honor—as she deserves—this marvelous woman, Nancy
Ellis.

Wednesday, March 20

BY THIS EVENING it will be spring. It feels like spring. I haven't
recorded anything for a couple of days. The days have flown
away. But I have been thinking a lot, of several things. One, of
course, is Nancy Ellis, who is always in my mind now since I
heard of her suicide and especially since I read her letters to
me, which were written in the mid-eighties. I want to remember something she said so cogently about *A Reckoning* and the
relationship between Ella and Laura, who are not, in the
book, lovers. She says:

> To make Ella and Laura lovers in *A Reckoning* would be
> to destroy something very special in the book. It may be
> that sometimes the human connection you describe oc-
> curs in some relation to passionate love, but not usually.
> The connection between Ella and Laura is a fellow-be-
> ingness which has been thought to occur only between
> men, as brothers. *A Reckoning* is important because you

show this connection between women in such fashion
that it cannot be denied to exist. Perhaps your critic has
not recognized that she is seeing something new. Perhaps she is trying to fit Ella and Laura into extant, famil-
iar categories which are inadequate to contain the phe-
nomenon you have written about.

It's quite true that very few novelists have dealt with friendship between women. I have done so—in *Kinds of Love* also
and scattered through the novels, importantly in *The Birth of
a Grandfather*, the seeds for which were my reading of Jung.
He suggests that in middle age people are apt to turn for
comfort and understanding to their own sex. This was true of
Sprig's wife in *The Birth of a Grandfather*.

I would like to take one more paragraph from the same
letter from Nancy Ellis—it's 1979. She says:

The effective assertion of self, power, if you will, that
comes through your journals reassures me because you
are doing, and have done, what I wish to do in my work
and what I wish for Amanda [her daughter]. But I am
ignorant, and uncertain where to look for others who
understand that a woman's power and achievements are
not won *from* men; they are won by her courage, and
sometimes, from herself. It is very painful and defeating
to uncover unconscious sexism in women who appear to
be "liberated," effective individuals.

There's something in the *Times* on March 19, yesterday,
which really sent me. So wonderful to read that some ecolo-
gists have learned a way to resurrect vanished habitats. This
was, I think, in an oak savanna somewhere in Northbrook,
Illinois. This has been engineered by the Nature Conserv-
ancy. It makes me eager to give them money. I hadn't been
sure of what they were doing. Through arduous detective
work restorationists tracked down species which had either

died out or had been sort of squeezed out. They fired the area
they were working on so that everything else was killed and
then sowed the seeds of the original grasses and flowers—
sowed them on the bare ground,

> and within two years a rich, evolving savanna ecosystem
> was well on its way to reassembling itself under the oaks.
>   Uncommon species of butterflies, like the Edwards'
> hairstreak and the Appalachian brown, appeared as if
> from nowhere to feed on the plants. A pair of Eastern
> bluebirds, long absent from the area, returned in 1989 to
> establish a family in what had become, for them, an ideal
> habitat.
>   The resurrected ecosystem is "so strikingly beauti-
> ful," says Steve Packard, the science director of the Illi-
> nois Nature Conservancy, who directed the project. "It
> was like finding a Rembrandt covered with junk in some-
> body's attic."

Isn't it just marvelous to think of this? The birds and the butterflies and the grasses? It came with a charming drawing of
some of the things brought back: sweet brown-eyed Susans,
starry campion, cream gentian, Indian grass, prairie fringed
orchid, large-leafed aster. So here is this treasure which we
can, if we care enough and take care, restore. If only we could
do the same thing with the homeless.

But there was also in the *Times* very good news, that the
Supreme Court has come down—I think it was the Supreme
Court or it may have been a New York court—with a new
examination of the law of what is your home. In other words,
the homeless living under a bridge own their goods and they
cannot be taken away. They have the right to defend their
homes—to be defended in their homes. So little by little we
are getting more intent on maintaining and on rebuilding. The
whole history of this country has been the opposite—has been

cutting down the trees, destroying the plains, filling the empty areas with too many people. I felt it always when I went back to Belgium and would see a tiny plot of land in front of a house with two rows of small lettuces in it—every bit of earth cherished—whereas here almost all the earth is just neglected or put into factory-sized lots as in the Middle West with wheat and corn and soybean.

Friday, March 22

IT FELT LIKE spring yesterday, because Diane came and spent the whole day. First, heroic work, cleaning out one side of the garage with the accumulations of ten years. But the great work, the one that was so spring-enchanted, was taking the hay off the flower beds, although she told me—when I went down to say goodbye in the afternoon—that the bed back of the house where I have two yellow tree peonies was still frozen. But right in front of the terrace, snow crocus is out along the edge, and everywhere the daffodils are coming up, although it will be a long time before spring is really here.

Yesterday Susan drove me to Portsmouth. What a welcome lift that was! I didn't have to drive it myself twice in one day, to have a new lining put in my "upper," as they call it, because it was slipping out. We had to go back at four and get it—the partial—with the new lining in. It's much more comfortable now and I'm delighted that it's done. While we were waiting around at Dr. Dinnerman's, the wonderful dentist, I told him he would be playing tennis soon. He laughed and said, "Well, I've lived in Maine a great many years and I've

now learned that although one thinks April is spring, it is not."
That's so true. That's why I always went off and did the lecturing and the reading of poems in April, hoping to get where spring was already in full swing. As I mentioned, spring was bursting out in Seattle when Nancy and I were there a year ago—at just about this time.

The big event so far in this week, I think, has been that we got the video of Marjorie Kinnan Rawlings. It's not her movie but a video made from her life, called *Cross Creek*, which is the name of the tiny village where she lived and on which she based her great book, which was a best-seller. It's always moving to watch a writer find her way. Rawlings started—which I hadn't known but I presume is true, it is in the film, at least—by writing Gothic novels, which were consistently turned down by Max Perkins. How lucky she was to have him as an editor!

She began to write letters to him about her life when she first moved into Cross Creek, knowing *nothing* about life in the country. She found infinite friendliness and help all around her. People just showed up and started working because they needed the work. Soon she had people helping her with the orange grove, which was completely neglected, and which she had bought with a ramshackle house. She had a wonderful young black woman as a cook and helper—a relationship which is beautifully shown in the film. The black girl defends Marjorie against any interruptions, saying, "She's *working*, sir." She's a dragon in front of the door. But every single character is vivid in the film. The major drama, as it is in Rawlings's novel, is the young fawn who grows to be a year old and therefore must be shot because otherwise it will eat the gardens, it will go wild and not be wanted. The father who has to shoot it had warned his daughter, had begged her not to make a pet of it for this very reason. Then comes the terrible day when the deer has to be shot. The barriers that were holding it in were too low, and the deer could jump almost anything. I felt for it newly because of all the damage deer did last year to my garden.

Now I count the days until Tuesday when I see the doctor who is my one best, last hope. Perhaps I'll get well. These have been very hard days all this week in spite of Susan's wonderful meals. We had such a delicious supper last night of halibut, creamed spinach, mashed potatoes, and baked apples, surely one of my favorite desserts.

Jerri has just come and given me my breakfast and changed the sheets on the bed and is gone. So now the real work day begins and I must get at rereading the journal right this minute.

Sunday, March 24

YESTERDAY WAS A terribly gloomy day, enlivened only by— sometime in the late morning—a *huge* blizzard which had enormous flakes, so large that I suggested to Susan that she try to photograph them. So she did, but that only lasted about half an hour and then it became sleet and rain—dismal. When it snowed like that it was like being inside one of those glass paperweights where it snows if you shake it around.

We had looked forward to and did enjoy seeing that marvelous Australian film *My Brilliant Career*. It gives one much to think about. This is a relentless film because you keep thinking that the protagonist *is* going to have a brilliant career, she is *so* determined. But the lesson, perhaps, if there is one, in this remarkable film—the photography is really won-

CREDIT: SUSAN SHERMAN

Sudden blizzard

derful, amongst other things—is just that this is a person with enormous ambition, without talent. I have known one person like that whom I called a genius without a talent. Nothing is more tragic. Here in the film we have the determination, the imagination, but she played the piano very badly, she couldn't draw. Apparently she did write a book called *My Brilliant Career* on which the film is based. It was quite an experience, which completely disappoints the watcher, since the watcher is made to sense that this is right but because it's a movie expects it to be a triumph, that in the end pluck and determination will win.

It's sad. I get so many letters from people who are determined to be writers—women, especially, often middle-aged

women, sometimes divorced or whose children may have left
home, and who suddenly feel: I can do what I want to do. In
very rare cases she can, but very rarely, because writing is a
craft and an art. It's not only having a good story to tell, it's
knowing how to tell it that makes the great writer. One always comes back to Chekhov's saying that if you want to describe a moonlit night, describe a piece of broken bottle shining on the path.

I've also had another experience of great art, other than
My Brilliant Career. This is a novel that was recommended to
me by Deborah Straw. I'm so grateful, because she does know
what's going on and I don't anymore. What's going on, and
I'm heartily in agreement with it, is a writer called Barbara
Kingsolver who is the best new writer that I've come across in
about ten years. She's apparently written two other novels,
one called *The Bean Trees.* This novel, *Animal Dreams,* is
laid in the pueblo country of Mexico. Every sentence counts.
Everything is extraordinarily vivid and true and uncompro-
mising. I have complained, perhaps not in this journal, but
I've certainly complained in talking with friends, of the fact
that one is getting very tired of descriptions of sex and of
lovemaking in novels. They are so crude and really so off-
putting. Well, Kingsolver has written one of the most beautiful love passages I've ever read in this book—just a marvelous
description of lovemaking between a man and a woman who
are extremely shy but terribly in love and who finally are able
to touch each other. The very depth and sensitivity of the
touch is what she manages to convey. I'm extremely grateful
for it. It's published by Harper Collins.

One interesting little sidelight on this. I have been—and
still am—an admirer of Rosamunde Pilcher, who wrote a
best-seller novel, *The Shell Seekers,* about which I was enthusiastic. I've now read almost everything she's written. They
are wonderful stories, very believable characters, but the
minute I started reading *Animal Dreams* I felt: This is art.

And I felt that *The Shell Seekers* somehow just isn't. It's a good read, and that's no small thing to be, but the difference is really immense. It's a difference between verse and poetry: the intensity, the awareness, the sense of style, the formidable personality one senses behind *Animal Dreams*. This is a modern novel, very modern, that does not shock. That is quite rare these days. It nourishes. I've said elsewhere in this journal how rarely does a book one picks up nourish.

Tuesday, March 26

A REAL SPRING DAY—and at last some sunshine! And light birds on the ceiling! But it seems to be a rather calamitous period in which nothing really goes right, so I'm constantly given blows to surmount. I feel a little like Sisyphus. Every time I push the rock up to the top and feel that I'm somewhat in control again of what's going on, something happens and everything crashes around me.

Yesterday I had a letter from Jerri, the charming young woman who has been coming two mornings a week, to bring me my breakfast, tidy up, and sometimes do a small laundry for me. She announced that she was leaving without notice because she could not take being screamed at. I have a terrible memory these days and I couldn't remember any occasion on that Friday when she was last here when I had screamed. In fact I remembered it as a very warm and loving morning. I found a stuffed tiger and a puppet lamb to send to her two little girls, who are two and six. I was rejoicing in what a happy and beneficent presence Jerry is. Then, apparently, something happened.

Luckily Susan did remember. The last thing I remembered saying to Jerri was that if the pajamas were not dry—
she was on her way to leave—to just hang them on a hanger
and Joan would iron them on Monday when she came. Apparently I went into the hall, and then of course I did remember
it. I screamed, "It's hell! It's hell!" What I meant was that my
life is hell because I had been waiting all morning—really
since way back around five—to dare to take a suppository. So,
"It's hell" was this waiting and the fact that I have to depend
so much on what the state of my digestion is. But Jerri evidently took it as an attack on her.

In her letter she says "I'm not a child" and so on. Of
course, I do know that people with chronic pain often have fits
of anger, frustration, and exasperation, but I have not shown
that to Jerry or anybody who works here. Poor Susan has had
it. Anybody who lives very close to me would experience moments when I am just on the edge of hysteria of one kind or
another—anger or tears.

That letter came yesterday, and I must admit that I was
terribly upset and I still am. I'm hurt. I feel in a curious way
like a pariah. I think a lot about Ruth Pitter's poem about her
people. Suddenly I feel European. I feel it's all right in France
to raise your voice but it isn't all right in America. Anger is
very bad—I know that. Of course, I've suffered from it for a
long time. I've been blamed for it for a long time. It's also the
energy back of creation sometimes.

I'm sure many people identify with this poem of Ruth
Pitter's, "The Lost Tribe":

> How long, how long must I regret?
> I never found my people yet;
> I go about, but cannot find
> The blood-relations of the mind.

Through my little sphere I range,
And though I wither do not change;
Must not change a jot, lest they
Should not know me on my way.

Sometimes I think when I am dead
They will come about my bed,
For my people well do know
When to come and when to go.

I know not why I am alone,
Nor where my wandering tribe is gone,
But be they few, or be they far,
Would I were where my people are!

Of course it brings back Belgium and Céline's *"Saperlipop-pette!"* What are you saying now? The fact is that most of the time our voices in her house were raised in discussions which were passionate and often called anger, but how life-giving! It makes me homesick for Europe—for the Continent, for French as a language. And it makes me sick with homesickness to live in a place where I feel that I am a pariah in spite of the letters that come every day telling me what I've done to help this person or the other person.

After I had swallowed that letter and cried—I'm afraid very bitterly—Penny Morrow came to give me a massage. It lasts one hour and is very relaxing and life-giving. I'm going to give myself two a month—that's all I can afford.

The expenses are very big now, and maybe it's a good thing that Jerri can't come, because that's forty-four dollars a week I'm saving. I've got to try and see if I can do it alone. In a way, of course, people coming and helping do interrupt something—that slow river of solitude when, for instance, I will not have to be ready at seven-thirty for someone to make my breakfast, when I will not get up much earlier than that and set the tray so that it's all ready for the person to bring it up. Change is what's difficult—abrupt change when experience has made a little groove, a little peace and harmony has been created. It's extremely painful when that is disrupted. It has been disrupted so many times this year that I should be able to handle it now quite well. But I am very nervous about being alone here from the 1st to the 18th of April, when Nancy will be on holiday and Susan back at school. At the end of April everything will be better and perhaps I'll feel better.

Friday, March 29

GOOD FRIDAY. I have been trying for two days to get myself together so I can talk about a radical change in my life. I am trying holistic medicine as the last hope to cure my intestinal troubles, which have been almost unbearable in the last two weeks. On Tuesday I saw Dr. Ferida Khanjani, a chiropractor and holistic doctor. I didn't know anything about the chiropractor part, but it makes sense, of course, since chiropractors believe that everything is connected. Unfortunately, that day I was not at all well and had horrible cramps. Because of some emergency cases she kept me waiting for quite a while, and I had gotten extremely nervous. But she was very warm. I had meanwhile filled out a long list of all the illnesses I've had in the last ten years and what medicines I'm taking now for my heart.

I liked her. She listened extremely carefully. She explained things—in spite of the fact that she was eighteen when she came to America from Iran and her English is not perfect—so clearly that it was a relief to listen and to understand. She then prescribed what is becoming my regular diet. It's at such total odds with anything I've ever liked to eat that it's really hilarious: no dairy products, no eggs, no margarine—which I don't like anyway—and for this first week no protein at all.

So what I've been living on is two tablespoons of chlorophyll and two tablespoons of aloe vera four times a day, and brown rice mixed with a steamed green vegetable. Last night I had steamed broccoli with brown rice, and it tasted very good. I had a half of an avocado—the only thing resembling a fruit if not steamed which so far I've been allowed to have. I'm seeing the doctor today and I hope that there may be a little more leeway over the Easter holiday, because the trouble is I feel hungry. What I can have is a slice of whole wheat bread with butter, and then I put a little honey on it because Dr. Khanjani said that I could have no sugar but I could have honey. It does taste awfully good without any other sweet thing at all. To change one's entire eating habits at my age is a terrific punishment, but it's worth it, for today I feel stronger. All of this is good news. I went down almost to the bottom but now I'm back up and with hope.

I feel better today. I'm seeing the doctor again. Nancy has kindly agreed to go with me to the vet to take Pierrot, who needs his shots. It is next to impossible for me to take him alone, so this is a real boon.

Sunday, March 31

EASTER DAY and I watched the sun rise—a dark orange. It rises now to the north. It's only in midwinter that it rises right in the center of the windows in my room—in the center of the ocean view. A perfectly glorious Easter morning.

I say to myself: *force et confiance,* strength and courage. I don't think I could have said that last week. I couldn't have said it until I started on this adventure of the holistic system and met Dr. Khanjani, who proves to be a very enlightening and helpful doctor. One thing I like about her is she laughs so much. She laughs at almost everything I say, but in a truly amused, kind way, not in a sneering way at all.

There is a great deal of good news. I have a wonderful woman now to replace Jerri. The extraordinary thing is that Nadine Wheeler had irritable bowel syndrome when she was eight years old and spent her childhood in and out of hospitals, in extreme pain. So she knows all about it, and that's very comforting. She also told me that chlorophyll, which I take four times a day, is the great answer to everything and it's going to do the trick. But I already feel far more strength. The bowel syndrome has not completely died down. I can't expect that in a few minutes, but Dr. Khanjani thinks that within six months I should be well. So it's worth it to eat almost nothing that I really like, although last night I had an excellent supper which consisted of a small slice of flounder, broiled with just a touch of olive oil and paprika on it; brown rice mixed with very small peas that come in a can (I shouldn't have done that, but they did taste delicious!); half an avocado, on which I squeezed some lemon juice; and then, most delicious, an apple baked with honey and cinnamon. So that was a real feast and I have nothing to complain about.

Last night at about seven-thirty Eleanor Blair called to tell me a little joke which much amused me. She said, "Martha and Mitzi and I have had a wonderful day." Mitzi is her cat. Who is Martha? I was completely in the dark until she laughed and said, "Martha Washington, of course!" I had sent her for Easter a Martha Washington geranium, because the florist out there didn't have any of the pinkish-red new geranium I wanted so much for her plant window. I didn't know that Eleanor's small, delightful plant window was in sore need of something to cheer it up. So Martha turned out to be a good choice, especially as Eleanor had never seen one before. Although she is legally blind she manages to see out of the corner of her eye and knew that the Martha Washington was red. She managed to write me a letter. I know the effort. Last night she had made two or three tries and torn them up. This was perfectly written, an example of what *force et confiance*, strength and courage, can do even if you're blind.

There's no doubt that I'm better, because I wake up looking forward to the day. This is the first experience I've had of looking forward, literally for months. I long to get up and get started, because partly the strength is still not very big and I know that in about an hour I shall be tired. I'm hoping—and this will be a real event if I can do it—to write a letter to Juliette Huxley, whom I haven't been able to write to for months. I am beginning to be able to write, though not yet on the typewriter. I don't know why that is. My typing has never been good, but at least I could do it rather fast. Now I simply clutter up the letters. I don't know whether this has to do with the heart medicine I still have to take or whether it is simply old age.

Tuesday, April 2

WE'RE HAVING bitterly cold weather, which everyone resents because we so long for spring. In my garden even the crocuses are pausing, shivering, and haven't really come out.

It's been quite a day today. I woke with very bad cramps, and I wonder whether it's due to the chlorophyll. I'm very faithful, had an excellent supper last night: delicious fresh flounder and brown rice mixed with spinach. So it was a good hearty meal, ending with a banana with some lemon juice and honey. Why do I wake up this morning with awful cramps? However, I see the doctor at two-thirty and she will surely give me some good advice.

Meanwhile I have managed to accomplish quite a lot this morning. The cat, of course, went out at four. At six I went down to let him in and remembered it's the day they come for the rubbish. I luckily had on a warm wrapper and so went out to the garage and dragged it out, filled the bird feeder, and hung it up. The squirrels had gnawed a hole already—although this one is almost new—but I managed to slip a knife with its bone handle between the outside wire grill and the inside plastic which holds the seed. They haven't gnawed through another hole, so it is better. The day I found it the feeder was empty at ten in the morning. They had simply eaten everything. Something gets eaten all the time. The deer have already eaten the shoots of the tulips. I planted none last fall because that's what happens. These were left from other years.

CREDIT: SUSAN SHERMAN

The bird feeder

After doing those chores I went back to bed with a hot-water bottle and finally got up and made myself some brown bread and honey and some orange spiced tea. Now I don't have quite as much pain.

It's so rare these days that true kindness brings tears to my eyes. A few days ago when I was at the big IGA there was a man in front of me in a wheelchair, pushing his cart. He had to wait a long time, and when suddenly a new opening occurred he insisted that I take his place. I said, "You've waited so long!" He said, "No, you go ahead." He did it in such a kind way that it made me smile all over. If only people realized what a smile or a little gesture of kindness can do!

I've been wanting to find a place in Kingsolver's wonderful book *Animal Dreams* which would give an idea of her style, of the kind of observing eye she has, her humor and her compassion. This may seem strange, but I think I've found the right one:

> In the middle of that gray month Emelina's youngest son learned to walk. . . .
>
> For quite a while now Nicholas had been cruising the perimeters of his world, walking confidently from house to tree to lawn chair to wall, so long as he had something to hold on to. Sometimes what he touched was nothing more than apparent security. Today I watched the back of his red overalls with interest as he cruised along a patch of damp, tall four-o'clocks, lightly touching their leaves. He had no idea how little support they offered.
>
> He spotted a hummingbird. It buzzed around the red tubes of a potted penstemon that stood by itself in the center of the courtyard. His eyes followed the bird as it darted up and down, a high-strung gem; Nicholas wanted it. For a long time he frowned at the brick path that lay between himself and the bird, and then he let go of the wall. He took one step and then more, buoyed up by some impossible anti-gravity. After two steps the hummingbird was gone, but Nicholas still headed for the air it had occupied, his hands grasping at vapor. It was as if an invisible balloon floated above him, tied to his overall strap, dragging him along from above. He swayed and swaggered, stabbing one toe at a time down at the ground, pivoting on the ball of one foot, and then suddenly the string was cut and down he bumped on his well-padded bottom. He looked at me and screamed.
>
> "You're walking," I told Nicholas. "I promise you it gets easier. The rest of life doesn't, but this really does."

I stayed out there with my book for the rest of the afternoon, surreptitiously watching as he tried it over and over. He was completely undeterred by failure. The motivation packed in that small body was a miracle to see. I wished I could bottle that passion for accomplishment and squeeze out some of the elixir, a drop at a time, on my high school students. They would move mountains.

I must now try to get hold of her earlier books. I am sad to be finishing this one.

Wednesday, April 3

AT LAST IT'S GOING to be a little warmer. Yesterday there was a bitter wind and I had a strange hollow sensation in my chest. I'm glad I'm seeing Dr. Petrovich on Monday. I overdid, not stupidly, but simply Tuesday is the day when nobody comes, so I had to do everything, including dragging the rubbish out from the garage. I'm happy to hear that Nadine may be able to come on Tuesday in a week or two, then she can do that chore for me. It's really not difficult. The carts are filled and I only have to pull them out. The thing that's so hard for me to get used to is that walking across the room demands an effort, so often I don't do something because I don't want to walk across the room! It's as simple as that.

Now that Nadine is gone, I have the day. I don't have to go and get the mail or the *Times* or any food in. So this is going to be a good morning, although it's already ten. But soon I'll be up at my desk. I think today I may get the tax off. It came more than a week ago but I just haven't had the gumption to put it in an envelope and send it.

The bad news which is now in the newspaper and was on *The Today Show* today is that of the numbers of adolescent suicides: five thousand already this year. It does seem incredible. But what is not surprising and came up on *The Today Show* is that the reason for a fairly large percentage of these is that the boy or girl is a homosexual, feels either that he's wicked, will not be understood by his parents or his peers, or will never be able to make a go of it in life and so decides to end it all. A mother spoke about her son who had committed suicide and said, "All I had to do was to tell him, 'I love you and I accept you as you are.' " This is still extremely difficult for parents. Gay-bashing becomes more and more the thing. In every city there are beatings of young men especially who are gay. There's something terribly wrong about it. It's hard to combat, and of course the extreme right is no help at all, in fact they are among the gay-bashers. It makes one so sad to think of these young people. I've written about one in *Mrs. Stevens Hears the Mermaids Singing* who discovers his homosexuality and has what seems to him a miraculous encounter with another man and *then* realizes he's done something way outside the bounds and becomes extremely depressed. It's time we faced the fact that there are a great many homosexuals who are very remarkable and giving people. By giving, I mean giving to society, whether as artists or social workers or teachers. There are literally thousands. How can we afford to shut out this very large number of good people? It's going to be a question for a long time to come, I'm afraid, because it's extremely difficult to educate and there is such a profound rejection of the idea of homosexuality.

Friday, April 5

NADINE IS HERE. She is so quick and helpful. The sun is out. It feels a little warmer. That's what we need. We need two or three warm days, then everything will spring out. Whereas the air is still wintry. That's what we have to bear in Maine.

Yesterday I had a tiring but good day. I had to get the mail myself and get a prescription. Then Karen K. came and took me rapidly to Portsmouth. We left here at a quarter to eleven and got back before noon, which is really miraculous. We went to the health food store there, which was really like becoming a lion in a cave of food for me, because here I am with a total change of diet. The only way to go about this is to regard it as an adventure. In that store I felt very excited seeing all the things that don't have sugar, or that I can eat. I went to get soy milk, quite a lot of it, to store away, because there's a law in Maine that it can't be sold. I don't know why. So I've got a large amount and we came back with various goodies. Then we went to the A&P, where I got two arti-chokes, one of which I hope to offer Maggie when she comes over the weekend. There are not an awful lot of fascinating vegetables now but last night I had brown rice with steamed carrots—the first time I'd had that mixture. I found it very good indeed.

Because I have to think about food quite a lot I've decided to think about it and use it as one of my games. So I decided to think about some of the best things I've ever had to eat. The first person who came to mind was my neighbor who was Mr.

Hare in my book *Miss Pickthorn and Mr. Hare*. He lived opposite me in a shack with his dog, and he went out the first day of trout fishing and, I'm sorry to say, caught for me four or five trout, surely below the size they're supposed to be, and brought them on a big fern leaf. They made the most delicious breakfast I've ever had.

Then, to jump from that tiny village in New Hampshire to Palavas[-les-Flots], a seaside town below Montpellier in the south of France. There, just after the war, Judy and I traveled with Jane Stockwood and Annie Duveen. We found a very plain little hotel called the Hôtel Moderne right on the beach—it's not a fashionable beach—where we had bouillabaisse every day. We were there for four or five days. It was the best bouillabaisse I've ever had, and I dream of it!

Then, miracle Maggie Vaughan, who is coming this weekend, makes the most marvelous applesauce I've ever had. Luckily I can have a little of that. She did an extraordinary feat of bringing me oysters at the hospital when I was there the last time. I don't know how she did it, but it was marvelous.

Andrea Rioux, who comes on Saturdays to help me, cooked a magnificent apple pie one day.

Then I go back to France, of course, the great place for food, and to Grace Dudley's Petit Bois in Vouvray. Grace loved carrot soup which her housekeeper made. I think it was made with potatoes and carrots, then put through a blender. It was absolutely mouth-watering. I must learn how to make it.

Finally, thinking of the Grand' Place in Brussels, there is the traditional Belgian meal of fried potatoes—french-fried, very thin—and those wonderful mussels. It's a great blessing that mussels have become fashionable. You can get them here. It didn't use to be possible.

I have kept forgetting to say that the peepers began about a week ago! Now at night—and last night the moon was almost full, on the wane but almost full—a chorus of frogs, of large bullfrogs and other frogs and peepers, was simply dazzling, if sounds can be dazzling.

Monday, April 8

Suddenly—yesterday or the day before—suddenly the crocuses in the warm sun *burst* open and there is a great line of them—really glorious—under the pine trees. Nadine, who was here on Friday, planted six primroses that had come by mail and I thought would be better packed, but I nursed them along, then she put them in and they seem to be doing quite well. So things are beginning and there is a lift to the spirits.

Unfortunately I had a bad weekend of pain. Maggie was here and such an angel. She always invents incredibly helpful things. For instance, fastening the knobs back on one of the drawers in the dresser in the guest room, which is an old mahogany dresser I bought for eleven dollars in Cambridge years ago! It does have big drawers, and the knobs have persistently fallen off. Now they are firmly *there*. Then she fixed two of the bird feeders, having brought the last time she was here replacements for the inner plastic cases that hold the seeds. They are what the squirrels bite into. They bite into the holes so that the feeder has been emptied in half a day. We had a very peaceful time. The only thing was we could do so little together.

The great news is that there's been a really *splendid* review of the new book *Sarton Selected* that Brad Daziel edited, in *Publishers' Weekly,* which is the single most important place, since it is read by all the booksellers. This is a fillip for me. It's about the best review I've ever had—a very comprehensive review of all my work.

Meanwhile the news makes one ache. I dread looking at the Kurds, the misery, and thinking of the real monster— when you think of what Hussein has succeeded in doing. It seems to be quite clear that he's if not actually committing genocide very close to it, because he's driving the Kurds out of the cities onto the roads. Meanwhile he has brought about the most damaging ecological disaster I suppose there has ever been—the oil wells which go on spewing out millions of tons of oil and polluting the air so that very soon—at least it seems possible to imagine—Kuwait will become uninhabitable, or that people will go in, stay a week to tend to the oil, and then leave. It's very frightening and makes one sick to see such wickedness prevail.

I'm discouraged that I don't feel better. But Joan, who came this morning, said, "You look better. You have more energy, I think." Which is true, so if I can conquer the lower regions I should be on the way to feeling a lot better than I have for a year.

Enormous piles of books have come from Norton, which is getting rid of some of the hardcovers where the paperback is in print. It's wonderful to have these to give away. One of them is *A World of Light*. Yesterday I read the chapter on Jean Dominique, because I wanted to find comfort, and it was so comforting to read. What an extraordinary kind of courage and charm she had! Both her friends who were her whole support when she went blind died before she did. Then she became totally dependent on strangers. A young family moved in to take care of her, and with grace and wisdom she managed to adopt them, to love them, including a brown poodle called Presto who slept under her bed. Of course, the faithful—*les fidèles*—still came constantly to see her.

Friday, April 12

THE SUN IS OUT but it's *awfully* cold. Yesterday the wind was cruel. I had to go to the optometrist and had tried a new laxative which was giving me terrible cramps, but I think it is going to work out. It's called Swiss Kriss and is made from senna leaves. I am more and more convinced that the holistic method is going to help, but the transition is causing me extreme pain. That's why I have not talked into this little listener for several days.

It was difficult at the optometrist's, though he's such a nice man—David Upton. I had to wait fifteen minutes on a very hard chair. It sounds like nothing, but I'm so frail now that I felt I was going to fall off and faint. I finally said, "If it's much longer we'll just have to go." Anyway he did look at my glasses, and I don't have any of the things that plague old eyes, so I'm lucky. Karen K. kindly drove me there. We stopped and got fish on the way home. She is a wonderfully dependable, dear person.

What a joy to have daffodils! I'm looking right now at a bunch I picked yesterday, but it was almost impossible to walk down along the woods because I was so shaky. I did pick a little bunch and now I am having the reward, because they are simply glorious with the sunlight on them.

Duffy, the photographer friend of mine who every year

CREDIT: ANNE C. TREMEARNE

sends me trailing arbutus, sent the most beautiful group of
them in a little basket yesterday. It's really like a dream. It
always brings back Nelson and the place I used to pick them.
So many things in the spring bring Nelson back. The trailing
arbutus grew on a bank near a lake. It was such a lovely place.
Sometimes I had to go two or three times because the flowers
weren't out yet; I sometimes got there too late. It's such an
elusive flower. I was trying to remember Emily Dickinson's
poem about it, but unfortunately it has escaped my *oublieuse
memoire*, my forgetful memory, as Jules Supervielle calls it.
"Pink—small—and punctual—" is all I can remember.

Susan comes this afternoon about four, and that is such a
relief and delight. She will help, and I must say these last days
I've needed help. Eleanor Perkins couldn't come yesterday
because her husband is dying of cancer. I am anxious about

CREDIT: SUSAN SHERMAN

Cybèle

her, because I know there isn't money, but I really can't begin to spend more. I have to pull in my horns just a little as expenses mount, now that Dr. Khanjani wants to see me twice a week. I think that is wise, because I need help in this transition period.

It's now in these days that spring in Maine is frustrating because so little is out. The greatest delight for that reason is the plum blossom that Nadine has picked for me today again, and did last time she was here, at my request. I put that little tree in in order to be able to pick it before the flowers were out. They are the most beautiful white, small, exquisite flowers along a branch. So that's one real sign of spring. The daffodils are on the way. What we need is some warmth. Yesterday's cruel wind made one shudder. Tonight they said it might go down very low, so I think I must cover the primroses again.

Saturday, April 13

THE WHOLE HOUSE is alive now with Susan and Cybèle here
and dozens of roses everywhere. I had forgotten how beautiful they are, these roses that she gets in New York, flown in
from Ecuador so they are absolutely fresh—unlike some roses
from Foster's which fade in about a day. These last—some of
them—two weeks. Now here they are—white, two pinks, a
pale pink and a deeper pink, and that wonderful heart-red,
and yellow. I have by my bed five glorious yellow ones. Of
course, now the daffodils are out it's hard to decide which to
put where. A great riches.

Yesterday was altogether a day of celebration, because
when Karen K., who kindly got the mail for me, brought it in
there was a big box from Norton. Lo and behold it was the
new book, *Sarton Selected!* It looks very fine, and I'm just
delighted to have it. I think the selection is excellent. There
are a great many poems that are not in the *Selected Poems*,
some of the best, and then the quotations from journals are
very good, and it was a real inspiration to end the book with
the first chapter of *A Reckoning*, of which the last sentence is
"Now for the real connections." Also Bruce Conklin's photograph on the back cover is really a masterpiece. I like it very
much, because it's rather detached and humorous and certainly does not conceal my age. I love to see on the lapel of my
jacket in this photograph the tiger that Janice gave me some
years ago.

I was able to go up to my desk for a little while yesterday.

I signed the contract for the option on *Kinds of Love* which is being taken for a television special or a movie. I'll get fifteen hundred dollars right away and a lot of money later if they do it. So this is very good news, I must say. That too came yesterday, so it was quite a day.

I also saw Dr. Khanjani at one yesterday. I felt better. I didn't cry as I had the last time I saw her. In the course of the treatment I heard myself saying, "I cried, you see, not from grief but from frailty." There's nothing right now that makes me unhappy in the old ways, when I was unhappily in love, or when someone died suddenly. So I said, "It's not grief that makes me cry, but frailty." This is true, because it's when I can't do something that I very much want to do that I find myself in tears. Sometimes it's a kind of shame for having so little strength, having to measure if I cross the room whether I have the strength to do it.

Anyway I did manage to get a bunch of daffodils later yesterday for Susan's room. That meant walking all the way down to the end of the edge of the woods where the daffodils are the first to open. There was a very icy wind.

I have missed the *New York Times* in the last days because I wasn't getting the mail myself and often forgot to ask whoever got it to go next door for the paper. But Susan luckily brought me the obituary of Cora DuBois which appeared yesterday. She was the one who called me, and so later on did Carol Heilbrun, who realized that this was a major loss for me. But it isn't, because Cora has not been herself now for years. She was in a nursing home and had suffered many times from pneumonia and from chronic bronchitis because she refused to stop smoking. I don't suppose she could smoke in the nursing home, but she did smoke at home—much too late. She was eighty-seven. I was in love with her for five years, but it was a long time ago. I realize more and more that there was something in her nature which was not good for me.

Fundamentally she was one of those women who may be drawn to women, but who really don't like them. She identified with men. In other words, she felt very much the way men do toward women—some men anyway—somewhat contemptuous. She could be extremely destructive. She once told me that as far as she could see, nothing I'd written had any value. Now this is an extraordinary thing to say to a writer even if you believe it—to a writer who is in love with you and with whom you are in love. It seems sadistic and was. But I have to add to this that I wrote some wonderful poems for her, including one of my favorites, "Der Abschied."

She was a great anthropologist, but she didn't fulfill the enormous promise of her classic book *The People of Alor*, which was her Ph.D. thesis and is one of the seminal books in cultural anthropology. She lived for two years on an island in the Dutch East Indies where she was a day's horseback ride from any town, lived entirely with a tribe there, and had someone from the tribe who interpreted for her. She was forced, actually, to be a doctor. Once a child was brought to her whose face had been terribly torn by some sort of sharp-pointed piece of bamboo, I think. She had to sew that together. The only medicine she had was aspirin, as far as I remember. So it took courage and fortitude and belief. Those she had to a large limit, but it was tragic that she was not able to finish what could have been the great work of her career: an examination of what happened to Bhubaneswar, an ancient religious city in Orissa, India, when it became also the head of the state government, so there were two cities: a bureaucracy and a religious city about three miles apart. Cora took many graduate students there, many theses were written there. She spent months of every year there for, I guess, about ten years. But she never wrote the great book. I think this must have haunted her and is tragic because it would have been extremely valuable and interesting.

Monday, April 15

WE STARTED OUT with a bright sky but apparently we are
going to get rain and it's bitterly cold! I must admit I feel full
of resentment against the cold when everything is ready to
come out and is being held back—just as I am ready to burst
out and being held back by illness, of which I'm terribly tired.
Today I feel really ill. I am so weak I can't summon an ounce
of whatever it is that means energy. I can't turn the light bulb
on.

All kinds of good things are happening, however. Connie
Hunting's book of poems, *The Myth of Horizon,* arrived. I
shall have an enormous pleasure in reading it. Unfortunately I
have an appointment with Dr. Khanjani at two-thirty, which
means I really won't be home until four as I also have to get
fish for my supper, and brown bread at Sesame Tree. That is
the end of the day for me as far as energy goes.

I'm happily packing up *Sarton Selected,* and it's a thrill to
be sending it out. I think Brad Daziel did a superb job of
choosing and organizing what should go in it and especially
like that there are so many poems.

The hard thing about today is that I'm waiting for a call
from Doris Grumbach, who was to have called yesterday to
see if I'm ready for a visit from them some time today. She
didn't call last night and she hasn't called this morning. It's
frustrating because I have books to mail and errands to do but
I don't dare move.

Dear Karen K. is coming to take the books to be mailed.

What a wonderful place we have here where they actually
pack and mail by UPS! That will take a big load off me, because I'm in no state to pack books—or unpack them, for that
matter. More and more copies of earlier books going out of
print pile in from Norton. They have given me an enormous
number of them.

I am somewhat better as far as digestion goes today, yet I
feel very ill. It's strange. I may be getting better, but at the
same time, as the whole digestive system gets accustomed to a
new diet, I also may be getting worse for a while. I try to
believe that any day now I'll feel a real wellness coming.

Now I must call Eric. It's such a strange thing to believe
that Eric is semi-retired! I called his home in Connecticut but
apparently he's on the way to work. His wonderful secretary,
Eleanor Crapullo, retired two weeks ago. She was so kind and
so efficient that she will be sorely missed by every one who
had a connection with Norton. I really must do something
about celebrating her. I must write to her.

Tuesday, April 16

THE SUN HAS NOW come out, and very soon I'm going to walk
down to the daffodils along the wood—what a wonderful moment—and pick some. They last so wonderfully and are magic
in the house. Meanwhile there are also the roses, so I'm in a
tempest of flowers.

It was wonderful to see Doris Grumbach and Sybil on
their way to what really feels like home for them, although

they winter in Washington. They are migrating birds who fly back to their home in the spring and stay until the late fall. I hope very much that Susan can drive me there, for, they say, they can put us both up. Doris was very excited because they found a place in Portsmouth where one can get Boodles gin! This made us all laugh—that they were able to get some and with all the books they'd managed to pile into the car they had also piled in a gallon or two of Boodles to regale them through the summer. Doris looked lovely—and younger. After we had talked for a while she suddenly said to me, "You know, you look beautiful to me, and I think it's because your face has now gone back to what it was when you were very young. It's thin and like a young girl's face." It also made me laugh because I'm so old. But several people have told me and seem to feel that I look beautiful. I don't know how that's possible, but I'm grateful for the compliment, of course.

Meanwhile we talked, Doris, Sybil, and I, about the Kurds, and about Bush, who seems a very limited man who plays politics but not humanity, if you will, who can go out and play golf and brush aside the babies dying in those mountains, in the mud, without food, and having to be buried with all hope gone for the parents. There is something terribly brutal about the way we are having to throw out of airplanes mattresses and badly packed packages of food. I fear that some people will have been killed by the packages which they were trying to catch. A lot of people would not have had the strength to get to where a package fell. It's so grim. One can't believe—Hussein seems unbelievable.

In the paper there was one bit of good news, however. That is that the English scientists who have been flying over the oil fields in Kuwait, and who thought that the whole atmosphere of the earth might be changed and a kind of nuclear winter set in this winter, say that this is not going to happen

CREDIT: SUSAN SHERMAN

because the pollution is not rising to upper levels. So although much of Kuwait seems to be night in the daytime, it's not going to spread all over the world. That is good news.

The other good news is Baker going back to the Middle East. If only some steps can be taken toward peace it will make the whole horror of this war just ended less horrible.

I'm disappointed in the book of reminiscences by David Cecil's friends. The trouble is there are only a certain amount of things you can say about a person. The fact that he was so voluble and so brilliant comes back in every single one of the essays, so that finally you feel, after reading six or seven of them, that you have had it. There was one very touching one where one of the footmen at Hatfield House lost his wife. This was after Cecil had lost his. David asked the footman to come and have tea with him. They sat and drank tea together and Cecil said, "Now you know how I felt." That's very touching. He was not a snob in any way. And oh, the most lovable, fascinating man! I keep going back to the portraits, because there are several very good ones in the book—something extremely fragile about him and yet tensile, able to surmount almost anything. Perhaps to some extent that's what wit does for you.

Thursday, April 18

IT WAS A HARD day yesterday. I really was in great discomfort for most of the day. But I did manage to do two rather difficult things at my desk. One should have been fun if only I had a little more wit about me these days.

Eric Swenson, who is my editor at Norton and vice president of the firm—my editor for I guess twenty years—has semi-retired and will be called editor emeritus. They are putting together a bound book with a page for each writer or friend to write something on. I did a page yesterday, which I've got to improve. One of the charming things about Eric is that he always makes one feel happy. He has the most wonderfully positive outlook of anyone I've ever known. The phrase used so much now, "Follow your bliss," perfectly applies to him as he followed his bliss as a sailor—he has a beautiful yacht—and as a publisher in a distinguished house. Whenever Eric calls me his voice is so vibrant and tough and so full of cheer it's literally like a shot of a drug—a drug of joy. He was not an editor in the sense of asking for a great many changes. In fact, he perhaps bent over backwards to respect me and my style and to ask very little. Sometimes I wanted a little more editing than I got from him. But it is surely infinitely better to be underedited than to be overedited, as often happens.

I have been frightened in these last days. I think I'm losing more weight. It looked as if I was down to ninety pounds this morning. That can only be from the lung lining and from cancer. I have less and less physical energy. That is frightening, and there's no way of overcoming the fear it creates and also the dismay.

Yesterday when I was feeling awfully ill I found a wonderful letter from Mary-Leigh about *Sarton Selected*. She has the greatest gift for writing a note of thanks or appreciation of anyone I know. It's done with such grace that it's always a big gift when such a note appears on my round table. Yesterday was no exception.

It's again bitterly cold and gray. There will be rain and drizzle. I think it's partly the weather that makes me feel so very low. There's no much better weather in sight. I understand very well why in the last years I've always managed to arrange a lecture trip in April. It is the most discouraging month of the year in Maine, because it stays cold and there is an east wind. That's the trouble now. Inland it's not too bad, but we have an icy east wind tormenting us.

When I go upstairs I must try to find a poem by Francis Jammes which I translated once. The first stanza is:

O mon ange gardien, toi que j'ai laissée là
Pour ce beau corps blanc comme un tapis de lilas,
Je suis seul aujourd'hui. Tiens ma main dans ta main.

It goes on addressing the guardian angel for five or six stanzas. I feel my guardian angel is still there, so many good things are happening, but that health does not concern angels very much, guardian or not.

Friday, April 19

STILL BITTERLY COLD, but the sun did come out today, and, oh, what a difference it makes! But I am frightened because I'm so terribly weak. It's the first time that I've felt unable to do things on will. For instance, I didn't have the strength to go out and pick daffodils this morning. I *never* thought in my life that I wouldn't have the strength to do that! But now, in the middle of the afternoon, I feel a little better. I've had a nap.

Dear Karen K. came and took me out to get fish for Deborah Straw, who comes tomorrow. I got a beautiful piece of halibut and some flounder for myself tonight.

Nancy is back! What a relief that is! When she walked in with the mail it did seem like a sunrise. She has just come from southern California and was appalled at the terrible ravages of that frost that killed whole orchards. Apparently it's a real disaster area.

Yesterday a wonderful thing happened. In the mail came a letter from a woman in Chicago saying she was sending me a flier. She had known John Porter, who worked with her in some business that she's in. She thought I would like to know that his son, a marine, was killed in the Gulf war and that at the funeral there was a flier with a moving photograph of Mr. Porter, a noble-looking black man, and beside it my poem "All Souls." This flier was distributed to everyone at the funeral. After my signature on the poem it said: "Farewell, my war-

CREDIT: SUSAN SHERMAN

The andromeda

rior son." And of course I burst into tears. It was so touching and moving that he chose that poem and wanted it to be in memory of his son.

The andromeda is out, although the daffodils are still slow. The andromeda is a bush that was here when I came. It's above the second stone wall and is greatly regarded by birds—as I knew in the first month I was here nearly twenty years ago when I saw a scarlet tanager in it. I've never seen another, and it was a great moment, I must say, only matched by the moment when, just behind it, I saw a giant moose!

The trouble is I've been in rather acute pain lately. I wonder if it will ever end? So what I keep saying to myself recently is: Swing low, sweet chariot—comin' for to carry me home. I feel I'm dying. I think it must be the lining of the lung that explains why I've lost again—two pounds—and the weakness is so overwhelming.

Sunday, April 21

WE'RE HAVING A WILD STORM of rain and wind—really wild! About three hours ago the lights went out, and of course there's no heat. I can't get hot water for my hot-water bottle. Luckily Deborah Straw, who was here overnight to take care of me and was a perfect dear, left just before the light went out. I think a tree may have fallen, and we don't know when it will be cleared away. Now that Central Maine Power has an 800 number they know very little when you call, don't know whether the men are working there or not. So it's a little dreary, but on the other hand, the light outdoors doesn't turn dark until about seven, so I can go up—as I'm going to in a minute—and do something at my desk.

I'm depressed by the winterkill in the garden. I think I could say that fifteen years of hard work and joy, love, and adventure in the garden have been really destroyed over this winter when we had no snow, almost none, not enough to make a cover; when the deer were ravenous and are now eating everything. Mary-Leigh told me they had eaten Beverly's wonderful daylilies. She has a great show of them. I noticed they had eaten iris in my garden. The worst thing is a huge pink rugosa, which was beautiful. I planted it fifteen years ago and it is now about four feet high—a great round magnificent sight when in flower as it was last spring. There is only one branch now which has a leaf. Everything else is dead. The other roses are dead, I think, but rugosas are so hardy I can't believe it's gone. It's heartbreaking. The daffodils, which have always been the glory of this place, and which were here before I came, in their thousands, are very measly this year. There are fewer of them, but I'm proud to say the best ones are those I planted. Of course, they are younger and stronger, I suppose.

It's a sad sort of day. I long for some warmth and heat. But Deborah did wonderful things for me. Amongst others, what has been haunting me is some tuberous begonias. They came as little *tiny* bulbs. I ordered them thinking they would be about the size of the ones I've been planting for years and which I started in March down cellar under lights. I've now bought a light that is up in the little library so I won't have to go down cellar. Deborah planted them for me and we got the light set up.

Penny Morrow's soup—a wonderful vegetable soup—we had for lunch today. I think it's one of the best soups I've ever had—every vegetable you can imagine in it, including turnips, carrots. I don't know what the seasoning was, but it is a hearty, magnificent soup to have on a day like this. We had halibut last night, delicious, and a baked apple. So my diet is quite possible.

I think that the new laxative, or cleanser, which is called Sea Klenz, spelled with a zed at the end, is doing what it's supposed to do, which is to clean out the colon. This may, after a few days, make me feel a lot better and have less pain. That's what Dr. Khanjani is hoping. So all is not lost, but I still am so frail it's a little scary.

Monday, April 22

WE'VE HAD A MONSTROUS STORM of wind and rain that I spoke about yesterday. The lights finally came on, very briefly, at two and then for good at four. What a blessing light is when you've missed it! I darted about the house turning lights off, plugging in the flashlights. They really are wonderful, those ones that keep themselves going and are ready when you need them. Maggie's two battery lights—the big ones—were invaluable yesterday.

When I went down when it was light I saw at once that the bird-feeder cable had collapsed. I thought: I've got to get somebody, and who can I get to do that? I went through my checks to try to find the name of the man who had replaced Chris Cote, who used to do my storm windows. I found his number only to discover—when it was about quarter to eight and I thought I could venture a call—that my phone was out of order. It's now back in order. Finally, I took my courage in my hand and called Glenn Simon, Vicki's husband. She had said that he would help me if I needed help. He's just been here—as has Mary-Leigh with the lease for next year to be signed. Glenn was able to fix the cable. It seems like a miracle. The birds are so eager for food that it was painful to see them flying about in the air looking for their seed.

Deborah Straw's husband, Bruce, has done a beautiful small special edition of Henry James's trip to Burlington, with one remarkable illustration. I don't know how he did this on a small press. No, she said he had to send it to England to be done, I believe. The shimmer of the water is extraordinary. He's a painter and a very good photographer. He did the photograph of me on *Sarton Selected*. He's now fallen in love with this press and is going to become a maker of special editions. That's a beautiful vocation to have, I think.

While I had my breakfast I unfortunately turned on the news. It's Earth Day and it seems that we in America pollute the air with carbon dioxide—seventy-five percent of it comes from America. It comes from our insane use of oil, which we won't cut down. In Bush's new plans for oil he's talking about digging for more. As it is we've ruined the whole topsoil in many places. We're destroying the earth. It's not believable that this should be allowed to go on.

So it was a gloomy start to the day, but now the birds have a feeder and I did manage to pick a few beaten-down daffodils for Ferida Khanjani, because it's her birthday, I think, on Wednesday.

The fish market says they will have shad roe today. That's big news.

Wednesday, April 24

THE WEEK IS SLIDING AWAY.

Yesterday was memorable for several reasons. One, strangely, was in an article in *Time* magazine. I was depressed after the news. Bush, instead of looking for ways to preserve and for alternative energy, asking for money to dig for oil in Alaska! It's shocking. So it was good to open *Time* and see the four marvelous people who have been given the

Goldman Prize for preserving the environment. One of them is a man who has done a lot for dolphins. He roused people against the use of nets.

The most moving was a young boy from Sweden, Roland Tiensuu, who learned from his teacher, who shares the Goldman with him, about the destruction of the rain forests:

"I thought, 'There must be something we can do,' " he recalls. "I saw a television program where people planted trees to replace some of those that had been cut down. But, of course, we couldn't do that because we lived far away in Sweden. Then I thought that instead we could buy the rain forest."

... Tiensuu and the rest of the class organized a bake sale in their small village of Fagervik and raised enough money to buy four hectares (10 acres) of rain forest in Costa Rica's spectacular Monteverde Reserve. Their campaign gave birth to Barnens Regnskog, or the Children's Rain Forest, a nonprofit organization whose young supporters in several thousand Swedish schools have bought 7,000 hectares (17,300 acres) of jungle with the $1.5 million they have raised so far. Schoolchildren in Germany, Japan and the U.S. have followed suit.

In appreciation, the Monteverde Conservation League, which maintains the reserve, has named part of the rain forest the Bosque Eterno de los Niños, or Children's Eternal Forest.

The other great event was a massage as a birthday present from Penny. She brought me a book, *On Dreams and Death*, of which I've read only the first chapter, with immense interest. It's by a colleague of Jung's, Marie-Louise von Franz. I've been having dreams lately, although I think none—I may be wrong—foreseeing death. I do not remember my dreams usually.

It's thrilling to have a book which demands as much as this

CREDIT: SUSAN SHERMAN

Everything is in bud

one does of the reader. It's so fascinating you can't put it
down. It gives me pleasure, because I find reading anything
that demands thought very difficult, but here I am doing it, so
maybe I am getting a little better. Let us hope.

Everywhere now the forsythia is glorious. I used not to be
very fond of it—that blaze of yellow with no leaves—but now,
because we've had such a sad spring, it really is cause for joy.
Suddenly there is spring in the air. Everything is in bud. What
we need is a few warm days. I noticed yesterday when I
picked a bunch of the early spring flowers—there were two
small hyacinths in it with their delicious smell—that a big
bleeding heart was being strangled by ground cover. I re-

leased it, but the outer leaves have been hit by frost. It was thirty degrees two nights ago. Last night it was supposed to go down to nearly thirty. But at last the daffodils are coming out in the field. The little Jack Snipes are so darling. I have some right here beside me.

Saturday, April 27

AT LAST WE'RE HAVING spring weather, although apparently there's going to be a cold wind this afternoon. The daffodils in the field are opening, and it's marvelous to see—everywhere I look. The two forsythias that I planted down below the house are in full bloom.

I had a good talk with Carol Heilbrun on the phone yesterday and told her something of the story of a recent experience that I'd had. She laughed so much and said I must put the story in the journal tomorrow. So I'm going to do it, with some hesitation and no name, of course.

I had a letter some time ago from a woman who asked whether I would read a manuscript—she regretted it was not yet in proof—of a novel that she thought I would want to blurb. I wrote back that I was too ill and not capable of doing this now. Whereupon I got a letter from her which was like an *attack,* in which she said, "You just *have* to do this. This is a wonderful book! I know that it will help it. I'm already planning a publicity campaign with the publishers." The publishers are publishing forty thousand, so it's already, by my standards, a success. I said so in my first letter. Anyway, I was angered by her second letter, in which she asked me for help with "hype" on something already successful. So I wrote her a letter—a short note—which said, as far as I remember; "Your assault on a very ill and very old woman *demanding* praise for a book seems to me singularly lacking in humanity." Well, I gave her my telephone number—that was the big mistake— and said perhaps we could talk about this. So she called me, and of course I was persuaded that I had to do it. I had not expected—in the first place she didn't tell me—that it was a six-hundred-page manuscript which would arrive in *loose leaf!* It was too heavy for me to carry upstairs. I had to carry it—Nancy was on holiday—one hundred pages at a time, read them, go back down with them, and take another hundred pages up.

This woman is a very good writer. She's published two books already. She writes well about family life, and there are three very interesting children in the novel. But it is like a cartoon of everything that is fashionable in novel-writing today—that is to say, horror, torture, rape, treasure hunting for huge amounts of money—everything you can imagine. I read almost four hundred pages and then, when torture was looming for one of the chief characters, a woman, I said to myself: I *don't* have to do this. I don't *have* to read this book. And I laid it down and wrote her a letter to say exactly what I've said here: that she's a very good writer but I was sorry she was going for the fashionable thing and that I couldn't possibly blurb it as my readers would not like it and think I was a little mad to have done so. I also, on the back of the envelope, said that it had been very hard for me to handle the manuscript and she hadn't sent any wrapping, postage, or anything to send it back.

Whereupon she proceeded to have it bound in six parts and sent them to me—the original being still here, so now there are two manuscripts, or were two until yesterday— with, I think, a ten-page letter explaining that Shakespeare has a lot of violence, murder, and so on and that she considers herself, hopefully, the sister of Shakespeare and of Virginia Woolf, who of course talks about it in *A Room of One's Own.* Incidentally, it's not a good comparison, because in the Woolf reference it is that the sister of Shakespeare won't get a break, won't have any place to write in, and certainly has no publisher who will do forty thousand in a first printing! This novelist says that she has based her novel on the Bible and Shakespeare, or at least they are her inspiration and her sources. She goes into a long explanation of the symbolism of the whole thing. It is, of course, about good and evil and all the rest of it.

I laugh about this story now, but the whole thing was like a heavy leaden weight on my head. I think I found the right answer, because yesterday I mailed her a letter which said simply: "I'm sorry you took the trouble to repack the novel too late. The only answer I can make to your letter is: Don't try to teach your grandmother to suck eggs!" In this I was particularly referring to a reading list which she appended to the letter, of things, especially in sixteenth- and seventeenth-century English literature, which refer to horrors or very dramatic episodes. *Now* I'm exhausted by putting this on the tape!

Today a woman is coming who might possibly be able to take over for Nancy. Edythe is coming, bringing me soup for lunch. Ms. Gammons comes at eleven, Edythe at twelve, so it's rather a lot for me as I've been feeling extremely tired.

Of course the chutzpah involved in the whole episode of the novelist and her manuscript is almost unbelievable. I have never asked a famous person—even good friends who are famous—to write a blurb for me, although I think my publishers may have. I can't imagine writing to Virginia Woolf and asking her to say something about a book of mine—"Of course, you're so famous you can make me, and so please do."

And have her answer, "I'm awfully sorry but I'm ill," and then proceed to bludgeon her with demands to do it. This seems to me incredible.

It happened that in the last days of all this, Nancy was back from holiday, and the woman who wrote the book called while I was out because I had said, when I refused to blurb it, that I didn't know how to get it back to her. She explained to Nancy that she was having it bound and sending it to me. Nancy heard herself saying more than once, "But May's ill! May's ill!" But the woman just kept right on talking. Nancy got so upset that after the phone call she went down and ate a whole white chocolate rabbit that was on my mother's desk! This is so hilarious—it's such an endearing story about Nancy—that it somehow makes the whole thing a little more bearable. The entire manuscript, which must have weighed about thirty pounds, has now gone back.

Saturday, April 28

I'VE BEEN THINKING about the holistic treatment and Dr. Khanjani. It's disappointing that I still have so much pain, but I think I am a little better. Mostly I'm a little stronger. The proof is that I can walk considerable distances—to pick daffodils, for instance. I couldn't have done that a month ago. Also I go up and down the stairs so many times and don't have to stop and catch my breath. But the main thing is that the morale is better. That is what Dr. Khanjani is doing for me. I felt abandoned by the doctors. Nobody was interested in my symptoms or even in trying to help me as far as diet. The very

fact that I see Dr. Khanjani twice a week means there is somebody jacking me up, if you will. I spend an awful lot of time
getting in the food I have to eat. I couldn't find any ripe avoca-
dos. I'm supposed to have one a day, and I haven't had one
now for two days. I have three that are ripening, so soon there
should be one.

Karen Saum comes today. I look forward enormously to
that. Deborah Straw was here last weekend, and I had from
her the other day the best thank-you note I've ever had. Also
it's a good example of what I mean by grace. I've talked a
little about how rare grace is today and how precious, so I
want to read this little note from Deborah:

> May,
>   We exchanged flowers and words of encouragement
> and appreciation.
>   We enjoyed good food and planted bulbs together.
>   It was, for me, a perfect visit.
>   Lots of love,
>   Deborah

It's a poem, isn't it?

In the mail came a lot of things—*The Q Journal* by Paul
Reid, who lost his friend Tom to AIDS last year and who has
been going through a terrible depression. He has AIDS himself, and this is the journal of his trying a new drug which is
not yet lawful. I'm very moved by this journal. Paul is a great
person.

I continue to read *On Dreams and Death* with consuming
interest. I now wonder whether the very vivid dream I had
about my mother about a month ago was not one of those
dreams foreboding or warning of death. I very rarely remember dreams, but I remember this one very clearly even now. It
was exactly as if she was alive and well and with me. I don't
remember what she said, but she led me into a house or an

CREDIT: SUSAN SHERMAN

Poeticus

apartment. It had four walls anyway, but *no* furniture, nothing, completely empty, no rug. She said, "You'll have to get used to it." That, of course, might be a premonition of death. I don't know. It's very interesting.

I do look forward to every day. Having the spring here at last makes a gigantic difference. There's always something to look at, to pick, to admire. The many different narcissi and daffodils always amaze me. Beverly once counted that there were forty different kinds! One of my very favorites is *po-*

eticus, also called Pheasant's Eye. It's a flat white narcissus with a little, low, round cup which is yellow and ringed in deep vermilion.

Pat Chasse came yesterday. I asked her to come to pick some daffodils. Then I had seen that one of those wild roses was strangling a low rhododendron that I had planted a couple of years ago and which was beautiful last year. It's only about three feet high and it's a fuchsia color. You couldn't even see the flowers; it was in the grip of this wild white rose, which is very thorny and ubiquitous on the place. I asked Pat if she'd go out and cut it down. It was a *frightful* job, and she was out there nearly an hour. But I think she enjoyed doing it. She said, "I love challenges." For me, of course, it was the greatest blessing.

Yesterday (I should have started with this first, perhaps) Judy Gammons, who may come in November to follow Nancy, came for an interview: a large, handsome woman with white hair. We got along famously. She seems willing to do almost anything. She was head of an insurance agency, so she knows all about accounting, and that I sorely need. She's a very good typist. I have decided when I finish this journal on my birthday next week *not* to stop keeping a journal but to go right on. She said she would be very able to transcribe. She's a woman who is, I guess, in her fifties, and she is going back to college. I love that. Her son is graduating while she's still an undergraduate! Nancy liked her too, and that's a good sign. So altogether this is a good day beginning.

Sunday, April 28

It's an absolutely beautiful day! We're suddenly being given the spring in all its glory. The daffodils, which I thought were going to be a tragedy this year, are marvelous. I made an exquisite bunch for Karen Saum, who is here overnight. She said, "Oh, they are so beautiful! Did Nancy pick them?" And I said, "No, I did!" So she thinks I am very much better from the last time she was here, which must have been two months ago, perhaps even more. That's encouraging.

We had a wonderful supper and wonderful talk—a wonderful supper of swordfish, which I'm not specifically allowed, but I had only a small piece, and rice with chives from the garden, cauliflower with lots of butter and parsley on it, and baked apples for dessert. It was truly a feast.

Karen is looking well and is always illuminating about political matters. She feels that the country has been going downhill politically really since Eisenhower. There have been so many sellouts. The latest thing is that Bush is now being accused of having secretly made an agreement with Khomeini not to let the hostages out until after the election. I always thought it was a dirty deal in some respect. Karen thinks it will finish him, but I'm afraid nobody pays that much attention.

Several things have been on my mind lately that I wanted to remind myself of. One of them is Simone Weil's statement which I've quoted very often—I think in "The Writing of a Poem" also: "Absolute attention is prayer." When you think about it, we almost never pay absolute attention. The minute we do, something happens. We see whatever we're looking at with such attention, and something else is given—a sort of revelation. I looked into the heart of a daffodil in this way the other day—deep down. It was a pale yellow one, but deep down, at the center, it was emerald-green—like a green light. It was amazing.

Today I'm looking through my old anthologies of poems I love which I've kept since I was a child. I came upon the perfect one for this morning, for this morning the birds were singing very loudly when Karen got up at five-thirty. It's a sonnet without rhyme by John Keats:

What the Thrush Said

O thou whose face hath felt the Winter's wind,
Whose eye has seen the snow-clouds hung in mist,
And the black elm tops 'mong the freezing stars,
To thee the spring will be a harvest-time.
O thou whose only book has been the light
Of supreme darkness which thou feddest on
Night after night when Phoebus was away,
To thee the spring shall be a triple morn.
O fret not after knowledge—I have none,
And yet my song comes native with the warmth.
O fret not after knowledge—I have none,
And yet the evening listens. He who saddens
At thought of idleness cannot be idle,
And he's awake who thinks himself asleep.

I seem to have no voice today at all. Perhaps if I take some deep breaths it will improve matters.

Yesterday was a wonderful day. Dear Penny brought another great bowl of her marvelous vegetable soup just as Karen and I were sitting talking before supper. We'll have that for lunch. In the mail came Deborah Pease's poems. She's

been writing a poem a day, quite spontaneously, without trying so hard, letting herself be open to what comes. It is like a
new life—a new life in poetry. They are extremely good, is all
I can say. It's been an event for me to have them. Deborah
was a student of mine at Wellesley, but I'm sure I never
taught her how to write these wonderful poems.

Tuesday, April 30

A GRAY DAY, which, in a way, is rather restful, but I feel pressured because of everything that's going to happen: Maggie
for lunch tomorrow, Susan over two nights, which of course
I'll enjoy, but it's getting all the food and planning things that
tires me. Today Nancy is going to drive me into Portsmouth.
We'll do a lot of errands all at once. That's good.

Yesterday a very moving thing happened that made me
weep. It was a call from Sister Jean Alice Crosby at the Carmelite monastery. I had written her at Christmas, because
she'd written me the best letter I had at Christmas and the
best present, really, because it was such a happy letter. She
has done her stint of six years as a prioress and now is able to
go back to her life of contemplation and gardening, which is
what she loves. But it was so warm and loving—the call. I had
been a little sad that she hadn't answered my letter which had
thanked her for her Christmas message and explained how
very ill I am. She said, "You see, I'm not good at writing, so I
felt the Lord wanted me to call you. I'm so happy to hear your
voice." So we talked as if we had met yesterday. She spoke of
what a wonderful time it had been when she came here a year

and a half ago, I guess. I felt holy joy—tears streaming down my cheeks. I asked about the whole community, which is just sixteen nuns now. "Everyone is well," she said, and—most precious—she said that she will call again. It meant everything to me—to hear her voice. It shows what a letter can do. I had longed for a word from her, but now here it is—to make my birthday very special.

I've been haunted by a passage in the wonderful book *On Dreams and Death*. This is a passage by Jung himself. It's about the fact that as one gets ready to die, one gradually gives up even affection, even love changes, because a great transformation is taking place. The ego and the Self are differentiated, and it is the Self which goes into death. Jung says:

> I had the feeling that everything was being sloughed away, everything I aimed at or wished for or thought, the whole phantasmagoria of earthly existence, fell away or was stripped from me—an extremely painful process. Nevertheless something remained; it was as if I now carried along with me everything I had ever experienced or done, everything that had happened around me. I might also say: it was with me, and I was it. I consisted of all that, so to speak. I consisted of my own history, and I felt with great certainty: this is what I am. "I am this bundle of what has been, and what has been accomplished."
>
> This experience gave me a feeling of extreme poverty, but at the same time of great fullness. There was no longer anything I wanted or desired. I existed in an objective form; I was what I had been and lived. At first the sense of annihilation predominated, of having been stripped or pillaged; but suddenly that became of no consequence. Everything seemed to be past, what remained was a *fait accompli*, without reference back to what had been. There was no longer any regret that something had dropped away or been taken away. On

the contrary: I had everything that I was, and that was everything.

This, when I'm going to sleep at night, is very much the feeling I have. It's strange, but personal relations do not mean what they did—there's no doubt. I am in some ways becoming very detached. It's possible that pain, to some extent, does this, but also that passage makes me understand something I've not understood all the years since my mother, the day before she died, said, "Take the flowers away." She had loved flowers so much. They were so much a part of her that it came as a terrible shock, and I knew that it was part of the final episode of her dying, but it hurt. Now I see that she was detaching herself almost by will.

Thursday, May 2

I CAN HARDLY BELIEVE IT—the day before my birthday! Susan arrived early—at five yesterday, and I was so pleased—bringing a great bunch of white lilac and—most wonderful—a little bunch of lily of the valley from a garden of friends of hers. The scent of lily of the valley always sends me into a kind of ecstasy. It has been, ever since I was born, my flower, because they brought it from the garden to my mother when I was born. I was born in the house at Wondelgem after a hard labor of twelve hours. A dreadful, brutish doctor who sat, with his feet up, smoking a cigar—cigar smoke made Mother feel sick anyway—and said, *"Poussez, madame, poussez,"*—push, madame, push. My father, who of course was young then, was not a natural nurse at all, and I'm afraid he was not much help. So the lily of the valley must have come as a particular blessing—as they did for me yesterday.

It's wonderful to have Susan in the house. Everything gets done almost right away. She brought the vegetable processor—a squeezer to squeeze masses of parsley and carrots that Dr. Khanjani wants me to have. I've decided that I'm not going to try to tackle it until Susan is here in June for the summer. Then we can work on it together, because otherwise I spend too much of my life thinking about food, shopping for food, shopping for special food. I must have more time at my desk. Things are piled up.

The great birthday news is that I'm feeling a little better since I've gone to Dr. Khanjani. I was wondering if going to her had been the right move. It was. So it's a real birthday celebration today.

Susan is off now with Cybèle to Westbrook College to participate in the celebration of my seventy-ninth birthday which is taking place there. Connie Hunting is going to talk about the poetry; Susan Kenney will also speak about the novels and journals. I'm so grateful to both Connie and Susie, because this is asking a great deal of someone, to take the time and trouble to think out praises of a fellow writer. I'm probably even older, I think, than Susie's mother. I've been very much out of touch with her and Ed. Susie has become famous since I first knew them. Ed, I hope, although I don't know it for sure, is better. He had a long, frightening struggle with cancer about ten or more years ago. It went on for years, was hard to diagnose, so they've come through hell. It's wonderful to see Susie a star now. I wish I were going to be there.

I've been opening about thirty cards and letters. Wonderful to hear from friends old and new. I've just read a birthday letter from Grace Warner, and I would like to put in the tale she tells about her life there in Nelson.

I let my ducks out about a month ago and I was brushing
one of my ponies the other morning real early, it was just
coming day light. I saw a fox grab one of my ducks down
near the edge of the field near the woods. I knew there
wasn't time to go to the house to get my gun, so I ran out
of the barn after the fox, chasing it through the woods
until it dropped my duck. I was yelling to our dogs but
they are old and pretty much deaf, so didn't hear me.
Anyway that duck was alright. . . .

That's so like Gracie! She's the most wonderful mother to all
her animals. She ends the letter by saying that she's got her
pig.

I got my baby pig on April 7th. It is a little black and
white one with some red. She is so cute and full of fun
and will follow me all over the place.

But eventually, unfortunately, although she is a pet, she will
have to be killed for food.

Friday, May 3

MY SEVENTY-NINTH BIRTHDAY. The great good news—and it's
something I didn't expect—the best birthday present I can
imagine—is that I seem to be better, really better, at last. I
haven't had a very bad attack of pain for three days. I think
I've found a solution of how to handle things—at least for the
present—by taking a suppository very early in the morning
and that takes care of the whole terrible digestive problem
and for the rest of the day I am not in pain. I was going to add

CREDIT: SUSAN SHERMAN

May on her seventy-ninth birthday

glory be to God, that's how I feel. Of course Dr. Khanjani, whom I saw yesterday, was very pleased.

Yesterday what I kept thinking about was the fact that although spring is so late in Maine and always seems dreary during most of April, suddenly then things begin to come, one by one. It's not a great burst as it sometimes is in Massachusetts, but here it comes little by little. For instance, yesterday when I went out to do an errand I saw the marsh marigolds were out. Oh that brilliant yellow—just wonderful, and a single magnolia in York that I had not seen before, and of course the white violets, which are suddenly bursting out in great glory.

Susan is here and sitting looking at sprays of white lilac she brought yesterday when she came to go to the great celebration of my seventy-ninth birthday at Westbrook College.

There was a very good, large audience. The room would only seat about sixty, but it was full of attentive, Susan said, really reverent people. She made notes, so I got a good idea of how splendidly I was praised.

I can't say that this has been a very good year I'm leaving behind. It's been a hard year, but it has also been a year of learning to be dependent, which is important. I'm so grateful to the people who help me now—to Nadine and Joan, who come and bring me my breakfast—to Eleanor Perkins, who has faithfully cleaned this huge house for years and years.

I wanted to end this year and end this journal with a poem by Haniel Long. That, of course, takes me back to the years in Santa Fe, where I met Judy, where I had so many dear friends who are all except one, except Beryl Asplund, dead now. But the air is still as it always was, I'm sure, and the Sangre de Cristo mountains still flare up in the setting sun. It makes me remember all those wonderful times with Haniel and Alice Long. It also is something I want to give today—to myself and anyone who may be reading me:

May Your Dreams Be of the Angels

The old men who lived two centuries since
In the great houses of New Mexico, aspiring
In the New World to the courtesies of the Old,
Would say to a guest at bed-time, I am told,
Smiling, yet meaning it, "May your dreams be of the
    angels."

These are the words they said in the patio,
Under the great apricot grown from a Spanish stone,
And full of moonlight or of distant lightnings.
The guest would enter his chamber;
Lying abed, looking through the wide low door
Where he could see the apricot better, its branches
Thrown wide, receptacle of heaven and fire,
He might compare it to those highway trees

Which cast so little shade, yet rise so high;
And might debate two different kinds of living—
The tree of a life that soars forever higher,
And the tree of a life that stretches ever wider;
The life that cleaves its way, the life that waits
Like a bowl, like a vase. And who then or who now
Knows whether knowledge and peace are to be striven
   toward,
Or a place prepared by us for them to come to?

With Navajo marauding, and the drought lurking,
And slaves and peons restless and resentful,
It was a good question to go to sleep with
For the Spaniard facing the terror of his New World;
As it still is for you or for me tonight,
Sleepless between our future and our past,
Sleepless between our furies and our demons.

Whichever is your answer, may your dreams,
Whoever you are, be of them, of the angels.
In these human hells we go through, it is sure
We are not alone; there are witnesses to it.
Our helplessness is but a receptacle, 'twill catch good ghosts.